W9-CAX-504

Thomas Hardy
and
the Proper Study of Mankind

VICTORIAN LITERATURE AND CULTURE SERIES

Karen Chase, Jerome J. McGann, *and* Herbert Tucker,

General Editors

Thomas Hardy
and
the Proper Study of Mankind

Simon Gatrell

University Press of Virginia
Charlottesville

First published 1993 by The Macmillan Press Ltd

First published 1993 in the United States of
America by the University Press of Virginia
Box 3608 University Station
Charlottesville, VA 22903

Printed in Hong Kong

Library of Congress Cataloging-in-Publication Data
Gatrell, Simon.
Thomas Hardy and the proper study of mankind / Simon Gatrell.
p.   cm. — (Victorian literature and culture series)
ISBN 0–8139–1435–3
1. Hardy, Thomas, 1840–1928—Political and social views.
2. Literature and anthropology—England.   3. Literature and society—
England.   4. Community life in literature.   5. Man in literature.
I. Title.   II. Series.
PR4757.P6G37   1993
823'8—dc20   92–24349
                                                                              CIP

For Tita and Clym

Contents

Preface

Several parts of this book are more or less altered from pieces published earlier, and I have in particular to thank Oxford University Press for putting no obstacle in the way of my including material from the introductions to World's Classics editions of *Under the Greenwood Tree, The Return of the Native,* and *Tess of the d'Urbervilles.* An earlier version of Chapter 4 appeared in the *Thomas Hardy Annual* Vol. 4 (1986), and I would like to take this opportunity to thank Norman Page, the editor of the *Annual* (and now of the *Thomas Hardy Journal*), both for his continuing service to Hardy studies and for his unfailing generosity to me, the latest example of which was reading and commenting on a chapter in this book. Dale Kramer, Karen Radford and Emily Hipchen have also read and commented on chapters of the book, and I am grateful to them for their patience and perception. I must also thank members of University of Georgia graduate seminars on nineteenth-century fiction and on Thomas Hardy, who listened to embryonic versions of parts of the book, and in discussing them helped me to shape them – in particular Kathy Agar, Suzanne Gilbert, Alice Kinman and Ryan Lankford.

A Note on References

Six of Hardy's novels are quoted with reference to the critically established texts of the Oxford World's Classics series: *Under the Greenwood Tree* (ed. Simon Gatrell), *The Return of the Native* (ed. Simon Gatrell), *The Mayor of Casterbridge* (ed. Dale Kramer), *The Woodlanders* (ed. Dale Kramer), *Tess of the d'Urbervilles* (ed. Juliet Grindle and Simon Gatrell), and *Jude the Obscure* (ed. Patricia Ingham). *Far from the Madding Crowd* is quoted from the critically established text of the Norton Critical edition of Robert Schweik. All other Hardy works are quoted from the Wessex edition of 1912–13.

The abbreviation *Life and Work* refers to *The Life and Work of Thomas Hardy* by Thomas Hardy, edited by Michael Millgate (Macmillan: 1984).

The abbreviation *Letters* refers to *The Collected Letters of Thomas Hardy*, ed. R. L. Purdy and Michael Millgate, seven volumes (Oxford: 1978–88).

Introduction

Know then thyself, presume not God to scan;
The proper study of Mankind is Man.
> (*An Essay on Man*, Epistle II.1–2, quoted from *The Poems*
> *of Alexander Pope* edited by John Butt, London, 1963)

Titles are important (indeed it is the first argument the reader will encounter in the pages that follow that Hardy's own titles are significant and have on the whole been too much neglected) and the proper naming of this book was achieved only days before copy was sent to the publisher. For a long time I tried to adopt some fragment of a note of Hardy's, first published in *The Early Life of Thomas Hardy*, which at every reading strikes me with the force of a revelation, as something often thought about his writing but nowhere so vividly expressed. It is dated 28 September 1877:

> An object or mark raised or made by man on a scene is worth ten times any such formed by unconscious Nature. Hence clouds, mists, and mountains are unimportant beside the wear on a threshold, or the print of a hand. (*Life and Work* p. 120)

Hardy is a magnificent writer about unconscious Nature. The English countryside was first brought to focus in my city-bred teenage imagination through the overwhelming rhetoric of the first chapter of *The Return of the Native*, and it was long before I could bring myself to recognize that when Hardy wrote – while he was still in the process of creating *The Return of the Native* – of mountains as relatively insignificant beside the humblest evidences of humanity, he was summarizing one of his fundamental beliefs, a belief expressed throughout his fiction and his poetry. For years I was in love with the trees and the hills and the heath in his novels, and saw the people as merely extensions of their environments. Now I think I know better, and this book is an expression of that better understanding. Thus for a while I tried 'The Wear on a Threshold' as a provisional title, and also 'The Print of a Hand', but neither seemed right. It was only when Providence, or fate, or

1

destiny, or senseless circumstance presented me, at a doctoral oral examination in eighteenth century literature, with the quotation that opens this Introduction, that I experienced the tingle of excitement that accompanies the finding of the true, the only, the real thing.

It will, I hope, seem eccentric to find in a poem of Alexander Pope the title for a book that considers aspects of the fiction of Thomas Hardy, and no-one should anticipate further comparison of the two writers than is found in this Introduction. As soon, however, as I reviewed in my mind (to the accompaniment of my colleague's questions about *Gulliver's Travels*) what I could recall of the 'Essay on Man', the classic quotable couplets, I recognized how one connection from high Augustan to late Victorian might be made.

In his examination of humankind Pope considers how individuals stand in relation to divine power, to Nature, and to each other; he also considers the fabric of human nature. It is my suggestion that Hardy considers essentially the same questions in his novels: what external to us causes things to happen – God, fate, destiny, the Immanent Will? how do individuals stand in relation to their environment? how do individuals stand in relation to society? and what part do individuals' own natures play in what occurs to them.

Unlike the secure certainties offered by Pope's poem however, any answers to such fundamental questions that are derivable from Hardy's fiction are often provisional and contradictory. They rarely form a single coherent argument from a consistent point of view. When, for instance, we try to work out why things happen to his characters the way they do, we are driven up against a jumble of Providence, fate, destiny, character, other characters, even the novelist overtly acting as providence. All we can do in the end is to shrug our shoulders and repeat that Hardy was not a philosopher, and that the novels as much as the poems are not consistent and represent only a series of seemings.

From *The Return of the Native* onwards the question of causality irritated Hardy's imagination more and more painfully, and by the time he came to write *Jude the Obscure* his fictional testing of the possible power of different agencies in the world led him to an overdetermination that threatened to destroy – some would say succeeded in destroying – his power to make his narrative in the traditional Victorian mode of close imitation of reality. Hardy seems to want to say that Jude Fawley knows despair and death because of his own nature, because society works to exclude him, because he was predestined to, because senseless circumstance wills that he should, because he met an unsuitable woman and caught a chill in the rain. Though many of us share such uncertainty, it is hard for a fiction of the kind Hardy felt he should write to sustain such a multiplicity of causality without breaking down, and it is a tribute to Hardy's imaginative power that we are deeply moved by Jude's pain whencesoever it comes, and accept whatever the novelist shows us in spite of such uncertainty.

There is much less provisionality in Hardy's account of change in society, in particular in rural society. I am not alone by any means in thinking that the idea of community permeates Hardy's fiction. Douglas Brown, Raymond Williams, Merryn Williams, George Wotton, Noorul Hassan and Peter Widdowson have all left commentaries on Hardy's conception of community and on the relationship it bears to the socio-economic realities of rural England. What I have to add to these commentators is a focus on the way Hardy's own sense of the stability of rural community altered through his fiction. His youth passed during a time when he could believe that country villages and small towns might absorb the shock of industrial agriculture, the growth of global markets and a gradual standardization of education and culture, and he reflects such a belief in *Under the Greenwood Tree*. By the 1890s he has changed his mind, and *Tess of the d'Urbervilles* and *Jude the Obscure* successively proclaim both his awareness that village culture as it had sustained and nurtured him had almost disappeared, and his understanding of the process of this change.

A recent study of the subject, *Reshaping Rural England: A Social History 1850–1925* by Alun Howkins (London, 1991), offers striking support for such a view of Hardy's work. Howkins holds that 1872, the year in which *Under the Greenwood Tree* was published, came at the end of a period of twenty or so years of harmony and stability in rural social relationships, the period through which Hardy grew up and in which he began to write. It is this time of calm and relative prosperity that Hardy reflects in the Mellstock of *Under the Greenwood Tree*, even though the action of the novel is set slightly earlier. Howkins then shows how in the 1870s and 1880s a combination of economic and social circumstances generated a series of crises: a run of bad domestic harvests and an influx of cheap wheat from America and Canada caused economic depression; the growth of education, religious nonconformity and unionization, together with rapid rural depopulation, destroyed the evidently fragile rural consensus. This phase of upheaval lasted, Howkins says, until around 1895, the year in which *Jude the Obscure* was published – in which novel Hardy traces the consequences of the decline of traditional community and the inability of modern community to be born. The accurate sensitivity with which Hardy responds to these social realities is reflected in the fact that at several places in his study, Howkins refers to Hardy's fiction for substantiation of some detail of custom or practice. Of all the images representing Hardy's shift of vision in this area, perhaps the most potent is dance, and particularly country dance. It is an emblem in his early novels of the flexibility of the community which fosters dance; and the collapse in traditional rural culture can be measured by the corruption and abandonment of dance in his later fiction.

Hardy is at his most distinctive as a writer when he observes individuals in relationship to their non-human environment. Through hundreds of metaphorical expressions we are, for instance, forced in reading *The Woodlanders* to see characters and man-made objects in terms of trees, and woodlands and orchards in terms of human individuals and societies, while through the novel's action – in which the symbiotic or parasitic relation of humans and trees is a continual narrative perspective – the reader is forced perpetually to confront what it means to be human in a half-tamed wilderness, and what it means to be a tree nurtured and destroyed by humans. Egdon Heath is notorious, Talbothays farm scarcely less so. In some novels Hardy traces similarly intense literal and metaphorical relationship between humans and buildings. I have attempted, in chapters on *The Return of the Native*, Hardy's middle novels, and *Tess of the d'Urbervilles*, to open out some of the ways in which Hardy's imagination responded to such insights.

If taken very far, the comparison between Pope and Hardy with which this introduction began serves most effectively to point to the wide gap in thought between the 1730s and the last quarter of the nineteenth century. Yet it is striking for a student of Hardy to note that in the climax of his poem Pope insists on the paramount importance of Virtue, Benevolence – what Hardy called loving-kindness – in the achievement of human happiness:

> Grasp the whole worlds of Reason, Life and Sense,
> In one close system of Benevolence:
> Happier as kinder, in whate'er degree,

And height of Bliss but height of Charity.

(Epistle IV.357–60)

It is striking, since one conclusion readily derived from a perusal of Hardy's love-stories is that, when we come to consider the relationship between individual and individual, the virtue the most highly praised, and the last to be consumed Hardy's ultimate bonfire of all the virtues, is loving-kindness:

> And though the Swithin who had returned was not quite the Swithin who had gone away, though he could not now love her with the sort of love he had once bestowed; he believed that all her conduct had been dictated by the purest benevolence to him, by that charity which 'seeketh not her own'. Hence he did not flinch from a wish to deal with loving-kindness towards her – a sentiment perhaps in the long-run more to be prized than lover's love. (*Two on a Tower*, p. 312)

Viviette Helmsdale, the object of this loving-kindness, feels such a reversal from despair to joy that her wasted constitution cannot stand the emotional upheaval, and she dies from joy. This same virtue is celebrated in early novels like *Far From the Madding Crowd*, and in *The Woodlanders* it is the only force which permits true understanding of one human being by another:

> The woman herself was a conjectural creature who had little to do with the outlines presented to Sherton eyes: a shape in the gloom, whose true quality could only be approximated by putting together a movement now and a glance then, in that patient attention which nothing but a watchful loving-kindness ever troubles itself to give. (p. 30)

In *Jude the Obscure* loving-kindness, Pauline charity, seems to die with Jude. Sue, filled by circumstance and her nature with self-concern, can quote the epistle to Jude, but cannot see that in abandoning him she is denying its meaning. It is Hardy's understanding that a fundamental loss in the dissolution of traditional rural community was the loss of this cohesive virtue. When the schoolmaster Phillotson permits his wife Sue to leave him and go to her beloved Jude, he acts out of pure loving-kindness. He is victimized for his charity, and in composing a letter several years

later in which he asks Sue to return to him he reflects on the way
modern society has abandoned the virtue:

> To indulge one's instinctive and uncontrolled sense of justice
> and right, was not, he had found, permitted with impunity in
> an old civilization like ours. It was necessary to act under an
> acquired and cultivated sense of the same, if you wished to
> enjoy an average share of comfort and honour; and to let crude
> loving-kindness take care of itself. (p. 379)

Hardy, like all of his contemporaries, rejected Pope's injunction
not to examine the nature of God, and he would have mocked
the suggestion that 'WHATEVER IS, IS RIGHT' as he mocked
in *Tess of the d'Urbervilles* Wordsworth's extension of the idea in
'Nature's holy plan'; but he would have felt at home with Pope's
final couplet:

> . . . VIRTUE only makes our Bliss below;
> And all our Knowledge is, OURSELVES TO KNOW.
>   (Epistle IV.397–8)

   In considering none of these issues is Hardy single-minded or
wholly consistent. He is an impressionist of ideas with a variety of
points of view at command, even in the same novel. This makes the
experience of reading his fiction both rich and contradictory. I have
attempted to reflect this multiplicity through a series of related and
chronologically sequential chapters that do not themselves propose
a single line of argument, or embrace a single critical approach,
but rather seek to embody the variousness of Hardy's creative
imagination.

Prelude: Hardy's Titles

Authors usually have some purpose when they choose titles for their works. For this reason, if interested in discerning some meaning within a novel's multifariousness, it is sometimes worthwhile taking into account its title. This is particularly so on those relatively rare occasions when the author has decided to alter the title at some time or other; and though tracing the history of a revised title, and considering the implications of its various versions, will not necessarily provide an entry to all or even the most compelling meanings the novel is capable of sustaining, yet such attention will certainly direct the reader towards something of importance.

Hardy is an interesting case in point for he paid close attention to his titles, and changed a number of them. Three of the chapters that follow, those which concern *Under the Greenwood Tree*, *The Mayor of Casterbridge* and *Tess of the d'Urbervilles*, take title-pages as their starting point, and the value of such an approach can be tested at length in reading these chapters. As an example of its potential I should like to look briefly at the title of a fourth novel, the one usually known as *The Trumpet-Major*.

When Hardy published the first installment of the novel in *Good Words* in 1880, the title was simply *The Trumpet-Major: A Tale by Thomas Hardy*, and this unadorned version persisted in the first edition of the same year, and the first one-volume edition issued a year later. Hardy revised each of these versions of his novel, and presumably saw nothing wrong with the title as a label for the story. When Hardy first sent the tale into the world he intended to emphasize the role in it of John Loveday, the trumpet major. He may well have seen such a title as a partial solution to the question of how to signal to the reader that John is the hero of the novel, though he doesn't get the girl, and though his heroic death was only introduced in the first edition (serial readers not caring for the unrequited death of the hero). It is also of interest that he chose *The Trumpet-Major*, and not *John Loveday*; he was writing historical romance, and wanted to suggest that John's function was as important to the novel as his character.

In 1895 Hardy came to revise the novel for its inclusion in the first collected edition of his writing, and he found himself faced with a tale that proclaimed its historical intentions by being, uniquely amongst his novels, set in an undisguised Dorset environment – Weymouth, one might say, standing for the Wessex Budmouth and Dorchester for Casterbridge.[1] King George III appears in it, as does Captain (later Admiral) Hardy.

During this year of intense scrutiny of all his writing Hardy was driven by the need to strengthen, unify, re-embody the half-real, half-ideal Wessex environment of which he saw himself so largely as recorder; to recreate it if necessary. Thus there was a conflict between his original conception of the novel as historical romance and his newly pressing fictional intentions. Not surprisingly the fresh motivation was the more powerful force, and so *The Trumpet-Major* was removed from Dorset and neighbouring regions, and absorbed into Wessex. Exeter became Exonbury, Weymouth became Budmouth. It was as a compensation for the blurring of the sharp historical context that, in the new preface that he wrote for the novel in 1895, Hardy spent so much time stressing the historical accuracy of his recreation of the period in the narrative. It was at this time also that a new and equally compensatory historical descriptiveness in the title-page first appeared. It now became, as it remains in editions universally read today: *The Trumpet-Major John Loveday A Soldier in the War with Buonaparte, and Robert his Brother, First Mate in the Merchant Service: A Tale by Thomas Hardy.*

Perhaps most significant is the balancing in the new title of the two brothers. We may imagine that the process of rereading and revision gave rise in Hardy to an altered sense of the effect of the novel, that he became less certain that Bob Loveday was unworthy, or that John was uniquely heroic. Once we are aware of the revision to the title-page, we can say that by such an alteration Hardy specifically drew our attention to Bob, demanded of us as careful readers that we consider as fully his nature as John's. He made no changes by way of revision to the characterization of Bob in 1895, but his role in the novel is thrown into a new perspective by his inclusion in the title page.

Further consideration of the new title-page suggests that its inclusiveness signals also an absence: why does Anne Garland not find a place on the title-page? Is her name omitted from the roll-call of primary characters because no picturesque historical detail concerning her occupation attaches to it? Or is her failure to be included a way of showing what Hardy regarded as her relative subordination in the narrative? If we entertain the latter explanation, then we at once acknowledge that the seeds of a feminist debate over the novel are already sown in its title-page.

Other elements in the title might be examined – the reference to Bonaparte, for instance, or the definition of the fiction as 'a tale'. There is certainly sufficient material in the several versions of the title, and in the differences between them, to form the basis of a satisfying account of the novel and of Hardy's changing relation to it. At any rate the following chapter attempts such an account with regard to *Under the Greenwood Tree*.

1

Under the Greenwood Tree or The Mellstock Quire?

UNDER THE
GREENWOOD TREE
OR
THE MELLSTOCK QUIRE
A RURAL PAINTING OF THE DUTCH SCHOOL

Hardy could not, it seems from the title-page, make up his mind what to call his novel. In a 1912 addendum to the preface of 1896 he wrote:

> The name of the story was originally intended to be, more appropriately, *The Mellstock Quire*, and this has been appended as a sub-title since the early editions, it having been thought unadvisable to displace for it the title by which the book first became known.

As a description of what actually happened, this contains at least one statement that is deliberately misleading, for the alternative *or the Mellstock Quire* first appeared in print as late as 1907 when the novel was first issued by Macmillan in the pocket edition of Hardy's works. The intentional aspect of Hardy's account is repeated with extra detail in his autobiography, written a few years later:

> The pages of this idyll – at first intended to be called *The Mellstock Quire* but altered to *Under the Greenwood Tree* because titles from poetry were in fashion just then – were dispatched . . . ' (*Life and Work*, p. 88).

If interested readers turn for confirmation of this description to the first page of the surviving autograph manuscript, they will find the following at its head:

The Mellstock Quire,
or
Under the Greenwood Tree – – –
A rural painting of the Dutch School.[1]

The first two lines are cancelled, but they are written in such a way
(placing on the page, relationship to printer's notation, penmanship,
lack of underlining) as to suggest the probability that they were
added as an afterthought at some uncertain date, rather than the
first element in an original composite title. The spelling of 'Quire'
also implies that this element in the title was been added at a
later date, since in the body of the manuscript Hardy's universal
spelling of the word is 'Choir'. Thus, though the manuscript title
appears at first sight to support Hardy's autobiographical account,
on closer examination it is possible to doubt whether at this stage
in the novel's development Hardy had 'The Mellstock Quire' in
mind at all, either as single or as part of a composite title. Quite
plausibly Hardy, in his sixties, with the weight of Wessex tradition
on his mind, felt that he should in 1871 have intended to call the
novel 'The Mellstock Quire', even if such was not actually the case.
Such a feeling would provide a motive for a modestly deceptive
addition and cancellation of 'The Mellstock Quire' at the head of
the manuscript some time after 1906, but most probably during the
process of writing his autobiography.

On the other hand, it is also possible that Hardy, in his two
statements about the title of the novel, recalled accurately his
earliest intentions, which were never inscribed on paper at the time
– or not at any rate on any that survives. The question remains an
open one, and on the side of Hardy's own statements is the powerful
argument that a transition from 'The Mellstock Quire' to 'Under the
Greenwood Tree' would represent accurately fundamental changes
that Hardy made to the structure of the novel while preparing it for
publication.

In the earliest version of the narrative that can be distinguished in
the manuscript, the affairs of the choir were predominant, and the
love-affair between Dick and Fancy (which I take to be represented
by the *Under the Greenwood Tree* element in the title) was primarily
Hardy's vehicle for bringing the reader into contact with a wide
range of local characters besides the choir: the witch, the butcher,
the innkeeper of the Ship, Mr Day and his trapper and his eccentric
wife. In fact in this early version the relationship of the lovers

was a simple matter of love at first sight, meetings, declaration, father's opposition, father's permission, and marriage. There were only three scenes in which Dick and Fancy were alone together: one on the road from Budmouth, and two others illustrating Fancy's rather provoking manner towards Dick – over the cup of tea at the schoolhouse, and the narration of the bird-snaring episode with Shiner.

By the time the manuscript reached the form in which it was sent to the printer the balance had shifted decisively. Fancy and her three suitors became considerably more prominent. The three chapters that include Maybold's proposal and its sequel were added, along with a whole range of hints and suspicions of his interest in her in the earlier part of the novel. Fancy and Dick were given almost twice as much time together, and in particular the nutting episode was added, offering Fancy a chance to become really frightened that she might lose Dick, and thus be forced to express her true feelings for him, and Dick a chance to establish some independence of view, to prevent him from becoming too ridiculously besotted with Fancy.

Through other additions Fancy became (in the new description of her at the tranter's party) specifically the heroine of the novel, and we are given, as a measure of her new importance in the plot, a summary by her father of her background and education. Day himself was also (though in later revisions) made more important in the rural social spectrum, and – so that he might be a more dangerous rival for Dick – Shiner was raised in stature from the landlord of the Old Souls Inn to rich farmer and churchwarden.

The effect of these changes is to bring the love element into the foreground of the novel, and though the first part of the novel remains most closely concerned with the choir, the romantic filaments now spread everywhere. The alterations increased the length of the novel by twenty per cent (adding about forty of the completed manuscript's 194 pages), and to emphasize still further the change that took place in the balance of the novel, it should be noted that some fifteen or sixteen pages were eventually removed from the scenes devoted to members of the choir. This whole process of radical revision may well be thought of as a movement from *The Mellstock Quire* to *Under the Greenwood Tree*.

What seemed the right thing to do in 1871, seemed by 1896 (when Hardy came to revise the novel for the first time as part of Osgood, McIlvaine's collected edition of his work), and even more clearly by 1912 (when he revised it a second time for Macmillan's Wessex

Edition), to have been the wrong thing. In the 1912 section of the preface Hardy wrote:

> In rereading the narrative after a long interval there occurs the inevitable reflection that the realities out of which it was spun were material for another kind of study of this little group of church musicians than is found in the chapters here penned so lightly, even so farcically and flippantly at times. But circumstances would have rendered any aim at a deeper, more essential, more transcendent handling unadvisable at the date of writing . . .

It is not hard to see that the suppression of the traditional church music at the hands of a modernizing, evangelical clergyman would have provided Hardy with a powerful image for the larger extinction of his own class and the culture it represented. A later treatment of the same material would doubtless have included some more or less bitter narratorial reflection on the event itself and on the forces which caused it, while an extra poignancy would have been added to such a new narrative by the reflection that, in terms of 'the realities out of which it was spun', three of the four displaced musicians were members of his own family. If the love-story were to have remained an element in the plot, then Hardy would have found further ironic material in the observation that the vicar was partially motivated in his decision by his sexual attraction to the young pianist who was to replace the bandsmen. We can imagine also that many of the experiences of the musicians recorded in Hardy's poems would have found a place in the narrative, adding, as a contrast to the bleakness of the social and moral analysis, fragments of 'the poetry and romance that coloured their time-honoured observances' (*Life and Works*, p. 17).

It would be a pleasant parodic exercise to write such a 'transcendental' account of the choir's story, and hints are offered by a number of revisions to the novel in 1896 and 1912 which do add small bitter or ironic details, such as the description (added in 1896) of the displaced bees which attack the honey-gatherers as being 'demoralized by affliction' (as the choir, in the novel as it stands, is not). The 1896 preface gives further assistance to such an enterprise by dealing exclusively with the 'realities' out of which the choir's strand of the plot was spun. With one exception, however, the novel remained in 1912 substantially what it had been in 1872, and Hardy's claim in the 1912 preface that 'The Mellstock Quire' would have been a more appropriate title applies only to the story Hardy imagined he might have written.[2] In fact in this preface Hardy, aged seventy-two, appears to allow his regret that forty years earlier he did not perceive the tragic essence and emblematic value of the church musicians' story to obscure for him the real achievement of the novel, an achievement to which the phrase 'Under the Greenwood Tree' provides a stimulating introduction.

The fifth scene of act two of Shakespeare's *As You Like It* begins with Amiens's song:

> Under the greenwood tree
> Who loves to lie with me
> And turn his merry note
> Unto the sweet bird's throat,
> Come hither, come hither, come hither.
> Here shall he see
> No enemy
> But winter and rough weather.

In 1872 Hardy did not believe that change in the rural society he was familiar with, and which he valued so highly, meant extinction rather than evolution. He was also not so certain as he became by the time that he wrote *Jude the Obscure* that the social framework of Victorian England was insidiously destructive of the exceptional individual. Amiens's assertion of social harmony in the forest of Arden is, with some discordant but not disruptive notes, borne out by the subsequent action and the resolution of the play in dance and marriage. In 1912 the implication of such a harmonious resolution in the title of his novel must have seemed to Hardy too much like pointing to the grin on the skull, so intimately was he aware of the vanished village culture of Wessex. But in 1872 he felt differently, and the novel which takes its title from the song also asserts social harmony, though also with the odd discordant voice, and similarly concludes in a marriage-dance. Rich farmer Shiner one night curses the choir, and the next is a guest at their Christmas party. The schoolteacher Fancy Day takes advice from the 'witch' Elizabeth Endorfield. Thomas Leaf the generic village idiot is given a starring role at the end of the novel. Only the trapper Enoch isolates himself from the community. Even in the presentation of the dismissal of the choir from their position as church musicians Hardy sounds the underlying note of social harmony.

It is clear enough that they feel their loss of occupation deeply:

> The old choir, with humbled hearts, no longer took their seats in the gallery as heretofore . . . but were scattered about with their wives in different parts of the church. Having nothing to do with conducting the service for almost the first time in their lives they all felt awkward, out of place, abashed, and inconvenienced by their hands. (p. 167)

The sadness in this is unmistakable and finely observed. Had he written the novel in the 1890s, Hardy might have made the choir view their new unaccustomed position, with or without resentment, as the result of social pressure or of the workings of fate – an instinctive response of rural peasantry to misfortune throughout Hardy's work ("'twas to be and none can gainsay it' on p. 18 is a characteristic example), one which Hardy always criticizes, and which he views as a root cause of the destruction of individuals and social groupings in rural society. In this instance, however, though the choir-members acquiesce in the vicar's plan, they do so not primarily as submitting to destiny, nor does the narrator suggest that they are bowing to an inexorable social force.

In Spring, Chapter II the choir meet to discuss the news that they are to be turned out. The tone of the passage is gently ironic on two levels – the choir themselves speak ironically about Maybold's misplaced evangelical enthusiasm, while the narrator views ironically the villagers' sense that his enthusiasm is misplaced. The mixture is very entertaining, but is abruptly abandoned with the words of William Dewy:

> 'Nobody will feel the loss of our church-work so much as I,' said the old man firmly. 'That you d'all know: I've a-been in the quire man and boy ever since I was a chiel of eleven. But for all that 'tisn't in me to call the man a bad man; because I truly and sincerely believe en to be a good young feller.' (p. 74)

The direct simplicity and honesty of this is in sharp contrast to the previous dialogue, and prepares the way for the tranter, who in rehearsing his speech as spokesman for the deputation to the vicarage, formulates the serious principle that underlies their attitude to the vicar's decision:

'Pa'son Mayble, every tradesman do like to have his own way in his workshop, and Mellstock Church is yours. Instead of turning us out neck and crop, let us stay on till Christmas, and we'll gie way to the young woman, Mr Mayble, and make no more ado about it.' (p. 76)[3]

The eventual confrontation doesn't go quite as smoothly as the tranter proposes, the narrator's main concern being to preserve the comic distance between the participants; but the choir's good-humoured acceptance of the compromise worked out between the embarrassed by-play is based not on Maybold's power as a gentleman to impose upon workfolk, but on their view that he has as much right to dictate affairs in his church as Mr Penny has in his shop. They accept the radical change in the pattern of their lives because they respect Mr Maybold's judgement about what is the right way to conduct the musical portions of the services in his church.

It is an important aspect of the harmonious operation of Mellstock society that in so many ways we are made aware of the significance of the right way to do things. 'Right' is in this context an inclusive word whose signification includes 'traditional', 'proper', and 'effective'. We are encouraged to consider the importance of the right way to make a shoe, take a bee, follow a dance, constitute a choir, perform church music, tap a barrel, make a spar, lift a kettle from a fire, conduct a wedding, tell a story, treat the village idiot, court a girl, visit a vicar, cope with an eccentric wife, and so on. And consequently we are encouraged to grant, as the novel's characters do, authority to those who have the necessary knowledge or skill.

It is also the case that this community is able to assimilate a high degree of individuality. We really discover very little of the thoughts, desires, or personality of anyone in the novel, but we do learn to distinguish characters by their distinctive actions and by their external idiosyncrasies – by the way they plant their feet when walking, the way they account for their china, their habitual tricks of speech – rather in the same way as a dweller in a wood learns to distinguish the characteristic voice of various trees.[4] But if it is the exceptional aspects of some characters that are given prominence (such as Jane Day's way of responding to the presence of Dick Dewy at mealtime or the marriage of her step-daughter) Hardy also indicates the essential supporting structure of ordinary existence:

After a little more preparation and modification, Mrs Day took her seat at the head of the table, and during the latter or tea division of the meal presided with much composure. It may cause some surprise to learn that, now that her vagary was over, she showed herself to be an excellent person with much common sense, and even a religious seriousness of tone on matters pertaining to her afflictions. (p. 101)

Mrs Day's strangeness, Elizabeth Endorfield's witchery, Mrs Penny's fixation about her husband's size, Thomas Leaf's inconsequentiality, are all accommodated within (or subordinated to) the larger images of social integration, and the most inclusive of these is the dance under the shade of the greenwood tree at the end of the novel, which shows the whole community celebrating the union of Dick and Fancy.[5] This pair provide further examples of Hardy's sense that the community is strong and flexible enough to accept and move with change. They represent in the novel perhaps the first generation of Mellstock natives for very many years whose ideas are a force for social upheaval. In some ways Dick has more in common with Fancy than with the older members of his own family: his speech has very little more dialect inflection or syntax than Fancy's, and he uses very few dialect words: if his language is contrasted with either his father's in Spring, Chapter VIII or Fancy's in Summer, Chapters I and II, this will clearly be seen. He has been sent 'to a school so good that 'twas hardly fair to the other children', he has a room of his own (an important distinction in a large family in a relatively small house), he is more conspicuous by his absence from the choir than by his active involvement with it; he is also on quite different terms with the vicar from the rest of the choir, if what he says in the penultimate chapter is anything to go by: 'I can't think . . . whatever 'twas I did to offend Mr Maybold – a man I like so much, too. He rather took to me when he came first . . . ' (p. 188). It is this educated modernness about Dick that allows Fancy in the first place to become attracted to him. But in this novel Hardy stresses that though they are separated by education and youth from its older members, Dick and Fancy are still part of the community, and they join with no sense of unease in the communal ceremonies.

However, they are differentiated in the novel from the other inhabitants of Mellstock by the attention which Hardy gives to moral issues that concern them, beyond the common interests of the community. The motive force of their strand of the novel is in part provided by the fluctuations of the romance itself, but a further theme might be represented in the ambiguity of the word 'good' in the questions of whether Dick is good enough for Fancy, and whether Fancy is good enough for Dick.

The first of these questions is easily settled. The social gradations in Mellstock are carefully established in the novel: Mr Maybold the vicar is (in the absence of the lord of the manor) the only representative of the gentry, and the discordant trapper Enoch enunciates the principle which differentiates the remainder of the characters: "'tis the money . . . For without money man is a shadder' (p. 146). In these terms Dick is clearly not good enough to marry Fancy, and everyone involved accepts it as so. Though his father's business is expanding, so too is keeper Day's, and as Reuben would be glad for Dick to marry Fancy 'her father being rather better in the pocket than we' (p. 109),[6] so Geoffrey is anxious for Fancy to marry farmer Shiner, who is richer still. Indeed in his private thoughts the keeper was aiming yet higher, for in a passage added at a late stage to the manuscript he says that his savings were intended to give Fancy financial equality with 'any gentleman, who sees her to be his equal in polish'.

The last sentence of this same manuscript addition, in which Dick wonders 'at his presumption in asking for a woman whom he had seen from the beginning to be so superior to him' (p. 154), embodies neatly the ambiguity in the concept of value that is at the heart of his relationship with Fancy. Though we recognize that, in a society operating the marriage-money equation as wholeheartedly as that which Jane Austen depicts, she should financially be out of Dick's reach, we might ask as perhaps the more significant question, 'Is she morally superior to him – or even his equal?' The answer has usually been no: Fancy, one might say, has had a bad press from critics, who stress her coquetry, her cruelty to Dick, her deceit – usually in an attempt to show how this novel bears the seeds of the greater tragedies to come. But another view is possible.

In his original conception Hardy had a literary model for Fancy, and though two of the three direct quotations disappeared before the novel was published, one in proof for 1872, the debt is still apparent. At first Hardy used the titular first line of Wordsworth's 'She was a Phantom of Delight' as a title for Spring, Chapter V; and when the chapter now entitled 'A Crisis' was first added to the

novel, it was headed 'A creature not too bright or good', another line
from the poem – which at that point runs:

> A creature not too bright or good
> For human nature's daily food;
> For transient sorrows, simple wiles,
> Praise, blame, love, kisses, tears and smiles.

This seems a reasonable summary of Fancy's nature.

Other fragments of the poem suggest situations in which we see
Fancy: the first verse mentions 'a dancing shape' and the second 'her
household motions light and free'. In the last lines she is described
as 'bright with something of angelic light', a phrase which may well
describe how Mr Maybold at first imagines Fancy. It is certainly
true that when he discovers that she is already engaged to Dick,
he understands that she 'was less an angel than a woman' (p. 174).
The vicar has seen a truth about Fancy; Dick at the end of the
novel has yet to find his disillusionment, but it will surely come.
Dick uses a phrase from the poem to describe Fancy: 'You perfect
woman' (p. 135), to which Fancy replies, 'Yes: if you lay the stress
on "woman"'. And this is a crucial piece of self-knowledge, for what
Hardy is trying to show, and the now disguised literary borrowing
makes it clearer, is the gap between Dick's ideal vision of Fancy and
her reality. For in truth, Hardy suggests, Fancy is very much like
other women.

This is a very man-centred book, and gender-hostility is the only
element of conflict in it. There are plenty of places where a man
expresses some kind of criticism of a woman in particular, or
of women in general; sometimes good-humouredly, occasionally
quite seriously. Women are seen as another and unfathomable
race who do not operate by the laws guiding men. Women like
to have little secrets, are bad at keeping time, are liable to waste
good nutting time in manufacturing attractions for the opposite sex;
they steal promising lads from the true path. And consider these
quotations: 'Shall anything saucier be found than united 'ooman!'
(p. 44); 'Doom is nothing beside a elderly woman' (p. 99); ''Tis a
talent of the female race that low numbers should stand for high,
more especially in matters of waiting, matters of age, and matters
of money' (p. 195).

The tone is one of resignation in the face of an ultimately unknow-
able enemy. When we see Fancy thinking, the narrator will not

commit himself as to what she is thinking about – perhaps because he just does not know; whereas he has no such hesitation with Dick or Maybold, or any of the other male characters of importance. No one can see into Jane Day's curious mind. The same perception of woman as a separate race pervades *Far From the Madding Crowd*, but there Hardy's narrator enters the consciousness of Bathsheba Everdene in a much more confident way, and in his later fiction he came to a clearer understanding of the woman's side of the argument – though conflict it remains, as Tess Durbeyfield and Sue Bridehead bear witness.

Fancy Day is not exempt from this distrust of womankind, but even in a passage that seems to condemn her, there is a positive detail to balance the criticism; the narrator describes 'those beautiful eyes of hers – too refined and beautiful for a tranter's wife, but perhaps not too good' (p. 188). The passage was originally without the 'perhaps', and it is clear that Hardy reconsidered his judgement, admitting that, in spite of her secret, the question of Fancy's moral goodness is still open.

And this change of attitude is only reasonable if we consider her deceit in more detail. Mr Maybold spreads before Fancy a vision of a life for which she has been trained by her education, a range of material benefits that she finds impossible under the pressure of the moment to resist; and he is at least subconsciously aware of his strategy in framing the offer in such terms, when he says: '"Don't refuse: don't . . . It would be foolish of you – I mean cruel"' (p. 171).

She retracts her promise of her own accord, after a night of self-scrutiny, in language that leaves us in no doubt that she will marry Dick of her own free will, out of her own love for 'a trusting and generous man, whom I love still, and shall love always' (p. 177). At two crucial moments Fancy expresses her consciousness of the gap in refinement between herself and Dick in what might seem a heartless way - one at the end of 'A Confession':

'And I love you always – and those times when you look silly and don't seem quite good enough for me – just the same, I do Dick!' (p. 132)

the other before the visit of Mr Maybold:

'I like Dick, and I love him; but how plain and sorry a man looks in the rain with no umbrella, and wet through.' (pp. 169–70)

These quotations are different in their effect, in that the first includes her ungenerous awareness of the effects of Dick's relative poverty within the embrace of her love for him, while the second keeps the two separate; but both contrive to confirm that love. The pattern is repeated on a larger scale in her series of responses to the vicar's proposal of marriage, and when she says in her letter of retraction to Mr Maybold that her wish to keep his proposal secret stems from her desire not to give pain to Dick, we are encouraged by the serious tone of the letter to believe her, whatever little excitement the concealment may bring her later, as she and her new husband leave their wedding-party.

Hardy, it will be remembered, gave to his novel a further descriptive subtitle. Some have seen *A Rural Painting of the Dutch School* as referring to the minutely detailed and lovingly finished cottage interiors of certain Dutch paintings, and there are certainly several scenes in the novel which could well be thought of as fictional interpretations of such a painting. It seems more pertinent, however, to propose that Hardy had in mind one of those busy, filled canvasses that set out to show a representative selection of a village population performing a representative range of rural occupations.

Such paintings are limited by the constraints of their form – by how much of a village society can be presented within the confines of one frame – and also by being frozen in time; so that although a great artist in this genre may show universal human qualities through the dress, gesture, and action of the chosen instant, still the viewer's response must initially be to that single chosen moment and the features of its life. So it is with *Under the Greenwood Tree*. We do not have described for us the whole environment or the total population of Mellstock, and Hardy fixes the community at a period in its development, perhaps the only period, in which the traditional and modernizing social forces which he is exploring were held in balance. Thus the metaphor of the novel as Dutch painting unites Dick and Fancy by the church door with the knot of folk around the shoemaker's shop.

There are, however, other potent agents of social and individual unity in the novel. The dance at the tranter's and the dance at the keeper's are physical embodiments of that harmony which is the dominant note of the narrative, and are explored in the following chapter. The explicitly seasonal framework, beginning in Winter and following the cycle through to a second spring, also embodies

Hardy's purpose in the novel; and within this framework it is the last two chapters which are of particular importance. They represent the turn of a new year to spring once more, and make it clear that Hardy is concerned to emphasize renewal at the end of his narrative. Chapter I of 'Conclusion' begins:

> The last day of the story is dated just subsequent to that point in the development of the seasons when country people go to bed among nearly naked trees, are lulled to sleep by a fall of rain, and awake next morning among green ones; when the landscape appears embarrassed with the sudden weight and brilliancy of its leaves; when the night-jar comes and strikes up for the summer his tune of one note: when the apple-trees have bloomed and the roads and orchard-grass become spotted with fallen petals; when the faces of the delicate flowers are darkened and their heads weighed down by the throng of honey-bees, which increase their humming till humming is too mild a term for the all-pervading sound; and when cuckoos, blackbirds, and sparrows that have hitherto been merry and respectful neighbours become noisy and persistent intimates.

And so vivid is this observation of regeneration of nature that we are encouraged to see the marriage of Dick and Fancy as a renewal of the village life. Although Fancy feels that the wedding-customs of her mother are outdated, she adopts them out of love for her mother's memory and in acceptance of the desires of the other members of the community; and in the same spirit of compromise the tranter wears his enormous gloves (p. 190).

The opening of the last chapter is equally significant in directing our attention to a central concern of the novel:

> The point in Yalbury Wood which abutted on the end of Geoffrey Day's premises was closed with an ancient tree, horizontally of enormous extent, though having no great pretensions to height. Many hundreds of birds had been born amidst the boughs of this single tree, tribes of rabbits and hares had nibbled at its bark from year to year, quaint tufts of fungi had sprung from the cavities of its forks, and countless families of moles and earthworms had crept about its roots. Beneath and beyond its shade spread a carefully-tended grass-plot, its purpose being to supply a healthy exercise-ground for young chickens and pheasants, the hens their

mothers being enclosed in coops placed upon the same green flooring.

This benevolent mutual cooperation in nature is matched by the sense of community founded upon similar relationships, a community that is tough enough to withstand winter storms, like the change in church music, and put out new growths, like this marriage in the spring. Both lovers and the choir show that though (remembering Adam's Fall) there can never be perfect harmony between man and woman and man and man, and though mortal men must not expect their own way entirely, good-will, loving-kindness, respect for each other's craft, suffice to sustain the community through adversity.

The canvas that is *Under the Greenwood Tree* captures the community at a moment when a loss such as that experienced by the Mellstock musicians was interpretable as part of a natural sequence of events cognate with the arrival of a harsh winter that would nevertheless be followed inevitably by a spring that would bring different but related social arrangements and relationships. When Hardy reread the novel in 1896 and 1912 he must most poignantly have regretted that his narrator shared and even reinforced the optimistic sense of the characters that their culture was organically renewable, like the foliage of a deciduous tree, or the seasons. By 1912 he knew that such an expectation of renewal was opposed by the greater part of his experience and by the thinkers he respected most; that the communal virtues embodied in the novel were fragile defences against dominant economic forces in the world and darker powers in the mind and spirit of man. If, to refer to the 'Apology' to *Late Lyrics and Earlier*, we are to see Hardy as an evolutionary meliorist, then this novel must represent the relative innocence which in his later fiction becomes blighted with knowledge, in order perhaps to evolve into some unimagined future innocence in which Tess Durbeyfield will not be violated, deserted, and hanged, and Jude Fawley will not be seduced, frustrated, and abandoned to die.

2
Hardy's Dances

Everywhere for W. B. Yeats, but most famously in 'Among School-children', dance symbolizes a desired unity of being:

> O body swayed to music, O brightening glance,
> How can we know the dancer from the dance?

In this vividly memorable couplet Yeats does (at least) two things. He sets at bay Cartesian dualism, and imagines the lived-body concept of existentialists and phenomenologists who stress the indivisibility of body, mind and spirit, refusing to see the body as mere instrument of mind or spirit. He also recognizes the power of dance to provide a pattern, a ceremony, for action (and by extension life), but goes further to say that the individual is integral with the pattern, so that the dance becomes a model for the harmonious society.

Yeats grew to maturity as a man and a writer during a time (say from 1890–1915) of intense development and experimentation in stage dance, from Loie Fuller to Isadora Duncan and the Ballet Russe. As far as I know Yeats was never a dancer himself (indeed in 'Imitated from the Japanese' he implies as much), but perhaps stimulated initially by that great fan Arthur Symons, he became an intense observer of dance, a study that climaxed in his own 'Plays for Dancers'. For Hardy, on the other hand, dance was part of the essence of growing up. He was, to quote himself, as a child passionately fond of dancing. There is very little else in his autobiography that stimulates such a strongly positive response. Aged nine or ten, at a harvest supper and dance:

> He being wildly fond of dancing, [the lady of the manor] gave him for a partner a little niece of hers about his own age staying at her house, who had come with her. (*Life and Work*, p. 24)

This enthusiasm endured until late middle age. Hardy records a newspaper account of a dance at Rushmore with the Pitt-Rivers's in 1895, and then comments:

> It may be worth mentioning that, passionately fond of dancing as Hardy had been from earliest childhood, this was the last occasion on which he ever trod a measure, according to his own recollection; at any rate on the greensward, which is by no means so springy to the foot as it looks, and left him stiff in the knees for some succeeding days. It was he who started the country dances, his partner being the above-mentioned Mrs (afterwards Lady) Grove. (*Life and Work*, p. 286)

It is not surprising then that for Hardy, as for no other nineteenth century novelist since Austen, dance was an activity of fundamental importance, and if we return from 'Among Schoolchildren' to *Under the Greenwood Tree*, we discover that what Yeats learned from observation, Hardy understood from practice.

It has been my contention that perhaps for the only time in his fiction Hardy in *Under the Greenwood Tree* considers the social forces within a Dorset village, and concludes that though there are potent, even irresistible movements towards change, change will not mean destruction. Of all the indicators Hardy uses to establish this conclusion, dance is the most powerful.

In the novel there are two dances, one at Christmas, the other at a wedding. In noting so much, there is already material for comment. In every society unaffected by an industrial revolution, and in many post-revolutionary societies, dance is a universal response to traditional festivals of a religious or social significance. In Mellstock Christmas dances have been held time out of mind, and although Fancy only just manages to commit herself to the custom of walking round the parish after her wedding (because it is what her mother did), she has no question about the rightness of ending her wedding-day with a dance; and although she imposes a modern propriety of behaviour on the company, the measures she dances are traditional country-dances, performed with great vigour and intensity.[1]

A country-dance, formally patterned but permitting individual variation within the pattern, structured with a combination of unison and individual movements, is a vivid symbol of the vital interactive dynamic and ordered society which developed it. For instance, the division of the sexes in line dances – men in a line from the top to the bottom of the dance facing their women partners in a similar line from top to bottom – is balanced by the alternation of the sexes in ring dances – each woman holding her partner's right hand in her left, and another man's left hand in her right. Figures in which men have the leading role are matched by those in which women dance the most. During the Christmas party in *Under the Greenwood Tree* Hardy describes a dance with a more particular social reference:

> The country-dance called the 'Triumph, or Follow my Lover,' was the figure with which they opened . . . . the comely, slender, prettily-dressed prize Fancy Day fell to Dick's lot in spite of some private machinations of the farmer, for the reason that Mr. Shiner, as a richer man, had shown too much assurance in asking the favour, whilst Dick had been duly courteous . . . . And so the dance proceeded. Mr Shiner, according to the interesting rule laid down – deserted his own partner and made off down the middle with this fair one of Dick's – the pair appearing from the top of the room like two persons tripping down a lane to be married. Dick trotted behind with what was intended to be a look of composure, but which was in fact a rather silly expression of feature implying with too much earnestness that such an elopement could not be tolerated. Then they turned and came back, when Dick grew more rigid around his mouth and blushed with ingenuous ardour as he joined hands with the rival and formed the arch over his lady's head, which presumably gave the figure its name:– relinquishing her again at setting to partners, when Mr Shiner's new chain quivered in every link and all the loose flesh upon the tranter (who here came into action again) shook like jelly. (pp. 50–51)

The dance embodies in its pattern, at the moment when Hardy describes it, Dick's fear (not unjustified) that rich farmer Shiner's evident attraction to Fancy will be reciprocated; that the event represented in the dance, his beloved Fancy being legitimately seized and made off with by his affluent rival, will be enacted in life. Hence Dick's expression.

This moment of erotic fear is, however, contained in the structured pattern of the dance. In the text of the novel this is all Hardy describes of 'The Triumph', because it is the correspondence between dance and life that he wishes to stress. But we also know it is not the end of the dance, and we are aware that in the normal progressive fashion Dick and Fancy will be thus separated and reunited up through the whole line of couples, and on the return down the line Dick will seize the partner of another man and carry her in triumph down the middle of the line, but each time returning to face his partner Fancy. We may well take such fluctuation as an emblem of any enduring human relationship, and certainly of the progress of that between Dick and Fancy as it is offered us in this short novel.

Mr Shiner here, quite properly according to the established custom of 'The Triumph', appropriates Dick's partner. However, in a subsequent dance Shiner has Fancy for his partner, and

'I'm afraid you didn't cast off,' said Dick mildly to Mr Shiner, before the latter man's watch-chain had done vibrating from a recent whirl.

Fancy made a motion of accepting the correction, but her partner took no notice, and proceeded with the next movement with an affectionate bend towards her. 'That Shiner's too fond of her,' the young man said to himself as he watched them. They came to the top again – Fancy smiling warmly towards her partner – and went to their places.

'Mr Shiner, you didn't cast off,' said Dick, for want of something else to demolish him with; casting off himself and being put out at the farmer's irregularity.

'Perhaps I sha'n't cast off for any man,' said Mr Shiner.

'I think you ought to, sir.' (p. 52)

If Shiner and Fancy cast off, it means Shiner has to release Fancy and turn away in an opposite direction to hers. He refuses to do this, wanting greedily to keep Fancy in his arms for as long as he can in defiance of the established pattern. In the course of the following argument, all sorts of issues are raised: Shiner's transgression of the rules marks him, as clearly as his rejection of the carol-singing quire, or his behaviour with Keeper Day's bees, as a social outsider. Fancy, accepting acknowledged authority, would admit error, but Shiner egotistically, autocratically overbears her and the rules. In making his criticism more forcibly, Dick appeals to one of the central ideas in the novel – that each workman, in order to do good conscientious work, must have authority over that work. Though the nameless dance, like an oral ballad, may well have had no single originator, nevertheless Dick's point, that 'a man has hardly any right to hack and mangle what was ordained by the regular dance-maker', is well taken from the point of view of the community of the dance, and the only response that Shiner can make is again to assert his ego against the accepted order. The notion of the social code of hospitality is brought to the foreground by Dick, and there balanced against his own instinct for hostility towards a sexual rival; but before any crisis can be reached, and after ineffectual attempts at mediation, the situation is defused by the host, whose stamping arrival with his partner sets the figure in motion again. The dance, like the society of Mellstock, is flexible and secure enough to absorb such limited individual disruption, and it endures.

Some forms of disruption, however, are final; and in some communities the harmony of purpose has broken down. The dances of such villages are no less images of society. In *Tess of the d'Urbervilles* Hardy describes a dance in a hay-trusser's barn in the decayed market town of Chaseborough. There is no particular occasion for this dance, it marks or seals no ceremony. The participants are the villagers of Trantridge who get up 'a private little jig' for their own purposes. The narrator comments: 'Every village has its idiosyncracy, its constitution, often its own code of morality. The levity of some of the younger women in and about Trantridge was marked, and was perhaps symptomatic of the choice spirit who ruled The Slopes in that vicinity' (p. 65). The dance in the barn is emblematic of that euphemistic 'levity':

> They coughed as they danced, and laughed as they coughed. Of the rushing couples there could barely be discerned more than the high lights – the indistinctness shaping them to satyrs clasping nymphs – a multiplicity of Pans whirling a multiplicity of Syrinxes; Lotis attempting to elude Priapus, and always failing. (pp. 66–7)

Hardy finds in classical mythology a characteristic way of evading Victorian censorship. It is a licentious parody of the country-dance, as different from the dance at the tranter's as the community of Trantridge is from that of Mellstock. All sorts of unnaturalnesses are associated with it: it is held in private because the sexual stimulus that inspired it is too nakedly obvious for the inn; there is no sound from the dancers' feet because the floor is covered with the detritus of peat and hay; they cough and their shapes are vague because the dust also fills the air; the fiddlers 'now and then varied the air by playing on the wrong side of the bridge, or with the back of the bow.' Though we know from the novel's second chapter that Tess likes to dance, the narrator's 'pure woman' must refuse to participate here. The climax of the dance is the ultimate disruption:

> Suddenly there was a dull thump on the ground: a couple had fallen, and lay in a mixed heap. The next couple, unable to check its progress, came toppling over the obstacle. An inner cloud of dust rose around the prostrate figures amid the general one of the room, in which a twitching entanglement of arms and legs was discernible. (pp. 67–8)

A chaos of collapse which perfectly mirrors the narrator's account of the moral state of the community. Tess's aloofness from the dance and its moral implications is no proof, however, against the community's ruling spirit. She encounters Alec d'Urberville immediately before reaching the barn, and upon this final violent farcical close it is Alec's laugh that sounds behind her in comment. A few hours later, and she has, in her own and in society's eyes, become another Lotis.

For Hardy the country-dance can symbolize the state of a specific fictional community; it is also, as an enduring, still vital survival of many centuries, representative of the continuation into an industrialized society of a set of rural certainties. Of the maypole dance at the end of *The Return of the Native* the narrator says:

> The instincts of merry England lingered on here with exceptional vitality, and the symbolic customs which tradition has attached to each season of the year were yet a reality on Egdon. Indeed, the impulses of all such outlandish hamlets are pagan still: in these spots homage to nature, self-adoration, frantic gaieties, fragments of Teutonic rites to divinities whose names are forgotten, have in some way or other survived medi[ae]val doctrine. (pp. 389–90)

The club-walking and dance at the beginning of *Tess of the d'Urbervilles* are seen as the direct descendant of the May-Day dance, and either as benefit-club or as 'votive sisterhood of some sort' the women of the village had walked and danced for hundreds of years. It is an important initial measure of both the community and of

Angel Clare that, an alien from a different intellectual and social culture, the traditional dance can absorb him for the time, though only for a brief time, after which he detaches himself, and leaves with a regretful glance at Tess, with whom he has not danced. Though it is not ritual or organized, perhaps the impromptu dance in *The Return of the Native* begun by Timothy Fairway and Susan Nunsuch among the ashes of the November the fifth bonfire is more vividly representative of the origins of western dance in a pagan past:

'Susy dear, you and I will have a jig – hey my honey? . . . '
  This was addressed to Susan Nunsuch; and the next circumstance of which the beholders were conscious was a vision of the matron's broad form whisking off towards the space whereon the fire had been kindled. She was lifted bodily by Mr Fairway's arm, which had been flung round her waist before she had become aware of his intention. The site of the fire was now merely a circle of ashes flecked with red embers and sparks, the furze having burnt completely away. Once within the circle he whirled her round and round in a dance . . . .
  The vagary of Timothy Fairway was infectious . . . and in half a minute all that could be seen on Blackbarrow was a whirling of dark shapes amid a boiling confusion of sparks, which leapt around the dancers as high as their waists. (p. 28)

Ruth Katz has related the difference between mid-eighteenth century enlightenment and early nineteenth century romanticism to the difference between what she sees as their characteristic social dance forms: as action within a fixed moral and social order gives way to individual responsibility for morality and action, so the formal, highly structured minuet gives way to the whirling sensuous unstructured closed-couple waltz.[2] This transformation, effected in the first decades of the nineteenth century in bourgeois and then in upper-class society, was, however, irrelevant to the rural peasantry in the eighteenth and nineteenth centuries, who never adopted minuet or quadrille, and who were slow indeed to accept waltz or polka. This reluctance may well have been because country dances of all sorts satisfyingly combine the formality of the minuet and the sensuousness of the waltz, intricate line-patterns with whirling turns.
  In a story of 1882, 'The Romantic Adventures of a Milkmaid'

Hardy brings the two traditions together. At some date in the eighteen-forties the milkmaid Margery Tucker saves Baron Xanten from killing himself, and he offers her a reward. She chooses to go to a Yeomanry Ball; the Baron asks her if she can dance:

> 'Reels, and jigs, and country-dances like the New-Rigged-Ship, and Follow-my-Lover, and Haste-to-the-Wedding, and the College Hornpipe, and the Favourite Quickstep, and Captain White's dance.'
>
> 'A very good list – a very good! but unluckily I fear they don't dance any of those now. But if you have the instinct we may soon cure your ignorance. Let me see you dance a moment.'
>
> She stood out into the garden path . . . [and] performed the movements which are even yet far from uncommon in the dances of the villagers of merry England. But her motions, though graceful, were not precisely those which appear in the figures of a modern ball-room.
>
> 'Well, my good friend, it is a very pretty sight . . . But you dance too well – you dance all over your person – and that's too thorough a way for the present day. I should say it was exactly how they danced in the time of your poet Chaucer; but as people don't dance like it now, we must consider.' (*A Changed Man*, p. 312)

This meeting between foreign aristocrat and English dairymaid is imaged in their ideas about dance. When the Baron says 'they' don't dance reels and jigs any more, or that 'people' don't dance as Margery does, he means people of his own class, the only people he has been accustomed to consider. The narrator is quite clear, however that rural working people do still dance like that, even in 1882.[3]

The next day, having made enquiries, the Baron further instructs Margery:

> 'Now reels and such things do not do. For think of this – there is a new dance at Almack's and everywhere else, over which the world has gone crazy . . . . It is really an ancient Scythian dance; but, such is the power of fashion, that, having once been adopted by Society, the dance has made the tour of the Continent in one season.'
>
> 'What is its name, sir?'

'The polka.' (pp. 313–14)

Country-dances may change in detail over a long period of time, and new figures may be added to the repertoire and old ones drop out, but there was, for at least three hundred years, a basic continuity in the dances of the English countryside. These dances were sometimes appropriated by higher classes, and there refined into the contredanse and others. But in the dances of the rural villages there was nothing of the rapid revolution that seemed essential in Society, and seems essential in most social dance today. Margery learns the new dance, and when they reach the house where the Ball is being held, they hear the music and the sounds of dancing:

> The tones were strange. At every fourth beat a deep and mighty note throbbed through the air, reaching Margery's soul with all the force of a blow.
> 'What is that powerful tune, sir – I have never heard anything like it?' she said.
> 'The Drum Polka . . . The strange dance I spoke of and that we practised . . . ' (p. 323)

Hardy understood well that the music was an integral element of the dance, indeed as a child some dance tunes touched him to the soul:

> 'He was of ecstatic temperament, extraordinarily sensitive to music, and among the endless jigs, hornpipes, reels, waltzes and country-dances that his father played of an evening in his early married years, and to which the boy danced a *pas seul* in the middle of the room, there were three or four that always moved the child to tears, though he strenuously tried to hide them. (*Life and Work*, p. 19)

This vivid scene provides also a central moment in one of Hardy's deceptively simple autobiographical poems:

> The Self-Unseeing
>
> Here is the ancient floor,
> Footworn and hollowed and thin,
> Here was the former door
> Where the dead feet walked in.

> She sat here in her chair,
> Smiling into the fire;
> He who played stood there,
> Bowing it higher and higher.
>
> Childlike, I danced in a dream;
> Blessings emblazoned that day;
> Everything glowed with a gleam;
> Yet we were looking away!

And he often comments in his fiction on the power of a tune to drive dancers to feats of endurance:

> As to the merits of 'The Soldier's Joy,' there cannot be, and never were, two opinions. It has been observed in the musical circles of Weatherbury and its vicinity that this melody, at the end of three-quarters of an hour of thunderous footing, still possesses more stimulative properties for the heel and toe than the majority of other dances at their first opening. (*Far from the Madding Crowd*, p. 186)

or

> The air was now that one without any particular beginning, middle, or end, which perhaps, among all the dances which throng an inspired fiddler's fancy, best conveys the idea of the interminable – the celebrated 'Devil's Dream.' The fury of personal movement that was kindled by the fury of the notes could be approximately imagined by these outsiders under the moon, from the occasional kicks of toes and heels against the door, whenever the whirl round had been of more than customary velocity. (*The Return of the Native*, p. 133)[4]

As the Baron and Margery approach the floor of the ballroom, Margery thinks it is made of black ice:

> the figures of the dancers appearing upon it upside down. At last she realized that it was highly-polished oak, but she was none the less afraid to move.'
> 'I am afraid of falling down,' she said.

'Lean on me; you will soon get used to it,' he replied. 'You have no nails in your shoes now, dear.' (p. 324)

The narrator stresses once more the huge social gap between Lord Quantock's dance-floor, the kind of floor that permitted the rapid advance of the waltz amongst the classes who had access to such relatively frictionless surfaces, and the freshly sanded floor of the Tranter's cottage. And, making specific the connection between the new dance and the romantic/industrial revolution, he adds:

A new motive power had been introduced into the world of poesy – the polka, as a counterpoise to the new motive power that had been introduced into the world of prose – steam. (p. 325)

We have been considering dance as an epitome of aspects of society, and there is no doubt that Hardy was aware of the potential of dance as social indicator, even as social criticism. But perhaps more important, and certainly more vivid to him, was dance as it affected the individual dancer. Though when seen from one angle varieties of dance and the practices of dancing can display truths about the society that engages in dancing, seen from another point of view it is possible to say that dance levels all social distinctions.[5]

Once the measure begins your social status, your wealth, your education cease to be important, and the lived body comes into play. Laura Dean said that 'Rhythm is the great leveler which brings us together' (quoted in Fraleigh, p. 193). The formulations of society are all suspended outside this intensely lived moment. Neither soul nor mind seeks any longer to tyrannize the body, for all are combined in communication through the movements of the lived body, in what might be considered an image for a new perception of the unity of being, of the indivisibility of the elements of our nature, an indivisibility innate, but only made palpable in dance. '[D]ancing requires concentration of the whole person as a *minded body* . . . the whole self is shaped by the experience of dance, since the body is besouled, bespirited and beminded' (Fraleigh, pp. 9, 11). Dance theorists have often seen the dancer's body as the instrument of the mind or spirit; Fraleigh is anxious to refute this, and Hardy provides intensely felt examples of that 'unity of self and body in action' (p. 13) which she eloquently proposes. Hardy perceives this unity in daily life, as well as in dance. Fraleigh writes that the body 'does not *have* a consciousness – rather, it *is* a consciousness. When we understand the body in terms of intentional consciousness, body and consciousness take on new meaning' (p. 15). Hardy, describing the way in which the people of Casterbridge unconsciously express themselves not just with the tongue as instrument of the mind, but with the whole minded body, has already seen that this is so:

Not to hear the words of your interlocutor in metropolitan centres is to know nothing of his meaning. Here the face, the arms, the hat, the stick, the body throughout spoke equally with the tongue. To express satisfaction the Casterbridge market-man added to his utterance a broadening of the cheeks, a crevicing of the eyes, a throwing back of the shoulders, which was intelligible from the other end of the street. (*The Mayor of Casterbridge*, pp. 61–2)

'We dance to assure our bodily lived freedom .... Dance frees us from the constraints of our practical lives and utilitarian movement' (Fraleigh, pp. 18–19). When Hardy enters the consciousness of a dancer he is vivid in his expression of the transformation in the relative relationships of body, reason and soul, all brought into a harmony that drives experience beyond the capacity of the features to express.

As a dancer, I am both universalized (like dancers in every culture and time) and personalized (I am my own unrepeatable body; I am my own dance) .... I move beyond the confines of persona (meaning mask or that which *appears* as evidently personal about me) to union with the larger aesthetic purpose of the dance and in communion with others. The magic here is that self is surpassed toward the dance and toward others .... The self that dances I is not the same self that thinks I, not the same self that ordinarily speaks and gestures I. Something changes my perception of myself and of my body as myself in the I that dances I. (Fraleigh, pp. 29–30)

Fragments of these insights are present in this account from *The Return of the Native* of Eustacia Vye dancing with Damon Wildeve:

Through the length of five-and-twenty couples they threaded their giddy way, and a new vitality entered her form. The pale ray of evening lent a fascination to the experience. There is a certain degree and tone of light which tends to disturb the equilibrium of the senses, and to promote dangerously the tenderer moods: added to movement it drives the emotions to rankness, the reason becoming sleepy and unperceiving in inverse proportion; and this light fell now upon these two from the disc of the moon. All the dancing girls felt the symptoms; but Eustacia most of all. The grass under their feet became trodden away, and the hard-beaten surface of the sod, when viewed aslant towards the moonlight, shone like a polished table. The air became quite still; the flag above the waggon which held the musicians clung to the pole, and the players appeared only in outline against the sky; except when the circular mouths of the trombone, ophicleide, and French horn gleamed out like huge eyes from the shade of their figures. The pretty dresses of the maids lost their subtler day colours, and showed more or less of a misty white. Eustacia floated round and round on Wildeve's arm, her face rapt and statuesque; her soul had passed away from and forgotten her features, which were left empty and quiescent, as they always are when feeling goes beyond their register.

How near she was to Wildeve; it was terrible to think of. She could feel his breathing, and he, of course, could feel hers. How badly she had treated him; yet here they were treading one measure. The enchantment of the dance surprised her. A clear line of difference divided like a tangible fence her experience within this maze of motion from her experience without it. Her beginning to dance had been like a change of atmosphere; outside she had been steeped in arctic frigidity by comparison with the tropical sensations here. She had entered the dance from the troubled hours of her late life as one might enter a brilliant chamber after a night walk in a wood. Wildeve by himself would have been merely an agitation; Wildeve added to the dance, and the moonlight and the secrecy, began to be a delight . . . .

Thus, for different reasons, what was to the rest an exhilarating movement was to these two a riding upon the whirlwind. The dance had come like an irresistible attack upon whatever sense of social order there was in their minds, to drive them back into old paths which were now no longer regular. (pp. 263–4)

Fraleigh says 'As the dance is fully realized it ceases to be an object of consciousness; it dissolves in perfected action. To understand the dancer as the dance is to understand a point of unification, which is a state of being when the dance is lived not as an object but as a pure consciousness' (p. 40). This is what Hardy means by 'the ecstacy and the dream':

> . . . by this time every couple had been suitably matched. It was then that the ecstasy and the dream began, in which emotion was the matter of the universe, and matter but an adventitious intrusion likely to hinder you from spinning where you wanted to spin. (*Tess of the d'Urbervilles*, p. 67)

Much depends upon the dance described in the passage just quoted from *The Return of the Native*. The remainder of the novel traces, amongst other things, Eustacia's alienation from her husband Clym, her self-questioning as to whether she loves Wildeve or cares for him enough to elope with him, and her death by drowning. It is unclear whether she falls into the raging weir-pool by accident in the stormy night, or whether she chooses suicide as a way out of her dilemma (or even whether her feet were directed by witchcraft to the weir). It is Eustacia's response to Wildeve's partnership in the dance alone in the novel which encourages the reader to imagine them united; it is at this moment alone that (despite suggestions of sexual intimacy before their marriage to others) there is a union of their lived bodies which implies that a future together is plausible. The more weight one lends to the power of this revelation over Eustacia, the less likely it is that she deliberately killed herself. Hardy has Wildeve drown also in a vain attempt to save Eustacia, so they are joined in death (for the living who remain, and Hardy says nothing here, as he does at a comparable moment in *Tess of the d'Urbervilles*, about the absence of an existence after death). Clym, we may notice, does not dance.

Something of the same is true in the climax of the dance at the tranter's house in *Under the Greenwood Tree*. It is here that the reader is given most vividly the sense that the love-relationship between Dick and Fancy has a physical as well as a romantic existence. They are joined in that transcendent union of mind and body as 'pure consciousness' which is only possible in the dance:

> Again and again did Dick share his Love's hand with another man, and wheel round; then, more delightfully, promenade in a circle with her all to himself, his arm holding her waist more firmly each time, and his elbow getting further and further behind her back, till the distance reached was rather noticeable; and, most blissful, swinging to places shoulder to shoulder, her

breath curling round his neck like a summer zephyr that had strayed from its proper date. Threading the couples one by one they reached the bottom, when there arose in Dick's mind a minor misery lest the tune should end before they could work their way to the top again, and have anew the same exciting run down through. Dick's feelings on actually reaching the top in spite of his doubts were supplemented by a mortal fear that the fiddling might even stop at this supreme moment; which prompted him to convey a stealthy whisper to the far-gone musicians to the effect that they were not to leave off till he and his partner had reached the bottom of the dance once more, which remark was replied to be the nearest of those convulsed and quivering men by a private nod to the anxious young man between two semiquavers of the tune, and a simultaneous 'All right: ay, ay,' without opening the eyes. Fancy was now held so closely that Dick and she were practically one person. The room became to Dick like a picture in a dream, all that he could remember of it afterwards being the look of the fiddlers going to sleep as humming-tops sleep – by increasing their motion and hum, together with the figures of grandfather James and old Simon Crumpler sitting by the chimney-corner talking and nodding in dumb-show, and beating the air to their emphatic sentences like people near a threshing machine. (p. 55)

Dance, Fraleigh says, is a potent force for communion:

While I cannot know the body of the other as he lives his own unique rhythms and energies, I can know the body of the other as he dances it when we are dancing the same dance. Then we are a common presence, bound up together in the rhythm, space, and present time of the dance . . . . This is an occasion for knowing my body as known by another and for knowledge of another through unified lived-body purposing. It is an occasion for mutual fulfillment. (pp. 193–4)

Judith Hanna, attempting to account for the potency of dance as communication, proposes a neurological/psychological rather than a philosophical explanation of what Hardy describes:

The communicative efficacy of dance lies in its capacity to fully engage the human being; it is a multidimensional phenomenon codifying sensory experience. Furthermore, it can lead to altered states of consciousness. Thus, there is a potential multisensory bombardment and saturation . . . . With its multisensory and flow or altered states of consciousness arousal, dance . . . may promote change by circumventing the loading process, our habit of keeping our minds so busy with familiar ideation that unwarranted thought processes have no chance of intruding. The arousal process involves altering central nervous functions. Dance may . . . facilitate right hemisphere dominance, resulting in gestalt, timeless, nonverbal experiences. These are distinct when compared to left hemisphere function.[6]

Of these general insights Hardy's account is a vivid specific example. How else but in the dance is the tranter's son going to experience this unity with the schoolmistress; how else are their mutual consciousnesses of their social differences to be set aside; at what other moment in the novel do we believe so fully in the lived potential of their social as well as their physical union? It is not that the world disappears in the dances Hardy has described, but that it contracts to the space and eternal present time of the dance while consciousness of self and the other expands through the lived-body experience to fill this whole world. The distance between the self and the others is closed as far as it can be closed. Such dances provide 'gestalt, timeless, nonverbal experiences' that change the perceptions of each other of Dick and Fancy, Eustacia and Damon, Donald and Elizabeth-Jane.

Indeed, if the idealizing tendency of the dance-descriptions in *Under the Greenwood Tree* and *The Return of the Native* is set aside, Hardy shows clearly that he believes dance has at its root the physical pleasure of energetic, social, but non-functional movement; and much more often than not, the stimulus of sex. Dancers like the Tranter are rare in Hardy: someone whose physical pleasure in the dance is an end in itself, whose virtuosity in varying the movements within the pattern of the dance is an expression of his imaginative and versatile individuality. For the most part dance is courtship, sexual selection, sexual fantasy. That it is so for Dick Dewy is made clear by his conflict with Shiner over the form of a dance, and the passage just quoted, though early in the novel, assures the reader that he will defeat that particular rival. There is certainly a heavy sexual charge surrounding the dance at East Egdon in *The Return of the Native*:

A whole village-full of emotion, scattered abroad all the year long, met here in a focus for an hour. The forty hearts of those waving couples were beating as they had not done since, twelve months before, they had come together in similar jollity. For the time Paganism was revived in their hearts, the pride of life was all in all, and they adored none other than themselves.

How many of those impassioned but temporary embraces were destined to become perpetuated was possibly the wonder of some of those who indulged in them as well as of Eustacia who looked on. She began to envy those pirouetters, to hunger for the hope and happiness which the fascination of the dance seemed to engender within them (p. 261–2).

The partnership of Damon and Eustacia feeds on this charge, though in the end it is not enough to move them to a life together. When Donald and Elizabeth-Jane Farfrae join hands in the dance after their wedding 'their emotions breathed a much subtler essence than at other times' (*The Mayor of Casterbridge*, p. 326). There is no escaping the sexual intent of the Trantridge dancers; indeed of all of Hardy's dances this has the slenderest formal veil over the potential of dance to become orgy, when cultural and social restraints are weak, and made weaker through the influence of alcohol. Hardy could not, at any rate does not, suggest directly that there was sexual intercourse going on in or around the barn, but several of his poems indicate that such dances could end in such intimacy:

After the Club-Dance

Black'on frowns east on Maidon,
And westward to the sea,
But on neither is his frown laden
With scorn, as his frown on me!

At dawn my heart grew heavy,
I could not sip the wine,
I left the jocund bevy
And that young man o' mine.

The roadside elms pass by me, –
Why do I sink with shame
When the birds a-perch there eye me?
They, too, have done the same![7]

Dancing is one of the activities at the heart of Hardy's Wessex. Wherever it appears it is powerfully symbolic. Dance is a religious or a social ritual: winter is rejected in an impromptu dance among the ashes of a bonfire, spring is welcomed in a dance around a flower-decked maypole, Christ's birth is celebrated in traditional dances; marriages and christenings are sealed by dances.

The patterns of the country dances Hardy's characters perform reflect life-patterns, most obviously in 'The Triumph', but also in the basic elements of hands-across, promenade, spinning, progressing up and down the complete line of dancers, shaping a square or circle dance, taking and breaking partners. Each of these fragments might separately be analysed to show how they symbolize aspects of human existence, from the promise of eternity in the ring-dance to the certainty of transience in the momentary encounter with another in a progressive dance, from the perception of life as a state of becoming in the measured progress of the pattern of the dance, to ideas of death and rebirth implied in the understanding at the close of an individual dance that, within the limits of performance it will be repeated on another similar occasion at another expected time, as the leaves of spring will be repeated after a desolating winter.

A country dance, Hardy shows, is a way of organizing and focussing the chaos of experience and in this is an image of the structures of the society that promotes it; it is a way of permitting the pleasurable exercise of the individual lived body, even of limiting as it stimulates sexuality within the confines of an accepted form. At the same time the engagement in the dance of the lived body at its sharpest intensity promotes exceptional clarity in the individual's awareness of others, and the dance provides a space-time environment in which all barriers to experiencing the other are for the moment dissolved.

Dancing in Wessex and everywhere is communication, of emotions especially, but also of information, as in clumsiness, smell, dress, dominance, conformity to pattern, experience: all sorts of things can be learned in the multi-sensory motion of dance that can be hidden in daily intercourse; or may be revealed in dance when latent in life – rhythmical acuity, physical intensity. Friends and enemies in the dance share hands, for the dance contains the whole society.

All this Hardy knew well at first hand, and his art makes live for us with a livingness beyond the reach of even the most intense theorist or critic.

3

The Return of the Native: Character and the Natural Environment

Everything, even in fiction, has to happen somewhere; but there is no place more remarkable in the rich history of the Victorian novel than Egdon Heath. Hardy wrote at the end of the great flourishing of the realistic tradition in English fiction, a tradition powered by the omniscient narrator; he felt himself bound by its conventions, but often chafed at the constrictions they placed on his ability to communicate his sense of the way the world worked. Most of his finest novels test the boundaries of the tradition, and in this matter of the importance of the place where the events occur in relation to the humans that inhabit it, the significance that Hardy grants in *The Return of the Native* to Egdon Heath comes very close to subverting the normal order of things in the Victorian novel. The heath is not only a vividly evoked environment, it also contains an energy which is felt by all those who dwell on it, an energy with the power to change the natures of those who are at all receptive to it.

When Hardy began work on *The Return of the Native* at the end of 1876, he was himself an imaginatively returning native, deeply stimulated by the decision to return in fiction to the country of his childhood. His perspective was that of a man of 36, married two years, experienced in life in London and Europe, fresh from a concentrated period of reading in contemporary science and philosophy, classical and renaissance literature; and he was creating, through the accounts of his narrator (who seems in this novel to share much of his perspective), and through the words of his characters, a version of the physical and social environment which had permeated his early years.

We are introduced to the heath before we are to any of the characters, and it is at once marked out for the reader as an environment
set apart, extraordinary, strange. And it is not surprising that we
find in this first chapter, and indeed throughout the novel, a curious
relationship between the childlike and the sophisticated, in which
the adult and the adolescent sometimes vie, sometimes coalesce
in the narrative voice. We might say that the child growing up
absorbed many of the elements out of which the novel is formed,
and the grown-up presents and explains them.[1]

Here, for instance, is the first sentence of the novel: 'A Satur-
day afternoon in November was approaching the time of twilight,
and the vast tract of unenclosed wild known as Egdon Heath
embrowned itself moment by moment.' The image of any stretch
of countryside in southern England as 'a vast tract of unenclosed
wild' is essentially that of a young child. To small feet wandering
over it, like those of Johnny Nunsuch, the heath must have seemed
interminable, like the Sahara or the Amazonian rain forest which the
description evokes. Part of the child's vision too, is the animation
of the heath, imagined here drawing darkness down upon itself.
These impressions of the child's mind, however, are made to seem
reasonable and unexaggerated by being presented in a measured
adult tone and vocabulary.

The famous opening chapter continues in part with other images
of childhood on the heath interpreted by the highly-literate adult
voice of the narrator: the child's fears of storm and ghosts and bad
dreams; the child's sense that time on the heath is different from
time elsewhere; that Egdon is not only boundless in extent, but is
the one unchangeable, permanent thing in his world, indeed that it
is in a sense *the* world. But interspersed with these intensifications
of childhood visions and anxieties there are sophisticated accounts
of the heath's emblematic quality as a pattern for modern man,
and of its place in geological and historical time, which only the
grown-up could have conceived, and which only such a fully
imagined environment could sustain.

The heath, throughout the novel, is like an island of heather in
a sea of agricultural land, and its inhabitants seem as distinctly
cut off from other society as the inhabitants of an off-shore island
would be. The island is inviolate, and inviolable. It is, we are
constantly reminded, full of life; a creeping, growing, observing
aggregation of plants and animals and birds. The rules which guide
experience on the heath are not quite those which do so elsewhere;

the heath has a language of its own which requires learning for full comprehension.

It was not until the revision of the novel in 1895 that this child's vision-illusion about a stretch of land in the midst of Victorian England began to fray at the edges. In a preface Hardy then added to the novel under pressure of a desire to assure his readers of the authenticity of the world he describes in the novel, he admits that Egdon was in fact a composite of many existing heaths, which, far from being unchangeable or inviolate, have long been fragmented by incursions of intensive agriculture and forestry. Thus he undermines the imaginative reality with which he has endowed Egdon by application of historical and topographical reality, a process which is enhanced by revisions to the novel itself over a period of years.

In no other attribute does the heath more fully demonstrate its separateness from ordinary experience than in its ability to control or ignore the effects of time. In the first chapter the narrator writes that 'the face of the heath by its mere complexion added half an hour to evening; it could in like manner retard the dawn' (p. 3), and later he notes that 'in the course of many days and weeks sunrise had advanced its quarters . . . sunset had receded . . . but Egdon had hardly heeded the change' (p. 105), and then there is the comment that 'on Egdon there was no absolute hour of day' (p. 130). Of the heathdwellers it is only Eustacia with her hourglass who seems particularly concerned with the passing of time; on Egdon minutes are too small a unit to be of value as dividers of time; indeed to Egdon the passing of the seasons is no more than a day: the 'flowering period represented the second or noontide division in the cycle of those superficial changes which alone were possible here; it followed the green or young-fern period, representing the morn, and preceded the brown period when the heath-bells and ferns would wear the russet tinges of evening . . . ' (p. 241). Moreover untouched Egdon encompasses all conceivable scales of time, from the geological to the hour by hour passing of each day. Clym at one moment in the novel finds himself in prehistory: 'The air was warm with a vaporous warmth, and the stillness was unbroken. Lizards, grasshoppers and ants were the only living things to be beheld. The scene seemed to belong to the carboniferous period, when the plants were few, and of the fern kind' (p. 206); lovers meet observed by the Celts buried in the mound on Blackbarrow; the heath is recorded in Domesday, by Leland, and it has not changed.[2]

It is not that the heath is a world outside time, but rather that time does not have the same significance that it does in Budmouth or Paris.

Thus Hardy has devised from his experience and his imagination an isolated, self-enclosed environment, where time itself is ambiguous – an environment he must have felt from the start was a particularly appropriate arena for the exploration of extraordinary passions.

For Hardy any landscape, however singular in itself, is ultimately only valuable for its human associations. It is worth noting how, at the end of the second chapter of the novel, the human figure on top of the barrow is seen in aesthetic terms as the justification of the whole composition; and this account stands also as a summary of Hardy's attitude to environment in general – that it only gains significance when brought into relation with man. But the interrelationship of man with Egdon is of a kind rarely found elsewhere. The Celts built their burial mound, but otherwise the heath has repulsed human attempts at transformation; even Wildeve's small patch of cultivated land on the edge cost the lives of two men before it could be established, and there is a strong sense that without intense vigilance the patch will return again to heather and furze. All occupations on the heath are concerned with the nurture and harvest of what naturally occurs there, furze and turf for the most part; and this labour hardly interrupts the slow continuous process of decay and regeneration that is Egdon's natural state.

Since this activity barely alters the heath, man's relation with it is a different sort of thing from the relation of those who cultivate land with their fields or orchards or woodlands. When Clym becomes a furze-cutter, he becomes a representative example of this symbiosis on the heath between man and nature, at times almost becoming a fragment of it; and there are moments when the heath seems to absorb the humans: Eustacia and Wildeve like horns on a snail, put out and then withdrawn, for instance, or in the same passage, Venn concealed beneath the turves. It *is* a symbiosis, not a domination. the heath cannot be dominated, it can only be co-operated with; Eustacia understands this, and finds it humiliating.

Egdon is a place where the temporal concerns of conventional Victorian society seem petty, almost irrelevant. Clym returns from the city with a countenance that is becoming worn with thought and concern; the heath provides an environment in which 'the incipient marks of time and thought' become smoothed out (p. 207). And yet paradoxically the attitudes and beliefs of Victorian society are the essential material of the plot.

Clym comes from Paris burdened with Comtean or socialist ideals; Eustacia comes from Budmouth with dreams of social splendour; Wildeve has trained somewhere as an engineer; Mrs Yeobright has the desires of an entrepreneurial social materialist; even Thomasin feels, in the face of Victorian convention, that she has to go through with her postponed wedding, despite her diminished affection for her future husband. It would seem at first thought that the heath would be an unfitting environment for the play of such ephemeral and passing concerns, and, indeed, we find by the end of the novel that Eustacia, Wildeve and Mrs Yeobright are dead, Clym is transformed, and Thomasin is widowed. And yet as the characters progress through the events that lead to this conclusion, we are made aware that the heath is the element in which the story moves, the element which has conditioned the formation of the characters (to a greater or lesser extent), and which is an agent in their ends. Again it is a matter of symbiosis: for better or worse they all pass their lives in the heath; the heath, for better or worse, assists in shaping those lives.

Hardy designed Clym and Eustacia as natures opposed in certain ways, brought together for disaster by catastrophic sexual passion. In no way does this seem clearer than through their attitudes to the heath: 'Take all the varying hates felt by Eustacia Vye towards the heath, and translate them into loves, and you have the heart of Clym' (pp. 175–6). Earlier in the same paragraph the narrator says: 'If anyone knew the heath well, it was Clym. He was permeated with its scenes, with its substance, and with its odours. He might be said to be its product. His eyes had first opened thereon . . . ' And yet he has been sent off to Budmouth and then Paris to become a rich gentleman; it has taken him a number of years to realize that such a life is intolerable to him, and he returns to Egdon with the atmosphere of these places clinging to him, stimulating Eustacia to hopes of release from the heath through union with him.

Eustacia, in a reverse pattern, spent her formative years in Budmouth, a seaside resort of fashionable society and considerable sophistication by comparison with Egdon, and she came to live with her grandfather on the heath after Clym had left it. Despite her background, despite her unwillingness to be where she is – ''Tis my cross, my misery, and will be my death' she says (p. 82) – it is accurate to say that Eustacia too is what she is at the beginning of the novel in large part because of the heath. She has been left free by her grandfather to wander at will across the heath, night and day; consequently (the narrator says) 'Egdon was her Hades, and since coming there she had imbibed much that was dark in its tone, though inwardly and eternally unreconciled thereto' (p. 64). Thus there is charted at once a conflict between the inhaled vapours, the darkness of the heath absorbed into her unconscious and bloodstream, and her conscious determination never to be reconciled to the heath; a permanent state of rebellion between parts of herself, and between herself and her environment. Clym, on the other hand, appears never to be out of harmony with the heath.

Eustacia knows nothing of the history of the heath, she hasn't learned its tongue. In her first proper conversation with Clym she says that she hates Nature, and cannot endure the heath (though she excepts its purple season, what Hardy in the first chapter had called the only time that the heath touched gaiety, an exception which emphasizes the opposition in her between her conscious desire for the brightness of high summer and her unconscious absorption of the darkness of the heath). She says she is unaware of the existence of any Druidical stones in her neighbourhood, but is aware of a Promenade in Budmouth. When she marries Clym, it is as if she is marrying the foreigner of the narrator's simile, consciously rejecting his language ('To dwell on a heath without studying its meanings was like wedding a foreigner without learning his tongue' p. 67–8); Clym's tongue *is* Egdon. To Venn (p. 89) she grudgingly admits that there is a sort of beauty in the scenery, but asserts that nonetheless the heath is a jail to her, a prison.

And yet it is quite possible to love or to hate someone whose language you do not trouble to learn. Eustacia is intimately familiar with the topography of the heath: her hatred of it doesn't result in her staying indoors and brooding all the time; she goes out, particularly at night (imbibing darkness), the feel of a path beneath her feet when she can't see it is as vivid to her as to any of the other heathfolk. She is calmed, in an image that seems significant, by the branches of the furze combing her hair – she'll do it again. She doesn't tear in angry rebellion at the brambles that catch her skirt, but leisurely untwists them. Against her will she finds herself instinctively in harmony with aspects of the heath, and this harmony fuels her conscious rebellion against it. This deeply buried harmony is also, though, the strongest thread of feeling that draws Eustacia and Clym together in sexual passion, and binds them one to the other.

Had Eustacia remained in Budmouth, she might, or even would have been quite unremarkable, one of dozens of pretty flirting girls milling around the soldiers and the gallants. The heath drives her inward, forces her to damp down the surface of her passionateness while intensifying the sexual energy within; it gives her a sense of her own dignity and makes her potentially a tragic heroine. The isolation and insulation of Egdon allows her to be superior as well as to imagine her superiority. And yet as a prison it makes her desperate; love in a prison can be satisfying only for a while. She and Clym live together for a couple of months in their Alderworth retreat in bliss; but as Hardy says, when you are driven against each other in such isolation with only each other as resource, then the initial sexually driven passion burns itself out at a rapid rate, and the surface of personality buried under the weight of desire is burned clear, and, if not softened by loving-kindness, may take shapes surprising to the beholder.

In the end Eustacia refuses to learn one lesson of the heath well understood by Clym, Thomasin and Diggory: patient endurance. The heath is in harmony with the storm and wind because its profile is low – heather, fern, furze – offering no points of resistance. Eustacia is full of points of resistance, and when the tempest at the end of the novel arouses Egdon, the heath, in harmony with it, becomes in Eustacia's mind most intensely her enemy. The narrator makes the point clearly in a contrast with Thomasin, to whom 'there were not, as to Eustacia, demons in the air, and malice in every bough and bush. The drops which lashed her face were not scorpions, but prosy rain . . . ' (p. 367). And so, resisting, despairing, we see Eustacia driven by her vision of the heath to her death, whether we hold it to be accident or suicide.

The novel leaves us on a fine summer afternoon with the figure of Clym standing on Blackbarrow, talking to Egdon folk about the importance of lovingkindness in personal relationships. We view him from a distance as Diggory viewed Eustacia in the same place at the beginning of the novel, and the narrator makes the point that the essential change in the scene is from darkness to light. Until the last book, much of the action of the novel has taken place in darkness; Egdon is a near relation of night; Eustacia is so fond of walking in darkness that the narrator calls her queen of night. With her death much of the darkness is removed from the novel, but so also is most of the passion. Egdon is calm and sunny and filled with flowers, Thomasin and Diggory contract a respectable marriage, Clym finds his muted vocation. But that restrained energy which Eustacia shared with the heath, which she used futilely in fighting it, has departed.[3]

4

The Trumpet-Major,
A Laodicean and
Two on a Tower: The
Man-Made Environment

In 1879, after the publication of *The Return of the Native*, Hardy seems to have felt that he could for the time go no further in his fiction in his exploration of the relationship between his characters and the natural environment, and in three middle-period novels he gradually evolves the notion that buildings might give form to the essentials of a narrative in the way that the Heath does in *The Return of the Native*. Buildings had sometimes been prominent in earlier novels, and the narratorial debate about the value of medieval barn, church and castle in *Far From the Madding Crowd* is one example of how they might carry thematic significance. But it cannot be said of any earlier novels that buildings – their literal presence and symbolic associations – are a structural element in them.

It would be eccentric to suggest that an exploration of the role that buildings might play in his fiction was a primary impulse behind *The Trumpet-Major*. He was interested, rather, in writing a historical novel, a novel of the period of the Napoleonic wars. It is, however, possible to show that the historical action is contained, and to an extent embodied, by the significant dwelling-places in the novel – Overcombe Mill, Oxwell Hall, the buildings of Budmouth, and the military camp on the down.[1] These structures, permanent or temporary, are at least half-integrated into the historical theme of the book, and are partially instrumental in defining character.

The nearest that Hardy comes to a statement of an idea of history in the *The Trumpet-Major* is when Anne Garland is in Budmouth and sees the King on the Esplanade. The narrator observes of her that she felt herself close to and looking into the stream of recorded history, within whose banks the littlest things are great, and outside which she and the general bulk of the human race were content to live on as an unreckoned, unheeded superfluity. (p. 111)

From time to time through the novel the reader is also an observer on the banks of this stream, visiting Captain Hardy, watching the *Victory* pass Portland towards the coming battle of Trafalgar, even seeing Anne dip a toe into it as she speaks with the King. But the moving-water metaphor finds an expression also in Hardy's summary of unrecorded history:

Thus they crossed the threshold of the mill-house and up the passage, the paving of which was worn into a gutter by the ebb and flow of feet that had been going on there ever since Tudor times. (p. 27)

The mill-house, like the family of the miller, is for Hardy a representative part of the unhistory of the country, what we now know as local history, and which many consider to be the most useful basis of any historical knowledge; in this, as in other things Hardy was ahead of his time. The common virtues of miller and mill are early established, and never lost sight of; their long-enduring foundations ('Miller Loveday was the representative of an ancient family of corn-grinders whose history is lost in the mists of antiquity . . . a vast body of Gothic ladies and gentlemen of the ranks known as ceorls or villeins, full of importance to the country at large, and ramifying through the unwritten history of England' [p.10]), their usefulness, their value to the community. We might to advantage compare both family and building with the Poysers and their farmhouse in George Eliot's *Adam Bede*. If this distinction between recorded and unrecorded history underlies the action, then the mill-house and its garden and river may also be seen to embody part of the action itself:

Overcombe Mill presented at one end the appearance of a hard-worked house slipping into the river, and at the other of an idle genteel place, half-cloaked with creepers at this time of the year, and having no visible connexion with flour . . . .

In the court in front were two worn-out millstones, made useful again by being let in level with the ground. Here people stood to smoke and consider things in muddy weather; and cats slept on the clean surfaces when it was hot. In the large stubbard-tree at the corner of the garden was erected a pole of larch-fir, which the miller had bought with others at a sale of small timber in Damer's Wood one Christmas week. It rose from the upper boughs of the tree to about the height of a fisherman's mast, and on top was a vane in the form of a sailor with his arm stretched out. When the sun shone upon the figure it could be seen that the greater part of his countenance was gone, and paint washed from his body so far as to reveal that he had been a soldier in red before he became a sailor in blue. The image had, in fact, been John, one of coming characters, and was then turned into Robert, another of them. This revolving piece of statuary could not, however, be relied on as a vane, owing to the neighbouring hill, which formed varying currents in the wind. (pp. 11–12)

The double nature of the building in this description is appropriate to the inhabitants of its partitioned state at the beginning of the novel, the idle Garlands and the busy Lovedays. As the two families grow closer, become united by marriage, so the external and internal dividing lines of the house become blurred and broken down. Discarded fragments of the mill machinery are found further useful functions to serve; and the weathervane, with its interchangeable figure that alters direction when the wind blows, anticipates accurately in its complication the relationship between Anne Garland and Miller Loveday's two sons. Even the final detail of its unreliability as a vane finds an echo by the end of the novel, in Hardy's demonstration that Anne's choice between the two sons is not made under the influence of any recognizable rational or moral breeze, but rather by the unaccountable breath of her own instinct, which proceeds from heaven knows where.

Both the mill and Oxwell Hall, the second important dwelling in the novel, were originally manor-houses, and both have undergone a social decline; but whereas the mill has turned from pleasure to fruitful industry, the Hall has become a farm through neglect rather than design, and its function as byre, yard and farmhouse is presented in terms of decay, at odds with the original grandeur. There has been no loving care, no conscious transformation, and it is as if old Derriman, whose home it is, camps rather than lives there. Both man and house are crippled by miserliness, and the house seems as clearly condemned to slow decay and ultimate destruction as Derriman. However the Hall still stands when the farmer dies, and the terms of his will, by which the heroine Anne Garland inherits the house, promise good hope of a regeneration and renewal.

If Derriman's occupation of Oxwell Hall seems impermanent, almost as if he were squatting, the third structure of interest is impermanence itself – not a building at all, but the tented camp of the soldiers on the down above Overcombe. The camp is the connection between the stream of history that runs through Budmouth for the span of the King's presence and the permanent unhistorical unmetaphorical streams that run past the mill and the Hall; it is on the fringes of both, it has a foot in either world, entertained by one, serving the other; temporary, movable, evanescent, the conductor through which Anne and others reach in to recorded history. It is the temporary home of Anne's temporary lover, whose temporary stay on the earth ends upon an indefinite but historical bloody battlefield in Spain. The transient nature of John's canvas dwelling balances the mercurial flighty nature of Bob Loveday, helping us to accept Hardy's choice for Anne.

It must be accepted that Hardy has not fully integrated his perception of the historical distinction between the two erstwhile manor-houses on the one hand and King George's Budmouth on the other, or of that between the mill and the Hall, into the thematic texture of *The Trumpet-Major*. But it seems right nonetheless to see in the novel the beginning of Hardy's feeling out of a way to express metaphorical relationships between buildings and his themes and characters.

It may have been that Hardy only realized how useful and important buildings might be for his purposes in the course of writing *The Trumpet-Major*. It cannot be coincidental that George Somerset, the hero of his next novel *A Laodicean*, is an architect. Unfortunately if it *was* Hardy's intention in *A Laodicean* to explore further the potential of buildings, the serious illness he contracted while writing the novel undermined his intention. It is only in the first two parts of the novel and at the very end that we can see how the approach might have developed.

When Somerset traces a telegraph wire through an arrow-slit in the wall of a feudal castle, the action becomes an occasion for reflection on the contrasts between new and old, between Victorianism and medievalism, couched at times in paraphrase of Matthew Arnold:

There was a certain unexpectedness in the fact that the hoary memorial of a stolid antagonism to the interchange of ideas, the monument of hard distinctions in blood and race, of deadly mistrust of one's neighbour in spite of the Church's teaching, and of a sublime unconsciousness of any other force than a brute one, should be the goal of a machine which beyond everything may be said to symbolize cosmopolitan views and the intellectual and moral kinship of all mankind. In that light the little buzzing wire had a far finer significance to the student Somerset than the vast walls that neighboured it. But the modern fever and fret which consumes people before they can grow old was also signified by the wire; and this aspect of today did not contrast well with the fairer side of feudalism – leisure, light-hearted generosity, intense friendships, hawks, hounds, revels, healthy complexions, freedom from care, and such a living power in architectural art as the world may never again see. (p. 22)

This contrast between new and old is taken up and reflected in other ways: the medieval castle belongs to Paula Power, the daughter of a successful entrepreneur; she lives only in a fragment of the structure, and when Somerset, in exploring Stancy castle, comes across her modernized rooms the narrator reflects that:

These things, ensconced amid so much of the old and hoary, were as if a stray hour from the nineteenth century had wandered like a butterfly into the thirteenth, and lost itself there. (p. 40)

She lives in the castle with the daughter of the last de Stancy to own his feudal inheritance, and just as the structure contains new and old, so Paula and Charlotte de Stancy represent new and old. Charlotte inherits the de Stancy face, and its feudal attitudes, but her father is very different, having accepted his social decline, and being insistent above all upon frugality. The house in which he now lives reflects this, and embodies the oppositions voiced in the first paragraph I quoted earlier. Initially the suburban villa is described in the language of an estate-agent's dream, in which the irony is unmistakable:

Genuine roadside respectability sat smiling on every brick of the eligible dwelling. (p. 47)

But in the following paragraph the tone changes dramatically; Somerset notices:

> a canary singing a welcome from a cage in the shadow of the window, the voices of crowing cocks coming over the chimneys from somewhere behind, and the sun and air riddling the house everywhere.

And this alternation of irony and appreciation continues throughout the description, so that in these first chapters of the novel we have modern pettiness and modern brilliance set against medieval splendour and medieval darkness and decay; and this theme operates through both characters and buildings, only to get lost in the search for incident to fill out episodes which became all that Hardy could cope with in his illness. But at the end of the novel it resurfaces in the destruction by fire of Stancy castle, and the proposal of Somerset, now married to Paula Power, to design a new house, eclectic in style, to stand beside the ruins of the old. And though they have made this commitment to the new but eclectic, the last words of the daughter of the quintessentially Victorian success, the railway entrepreneur, are: 'I wish my castle wasn't burnt; and I wish you were a de Stancy.'

In *A Laodicean* we can see what Hardy might have done; in *Two on a Tower* the symbolic substructure of the novel, based on buildings, is as successful and multifaceted as that based on Egdon Heath in *The Return of the Native*.

The novel begins rather deceptively:

> On an early winter afternoon, clear but not cold, when the vegetable world was a weird multitude of skeletons through whose ribs the sun shone freely, a gleaming landau came to a pause on the crest of a hill in Wessex.

The detail from the vegetable world and the mention of Wessex seem to suggest that this might be the first sentence of a book like *The Woodlanders*; but the presence of a gleaming landau represents the true note of the novel more accurately; even though Mrs Charmond might have possessed such a carriage, one cannot imagine Hardy beginning *The Woodlanders* with a reference to it. The mention of Wessex is especially misleading, for *Two on a Tower* shares little of the community of spirit, place and culture implied in that name. The novel could have been located anywhere, and the precise topography of its action in relation to any map of Wessex remains uncertain. It is only in the occasional presence of rural workfolk that Wessex surfaces.

Clearer, and important in the novel's symbolic structure, is the relative location of the significant buildings described in the narrative. The salient features are two groupings: the tower on Rings Hill, the temporary hut built at its foot and the farmhouse in Welland Bottom, which lie to the north of the turnpike road, and Welland House and Church to the south. Thus the crest of the road on which the heroine of the novel causes her landau to be halted divides her great House from the column in which the following paragraphs show her to be interested. This physical division is echoed in the structure of the novel.

The tower is a very ancient and a very potent symbol, and most critics who have said anything about *Two on a Tower* have discussed its significance. There is at the outset a relationship between Viviette Constantine's husbandless state and the phallic shape of the tower. Though the conscious reason for her interest in it is the broad view obtainable from its summit, yet it seems probable that the subconscious motive is sexual in origin. And when she has been jolted across the arable land in her carriage, has climbed the hill, and reaches the foot of the column, Hardy provides a description which possesses a phallic charge of some strength:

> The gloom and solitude which prevailed around the base were remarkable. The sob of the environing trees was here expressly manifest . . . some boughs and twigs rubbed the pillar's sides . . . . Below the level of their summits the masonry was lichen-stained and mildewed, for the sun never pierced that moaning cloud of blue-black vegetation. Pads of moss grew in the joints of the stone-work, and here and there shade-loving insects had engraved on the mortar patterns of no human style or meaning; but curious and suggestive. Above the trees the case was different: the pillar rose into the sky a bright and cheerful thing, unimpeded, clean, and flushed with the sunlight. (pp. 3–4)

And it is indeed true that she finds sexual satisfaction as a result of entering the tower; but Hardy's symbolic design is subtle and complex, and before that occurs we are invited to read the passage

I have just quoted in a slightly different light, and the tower sheds its sexual role, as will be seen later. In the meantime it is worth examining the other external symbolic burdens that the tower carries in these introductory chapters.

In describing its situation the significant words that Hardy uses are 'isolated' and 'insulated'. In modern usage we would, I think, consider these two words related, but distinct in meaning. In 1800 this was certainly not the case. Both words are relatively recent additions to English. 'Insulate', a characteristic renaissance formation from the latin *insula* or *insulatus*, meant originally 'to make into an island by surrounding with water'. The first figurative uses of the past participle are recorded early in the eighteenth century, with the meaning 'standing apart' or 'solitary'; it is more difficult to know when its present primary sense (deriving particularly from use in connection with electricity) of 'prevention from escape by a surrounding medium', became current figuratively.

'Isolate' is a still more recent acquisition; the verb is in fact a back-formation from 'isolated'. This entered the language through the use in the later eighteenth century of the French *isolé* to represent the figurative use of 'insulated' which was growing at the same time. By 1800, the *OED* reports, a publication called *The British Critic* could write 'The affected, frenchified and unnecessary word *isolated* is not English, and we trust never will be.'

It seems clear from Hardy's use that he did consider them distinct, and I believe that this distinction is important for him. The tower, we are told in the first page, stands upon a circular isolated hill, amidst an extensive arable field, with no track, let alone a road, approaching it. It appears, as Norman Page has pointed out, like an enchanted castle whose access is surrounded by tests of the seeker's endurance.[2] It is one of the thematic ironies of this novel that the conventional pattern of sexual relationships is reversed, and it is so in this aspect as elsewhere. The traditional fairy-tale arrangement is inverted, and it is the princess who is in quest of adventure, perhaps erotic adventure, and who stumbles on a beautiful youth in a tower – Swithin St Cleeve, guardian of the key to the column, and passionate astronomer, who has set up his telescope on the summit. That the tower is isolated by the field allows them to keep their meetings there secret; that it is insulated by the field preserves the charge of emotional and spiritual love that is generated within it. These qualities of isolation and insulatedness remain in force in some measure to the end of the novel.

As well as a phallic image, and an enchanted dwelling, the column also looks from a distance like a telescope; it is built in the plain unfluted Tuscan Doric order of architecture to make the resemblance stronger, it is itself a hollow tube pointed at the stars, and the fittest place for Swithin's observatory. For John Bayley in his fine essay in the first volume of *The Thomas Hardy Annual* (London: 1982, p. 64) 'It is the tower that is in the imaginative foreground, and the tower is only incidentally an observatory. In one aspect it is a strange man-made object in its natural setting: in another, a symbol of marriage itself. Or at least of a love-relation involving marriage.' It seems to me, though, that love and looking at the stars are fused in the symbol of the tower rather than separated.

Once we gain the interior of the tower, once we see the relationship between lady and astronomer grow, the pure exteriority of the symbol fades and in its place comes what Yeats (with his genius for symbol) represented by tower and winding stair, the union of masculine and feminine, direction and indirection, aspiration and emotion, body, perhaps and soul – as Bayley says, a symbol of marriage itself. Hardy refers often enough to the spiral staircase to make this anachronistic connection with Yeats not merely an intellectual exercise. And as we see the growth of love within the tower, Hardy disentangles the sexual element of the relationship between Swithin and Viviette from the emotional and spiritual, and locates it at the foot of the tower, in the darkness of the plantation. It is at the foot of the tower that Swithin is enlightened by the gossip of the workfolk, but it is outside the tower, in the hut that Viviette has paid for, that the physical expression of their relationship is centred. And the opening description of the tower quoted above takes on a different aspect in the light of this development, contrasting as it does the brightness and clarity of the tower's summit, with the suggestive darkness of its base.

The hut is built near the foot of the tower so that Swithin can have somewhere to sleep after late nights at work at the top and not disturb his grandmother in the farmhouse at Welland Bottom. At the same time as he recognizes his love for Viviette, he (as far as the novel is concerned) abandons the farmhouse; and the only shelter for his body that we are told about until Viviette sends him away from her, is this cabin. It is thus directly connected with their relationship; it is as Swithin says the 'palace' to which he brings Viviette back from their wedding at Bath (with its proleptically ironic reference to Viviette's subsequent marriage to Bishop Helmsdale and his palace), it is their bridal chamber, and later it is where their son is conceived. Its relation to the tower is indicated again on the morning after the lovers' first night together: they sit outside eating breakfast while

> at their elbow rose the lank column into an upper realm of sunlight which only reached the cabin in fitful darts and flashes through the trees. (p. 150)

The passage consciously echoes the first description of the tower, and directs the reader to the separation that has taken place of the physical and the spiritual aspects of love. They never make love on the tower, and when, in a 1912 revision, Viviette makes time to visit Swithin after their marriage and the resumption to outward appearances of their separate lives, it is in the hut, not the tower, that they meet.

For a while the tower and the hut are bound together in the gloomy and passionate darkness that surrounds them, and though hidden, the lovers' relationship is whole. But eventually circumstances combine to drive Viviette to sacrifice her happiness to Swithin's future, one might almost say to his ambition, and to send him abroad to study the strange stars of another hemisphere. The idea, the spirit of their love survives, as the tower survives, but the physical reality of their relationship is broken, as the hut is dismantled on Swithin's departure. And more: as it is dismantled, Viviette has the timbers numbered so that it can be re-erected in exactly the same form as before, when Swithin returns, just as she hopes that when he comes back he will help to reconstruct their relationship on the same terms as before. The cynical remarks of the workmen who take down the cabin relate to both the hut and what it symbolizes:

> the young man would as soon think of buying a halter for himself as come back and spy at the moon from Rings-Hill Speer, after seeing the glories of other nations and the gold and jewels that were found there . . . (p. 271)

For Swithin the tower has always been an observatory, and only passingly the vessel of his emotional awakening; from time to time Hardy has shown us Swithin in the character of the scientist with no horizons beyond those he scans; even in love he has none of the emotional surcharge that fires Viviette – he remains practical and as nearly detached as eagerly loving permits. They only marry so that his work may continue without interruption from the frustrations of unsatisfied love. The tower, as I have said, looks like a telescope, and in its role as aspirational structure it is the fit home for intellectual activity – this has been recognized from Milton's philosopher in *Il Penseroso* to Shelley's Prince Athanase. Yet Hardy is ambivalent both about science and the scientific temperament as it is embodied in Swithin. In one sense it is admirable, expressing Man's great desire to expand his knowledge beyond its perceived bounds, to increase thereby his stature. But at the same time it can be arid and inhuman when measured by other criteria, and Swithin is saved from this aridity by Viviette, saved from excluding from his life human relationships, and love the intensest of those relationships, in order to stretch human knowledge. Thus, as I have said, the symbol of the hollow tower twined by its winding stair. And when Swithin abandons Viviette to take up his legacy and sails for South Africa he leaves that saving grace behind.

The tone of the narrative towards his astronomical work at Cape Town is altered quite substantially from the eager interest that both narrator and Viviette show towards his activities on the tower's top. This is made clear discursively, and through image and symbol. As he receives Viviette's letter explaining her marriage to the Bishop, his response is:

> as one who suddenly finds the world a stranger place than he thought; but is excluded by age, temperament and situation from being much more than an astonished spectator of its strangeness. (p. 296)

At the end of three years work in Cape Town Swithin has achieved much; but the narrator chooses to commence the account of his achievement thus: 'His memoranda of observations had accumulated to a wheelbarrow load . . . ' (p. 299). And at the end of a description of the nature of his work there is this:

> In these experiments with tubes and glasses, important as they were to human intellect, there was little food for the sympathetic instincts which create the changes in a life . . . . Swithin's doings and discoveries . . . were no doubt, incidents of the highest importance to him; and yet from an intersocial point of view

they served but the humble purpose of killing time, while other doings, more nearly allied to his heart than to his understanding, developed themselves at home. (p. 300)

That the attitude to the scientific work is dismissive seems evident, more vividly so in the image of the wheelbarrow than the succeeding generalization perhaps. Still more interesting in this context is a slightly earlier passage that describes the setting up of Swithin's telescope at the Cape:

Unable to get a room convenient for a private observatory he resolved at last to fix the instrument on a solid pillar in the garden; and several days were spent in accommodating it to its new position. (p. 297)

In abandoning Viviette, putting his astronomy before his human relationship, he has caused the tower to harden and diminish, becoming 'a solid pillar', excluding the possibility of 'intersocial' activity, remaining aridly functional.

When he does return to Welland it is only because he has finished his work, not because Viviette is again a widow, or because she has also returned. There is no hut for him, and he comes back to the farmhouse in the Bottom, where amongst others, he meets Tabitha Lark, of whom more below. Intending, the day after his return, to visit Viviette at the great House, his attention is attracted to the tower by a transitory effect of light, which shows a figure at its summit. He changes direction towards it, 'for the spot seemed again like his own'.

When Swithin re-enters the tower he finds Viviette and their son at the top. As the narrator points out, 'the Swithin who had returned was not quite the Swithin who had gone away', and he is shocked by her faded aspect into silence, which she interprets accurately and tells him to leave her: '"Swithin, you don't love me," she said simply.' And it is true. But what Swithin has to offer her is marriage, not in the same spirit of passionate love symbolized by the combination of tower and cabin, but in the spirit of loving-kindness, of which the narrator says, that it is a sentiment perhaps in the long run more to be prized than lover's love. Swithin turns on the stair, reascends and embraces, kisses Viviette; but she cannot survive the intensity of her passionate renewal of joy and dies in his arms.

It then becomes a question of whether the novel is in part at least not another of Hardy's essays on the destructiveness of lover's love and of the value of loving-kindness; of whether in this context the tower is not also in opposition to the cabin, the light to the darkness. As I said earlier the complexity of Hardy's symbolism in this novel is greater than one might imagine.

And even this is not the last word from the tower; in an addition to the last paragraph of the novel made in the first edition, Swithin looks up for assistance with the insensible Viviette and sees

> Tabitha Lark, who was skirting the field with a bounding tread
> – the single bright spot of colour and animation within the wide
> horizon. (p. 313)

She is 'skirting the field', she has nothing to do with the tower, and yet it has been made sufficiently clear to us, even without this final hint, that Tabitha is a much more appropriate mate for Swithin. We may, though, imagine that he will never experience with her the union of body and spirit that the tower and cabin have symbolized; nor will he experience the destructiveness that the union can bring.

The buildings on and near Rings-Hill, however, are only half of the careful pattern, half of the significant structures in the novel, Swithin's domain, penetrated at times by Viviette.[3] Set against them are Viviette's realm, Welland Church and House, where occasionally Swithin is found. The first description we have of the church is at sunset:

> The heavy, many-chevroned church, now subdued by violet
> shadow except where its upper courses caught the western stroke
> of flame-colour, stood close to her grounds . . .

and a paragraph later, as Viviette enters the church:

> The semi-norman arches with their multitudinous notchings,
> were still visible by the light from the tower window, but the
> lower portion of the building was in obscurity . . . (pp. 83–4)

The most striking feature of these passages is the deliberate way in which they echo the first description of the tower, the darkness of the lower part shaded by trees and the brightness of the upper, flushed in sunlight. When revising the manuscript Hardy was perhaps worried that this parallel might escape his readers, and so in the second passage he altered 'visible by the light from the west window' as it originally read, to 'visible by the light from the tower window'. This church is Viviette's spiritual, aspirational home, as Rings-Hill Speer is Swithin's, its tower standing up to Heaven as the column stands up to the heavens, its roots in the Christian burial ground which joins it to Welland House, as Speer and cabin are rooted in the prehistoric pagan burial ground on which they are built. This parallelism is best shown within the two characters by comparing the extasis that Swithin experiences when examining and pondering the stars with this description of Viviette's experience in church:

> She knelt till she seemed scarcely to belong to the time she lived in, which lost the magnitude that the nearness of perspective lent it on ordinary occasions, and took its actual rank, in the long line of centuries. Having once got out of herself, seen herself from afar off, she was calmer . . . (pp. 84–5)

It is further evidence of the conscious intention within this passage that 'seen herself from afar off', the core of the connection with Swithin's seeing himself in relation to the far-off galaxies, was only added in the first edition.

The parallel is inescapable; but once it has been established, Hardy is mainly concerned to show the basic contrast between the two. Even in its darkness the tower has life and energy associated with it: the church is associated with oppression and death.

In the description of the church quoted above there were other revisions in the manuscript: the opening words 'The heavy, many-chevroned church, now subdued by violet shadow', with their emphasis on *heavy* and *subdued*, originally read 'The quaint and handsome church, now bathed in violet shadows' with a quite different effect. The church is also described at the time of the confirmation service; the girls in their white dresses

> lighted up the dark pews and grey stonework to an unwonted warmth and life. On the south side were the young men and boys, – heavy, angular and massive, as indeed was rather necessary, considering what they would have to bear at the hands of wind and weather before they returned to that mouldy nave for the last time. (p. 175)

And again the emphasis is on heaviness and death, an emphasis which here too has been reinforced through an alteration to the manuscript: the 'warmth and life' that the girls bring to the dark pews, with its implication that without them it is cold and dead, was originally merely 'gaiety'.

When Viviette goes into the church in chapter eleven, intending to resign Swithin to 'some maiden fit and likely to make [him] happy', she is saved from her sacrifice and her sin in one stroke by the news that she is a widow; but it is no coincidence that playing the organ as Viviette sits beneath the tables of the law, is Tabitha Lark, the 'fit' maiden. At Swithin's confirmation service in the church, representing the visible triumph of Viviette's emotional Christianity over Swithin's instinctive scientific paganism, the narrator insistently makes the same point:

> Handsomest woman in the church [Viviette] decidedly was; and yet a disinterested spectator who had known all the circumstances would probably have felt that, the future considered, Swithin's more natural mate would have been one of the muslin-clad maidens who were to be presented to the Bishop with him today. (p. 175)

And though Tabitha is not being 'presented', but is again playing the organ, Swithin has more direct and intimate contact with her during the ceremony than with Viviette, who is now his wife.

These two passages might be held coincidental – after all an organist is likely to be found in the church – were it not that in the first the organist was originally the schoolteacher, and only in a revision Miss Lark, and in the second the incident in which Swithin and Tabitha converse during the confirmation service is heavily revised to augment the solicitude with which he attends to her distress. And were it not also that there is a third scene in the church in which Hardy is drawing still more deeply upon the parallel symbolism I have noted. While Swithin is waiting for an appointment with the Bishop in the graveyard, he enters the church and ascends the tower in order to see what is going on in the adjoining garden of Welland House. As he observes Viviette together with her brother and the Bishop, and is in the dumb-show of receiving blown kisses from her, Tabitha Lark suddenly appears at his side on the tower. Swithin is surprised, and with some reason. Though she says she has come to play the organ, still, her motive in ascending the tower can hardly be the simple curiosity to know what he was looking at that she suggests it is. And this is underlined by their conversation, which takes a turn equally surprising to Swithin and the reader:

> 'The Bishop is a striking man, is he not?'
> 'Yes, rather,' said Swithin.
> 'I think he is much devoted to Lady Constantine, and I am glad of it. Aren't you?'
> 'O yes – very,' said Swithin, wondering if Tabitha had seen the tender little salutes between Lady Constantine and himself.
> 'I don't think she cares much for him,' added Tabitha judicially. 'Or even if she does, she could be got away from him in no time by a younger man.'
> 'Pooh, that's nothing,' said Swithin impatiently. (p. 197)

And with this rather inadequate remark the dialogue terminates. The tone and intention here are hard to assess. It almost seems that Tabitha is teasing Swithin, and Swithin perhaps suspects it; but either way the conversation suggests a greater intimacy between the two than we might otherwise have suspected.

Thus, as far as the reader is concerned, the relationship between Swithin and Tabitha (such as it is) is seen until the end of the novel entirely within the context of the church, the church which is Viviette's spiritual resort, and which by thus promoting encounters between the man she loves and another, younger woman, may be seen ultimately to betray her. If the church is seen also as the traditional place for weddings, it seems reasonable to suggest that Hardy is implying that the future of Swithin and Tabitha is to be joined there in matrimony; and the last pages of the novel can only reinforce this impression. 'Lady Constantine was,' the narrator explains, 'necessarily either lover or *dévote*'; but we might consider that for most of the novel, she is both. And there is a third strand to her temperament: the woman of convention who is responsive to the codes of society in general and her own class in particular. It is this aspect of her nature that insists upon keeping the marriage with Swithin secret, and it is this side of her character that is embodied in her House, her retreat, almost empty, dark, secure.

There is a revision in the manuscript near the beginning of Chapter 38 which illustrates Hardy's awareness of the potential of this connection between Viviette's commitment to Society and the great houses which it inhabits. She is sitting in a train taking her to Southampton, where Swithin is, as she thinks, on board a ship about to leave harbour. In the first manuscript version the narrator indicates her anxiety by commenting that 'The lovely scenes through which she was dragged had no points of interest for her now.' But in reconsidering the passage Hardy realized that he could express the same anxiety in a way that also directed the reader's attention to her major underlying preoccupation; and it becomes: 'The changeful procession of country seats past which she was dragged, the names and memories of their owners, had no points of interest for her now' (p. 275).

Welland House, then, symbolizes Viviette's sense of her position in the county, about which she is extremely sensitive; and it represents a refuge to which she can retire if she wishes, when her strength outside is insufficient to resist the forces attempting to break down her allegiance to the county code.

The central action of the second half of the novel is Viviette's decision to postpone her remarriage to Swithin for five years so that he can enjoy the fruits of his legacy and advance his position in astronomy. The narrator sees this as heroic self-sacrifice, almost martyrdom; and stresses the way in which the essentially christian virtue of altruism, self-sacrifice, conquers both her desire for Swithin, and her desire for social conformity: 'Thus she laboured, with a generosity more worthy even than its object, to sink her love for her own decorum in devotion to the world in general, and to Swithin in particular' (p. 257). The human greatness of this act is beyond doubt, but its relation to the building symbolism already established, and to subsequent events, undermines the premisses upon which it was built.

Her renunciation might be seen as wrapped around with betrayal; it is in the cabin which has been their bridal chamber that Viviette comes upon the document which leads to their separation; it is in the Great House which represents in such tangible form her commitment to the values of her society, that she decides to set aside those values; we have already seen how the church, whose moral teaching she is following here with such pain to herself, is offering Tabitha Lark as her replacement. Hardy admires her action, recognizes the love that inspires it, but believes that it is fundamentally misguided.

It is not chance that leads Viviette and Swithin to make love in the cabin on the night that they part for good, nor is it accident that Viviette becomes pregnant; it is the expression of their need for each other beyond considerations of wealth or ambition, and as such must have a powerful effect upon their lives; it is, one might say, the cabin's amends for its previous betrayal.

As soon as she realizes she is pregnant, her need for marriage for social conformity, increases beyond the power of her altruism to inhibit it, and she frantically tries to reach him before he leaves – but in vain. At approximately the same time the Bishop of Melchester renews his offer of marriage to her (urged by Viviette's brother), and she accepts him. Her need to conform to social convention might be seen as the revenge of the House on the morality of the church.

In all this the tower has remained inviolate; the observatory has been removed, but the walls and the winding stair within do not change; it is still the seat of that love which goes beyond the physical, and which Hardy believes to be the most important element in human life. He has examined scientific aspiration, social codes, religious morality, and found them all insufficient without that community of two people in loving-kindness that is symbolized by the tower. Viviette has shown her greatness of spirit throughout the novel, but Hardy has shown that it is based on wrong assumptions. By herself she is not strong enough to move beyond the conventions which she acknowledges, and Swithin is too weak to help her. He accepts her decision that they should part half through ambition, half because he has no will to oppose hers to the end. Thus it is right that they should meet for the last time on the tower, and it is beyond doubt right that she should die from joy – it is the most generous ending that Hardy could conceive. Swithin is simply not great enough for her, as Damon is not for Eustacia.

I began this discussion by pointing out the isolation of the tower; one might say that isolation in this novel is pervasive, and in this respect the novel anticipates *Jude the Obscure*. We are confronted with human isolation in face of the stars; Viviette is isolated in her House from all that she is accustomed to; indeed Welland itself is isolated. In face of all this isolation Hardy proposes that it is only the human loving relationship that keeps this isolation at bay; and without that, science, society and religion are sterile, even deadly.

5

The Mayor of Casterbridge: The Fate of Michael Henchard's Character

In editions read today the title-page of the novel always identified as *The Mayor of Casterbridge* in fact reads *The Life and Death of the Mayor of Casterbridge: A Story of a Man of Character*. This is a complex announcement, almost every substantive element of which rewards inspection, but it is perhaps more appropriate to begin further back historically, for, as with other novels, Hardy only gradually came to this fully-fledged description of his fiction. The earliest version of the title, written at the head of the holograph manuscript and used for both English and American serializations in 1886, was simply *The Mayor of Casterbridge*. There are also two intermediate versions to consider. When Hardy revised the text of the novel for the English first edition towards the end of 1886, he decided to provide a more elaborate title: *The Mayor of Casterbridge: The Life and Death of a Man of Character*. Contemporary reviewers found material in this statement on which they could base a critical discussion of the novel, and in one of those characteristic responses to the fooleries of critics to which Hardy found himself throughout his life only too prone, he reduced this version when the novel was first reprinted in 1887 in one volume to *The Mayor of Casterbridge: A Story of a Man of Character*. It remained thus for Osgood, MacIlvaine's collected edition, and Hardy only reintroduced the 'Life and Death' element, in the form we now know it, in 1902 when Macmillan printed a new title-page for their issue of an impression of the Osgood plates.

To return, then, to the earliest, simplest title. The first question it provokes is why *The Mayor of Casterbridge*, not *Michael Henchard*? Why is Henchard's function more important than his name? The force of this question is intensified when it is remembered that he is mayor for less than half of the novel. A partial reason for the choice is probably to be found in one aspect of the novel's supporting structure of reference and allusion – classical and medieval theories of tragedy (almost purely Aristotelian, as Dale Kramer points out),[1] which demand that the tragic hero shall be a man of high social status, for whom the wheel of fortune will turn downwards. One of the novel's major topics is the nature and function of the town of Casterbridge (as the early title also suggests), and the mayor of the town is its first citizen under the crown. Although in England appointment or election to an important but temporary office does not for the most part entitle the holder to use the title for the rest of his or her life, nevertheless to have been mayor provides sufficient social status for the operation of the rules of tragedy in Henchard's rapid and inexorable decline from that status and what it implies.

Conformation with the conventions of tragedy is, however, a superficial justification for Hardy's apparent concentration on Henchard's office; the name mayor means more to Henchard than it would to most others entitled to use it. To explore a little further it is useful first to go back eight years to *The Return of the Native*, Hardy's first attempt at an overtly tragic novel. The chapter entitled 'Queen of Night', the seventh of the first book, is the narrator's major attempt at defining Eustacia Vye, the tragic centre of the novel. Like the whole novel (and *The Mayor of Casterbridge*) the chapter is a chaos of references and allusions, but the tendency of the whole is expressed in the first paragraph:

> Eustacia Vye was the raw material of a divinity. On Olympus she would have done well with a little preparation. She had the passions and instincts which make a model goddess, that is, those which make not quite a model woman. Had it been possible for the earth and mankind to be entirely in her grasp for a while, had she handled the distaff, the spindle, and the shears at her own free will, few in the world would have noticed the change of government. There would have been the same inequality of lot, the same heaping up of favours here, of contumely there, the same generosity before justice, the same perpetual dilemmas, the same captious alternation of caresses and blows as we endure now. (p. 63)

By raising this image of Eustacia ruling the world, Hardy deliberately draws attention to his insight that it is in part frustration at her lack of power in any area of life save the sexual, at her lack even of the possibility of ever obtaining such power, which drives Eustacia to the actions that lead ultimately to her death. Hardy intensifies this frustration by placing her in an environment where even her sexual energy and authority have an extremely limited range of potential subjects to subdue and control.[2]

In some interesting ways *The Mayor of Casterbridge* can be seen as a sequel to *The Return of the Native,* and in the current context it may profitably be suggested that if, in the preceding quotation, feminine nouns and pronouns were changed to masculine, and 'Eustacia Vye' to 'Michael Henchard', the passage would (in isolation) remain effective. The essential difference between the two characters is that, being a man, Henchard has the freedom and the opportunity, as he certainly has the desire, to attain power, to achieve a certain amount of control over a small section of earth and mankind. On the other hand, when we first see him he faces, in his class, another disabling obstacle (while he believes he has a second in his wife and child). The young Michael Henchard, like Eustacia Vye, is deeply ambitious, but Hardy chooses not to show the process by which, having shed one supposed impediment at Weydon, he manages to transcend the other in Casterbridge and reach his limited but real as well as symbolic power as Mayor. The narrator tells us that it is his great energy that has subdued others, made him rich, and persuaded the ruling class of Casterbridge that they would do well to let him, rough as he is, run their Town Council. We may, on reflection, not feel that such an explanation is fully adequate, but the fact that we are habituated to calling the novel *The Mayor* substantially helps Hardy persuade the reader to credit his brief account. It is almost as if we are persuaded to believe that the office was Michael Henchard's birthright.

It is not only his crossing of social barriers and his rise to power which are handled cursorily, but also his wielding of power. We are presented with no real evidence about what difference it made to any aspect of Casterbridge that Henchard was mayor. In part we accept that it is Henchard's wealth that represents his real power, and that his mayoralty is a sign of his power rather than an addition to it; but it is also true that Hardy is much more interested in the personal than in the political or social uses of power. It is further true that if the desire for the power that wealth and office can bring were all that motivated Henchard, if to be Mayor of Casterbridge sufficed him, then however tragic his fall, Hardy would scarcely be interested in him.

When Henchard has finally told Elizabeth-Jane that she is his daughter the narrator comments:

> He was the kind of man to whom some human object for pouring out his heart upon – were it emotive or were it choleric – was almost a necessity. The craving of his heart for the re-establishment of this tenderest human tie had been great during his wife's lifetime, and now he had submitted to its mastery without reluctance and without fear. (p. 125)

At this stage in the novel the desire to love is as strong in Henchard as the desire for power; and there is a further connection with *The Return of the Native*. In the same chapter as that already quoted from, 'Queen of Night', the narrator announces concerning Eustacia Vye: 'To be loved to madness – such was her great desire' (p. 66). We can adapt this announcement also to Henchard thus: 'To be permitted to love to madness – such was one of his two great desires.'

Vye's method of ruling others is through their passionate enslavement to her, it is her only available way to power; seen thus simply, she is what many contemporary readers of the novel would have called a bad woman. Henchard wants to subdue others through his passionate devotion to them. The fragment from p. 125 quoted above refers to Elizabeth-Jane, but it could apply equally to Farfrae earlier in the novel. Henchard's relationship with Farfrae is complicated, however, by his other desire. While Henchard still retains his office and his wealth, his desire for the power they bring remains strong, but (once an appropriate object appears in the person of Farfrae) his latent and perhaps not quite so strong desire to be allowed to love comes into conflict with his desire for power. It is not inevitable that it should do so: Farfrae might have been a woman (though Henchard's rather remote affair with Lucetta is all the evidence we have that he can be moved to love a woman as he loves Farfrae), in which case love need have been no obstacle to the maintainance of Henchard's power; he might have been a doctor who cured him of some obscure illness instead of curing his wheat, in which case, similarly, there need have been no opposition between Henchard's twin desires. But as circumstances (or the novelist) would have it, Farfrae's arable knowledge and his economical efficiency, his very qualifications for the position of manager, bring about a conflict in Henchard between his desire to maintain his status, and his desire to love Farfrae.

When the crisis comes, when it is apparent that Farfrae's authority in business carries more weight with the farming community than Henchard's, when Henchard perceives himself in danger of being 'honeycombed clean out of all the character and standing that he's built up these eighteen year' (p. 107), the narrator carefully points out that it would be possible for Henchard to compromise by getting Farfrae to marry Elizabeth-Jane, and (by implication) for him to retire gracefully from active business, providing the cash to finance his son-in-law's success. The firm would still be Henchard and Farfrae, and he might mellow into a Casterbridge landmark. But Henchard cannot voluntarily mingle and thus diminish his two desires; they will remain incompatible and in conflict so long as the obstacle to one is the object of the other.

From this crisis in the narrative the sequence of Henchard's attempts to love is rapid. Abandoning Farfrae as an object of love he turns to Elizabeth-Jane, only to find that she is not his daughter, and that the kiss of her cheek 'he had prefigured for weeks with a thrill of pleasure' tasted of dust and ashes. Abandoning Elizabeth-Jane he turns to Lucetta, only to find that she has turned to Farfrae. In his bid to retain the power of wealth and status he drives to economic and social ruin. The graphic emblem of his defeat is the replacement of his own name by Farfrae's on the sign above his old headquarters, but Farfrae has not only taken over Henchard's business, he has also married the woman Henchard intended to marry, and has pretty well bought all that Henchard possessed. When Farfrae becomes mayor the reversal is complete, though Henchard's desire for power is not yet fully quenched.

Abandoned by Lucetta he turns inward and to drink. His first act, though, under the renewed influence of alcohol is to force the church choir to sing the commination psalm at Farfrae; such hate is only the obverse of his love. Farfrae now treats him patronizingly as an object for charity, unable to recognize him as the same man who befriended him at the beginning of his time in Casterbridge; this patronage provokes Henchard to competition once again, first to test (at the royal visit) how far his once secure power still resides with him and then (after his social powerlessness is made evident even to him) to demonstrate that his physical strength will provide him with another kind of power over Farfrae. But beneath this hostility to Farfrae is the abiding love.

He wrestles Farfrae, and has him at his mercy. Farfrae says he should take his life: 'Ye've wished to long enough.' Henchard's reply, as their eyes meet, their bodies in a close violent embrace, is (bitterly) 'O Farfrae – that's not true . . . . God is my witness that no man ever loved another as I did thee at one time . . . . And now – though I came here to kill 'ee, I cannot hurt thee! Go and give me in charge – do what you will – I care nothing for what comes of me!' (p. 273). The sequel makes it clear that the desire to be allowed to love Farfrae is by no means yet dissipated: after Farfrae goes Henchard was so thoroughly subdued 'that he remained on the sacks in a crouching attitude, unusual for a man, and for such a man. Its womanliness sat tragically on the figure of so stern a piece of virility' (p. 274).

Why is the posture of submission womanly? Perhaps because it is conventionally the role of the woman to play the weaker part, to long for reconciliation, for reinstatement of regard, of affection, to want to sue for the return of love. Henchard murmurs to himself: 'He thought highly of me once . . . . Now he'll hate me and despise me for ever', and the narrator continues: 'He became possessed by an overpowering wish to see Farfrae again that night, and by some desperate pleading to attempt the well-nigh impossible task of winning pardon for his late mad attack'. When Henchard does find him he says: 'Oh, Farfrae, don't mistrust me – I am a wretched man, but my heart is true to you still!' (p. 286) Henchard, the bull-like man, the man of strong appetites, powerful desires, apparently thoroughly masculine, overturns the conventional expectations of the novel's Victorian readership; his passion is in submission rather than domination; he wishes to give love, to adore, rather than to be adored. Like Eustacia Vye, he is in erotic terms a character subversive of the norms of the dominant culture.[3]

Farfrae, the representative of that culture in the novel, doesn't believe him, probably cannot comprehend him. He has insufficient imaginative sympathy to understand the complex of desires in Henchard, he cannot respond to the richness and power of a phrase like 'my heart is true to you still' in the mouth of a man.

The episode has finally buried Henchard's desire for power, and he finally ceases to be mayor. His desire to love is all that remains, and Elizabeth-Jane is now the only possible object for that desire. Under pressure from overpowering need, in a characteristically impulsive moment, he tells Newson that his daughter is dead. From that moment of radical deception he is loving on borrowed time.

He sees Elizabeth-Jane and Farfrae often together: he hates the possibility of their union, he cannot accept that such a marriage would be good for her and for him any more now than he could when he and Farfrae first began competing commercially. The narrator says that uncompromising powerful impulsive desire is 'the idiosyncracy of Henchard's which had ruled his courses from the beginning, and had mainly made him what he was. Time had been when such instinctive opposition would have taken shape in action' (p. 304), but now the 'netted lion' schools himself in restraint as he tries to hang on to Elizabeth-Jane. Henchard is to the community of Casterbridge dangerous like a wild animal; thus the network of allusions connecting him with the bull that threatens Lucetta and Elizabeth-Jane, and the references to his 'tigerish affection' (p. 91), and (after his defeat) to himself as a 'netted' and 'fangless' lion (pp. 303, 309). So long as his energy and strength can be harnessed safely for the good of the community it is prepared to give him the right he craves to assume power as mayor and to use for its benefit that energy and strength. Casterbridge is, however, relieved when, through Henchard's misjudged application of those energies in his commercial competition with Farfrae, it can deprive the barely controllable individual of power. And now he suppresses his instincts and desires in subjection to the perceived will of the beloved.

Later on the same page the narrator comments further on Henchard's subjection: 'The *solicitus timor* of his love – the dependence upon Elizabeth's regard into which he had declined (or, in another sense, to which he had advanced), denaturalized him.' It is a decline because though he needs desperately to be allowed to show human affection, he has up to now never submitted his own will or need or desire to any object of his affection, has never sought to alter his nature in order to retain affection; it is an advance because his life (and those of others) might have been less painful if he had tried earlier to alter his nature, and now at the last gasp he is beginning to see that there are communal needs and rights which in ordinary human intercourse, let alone loving relationships, require respect. In his bare need, perhaps for the first time in his life, the desire to be loved is equal in him with the desire to love.

Once we develop from the narrator's hint these alternative views of Henchard's dependence on Elizabeth-Jane, we are also forced to consider our response to the transformation that he has effected. Do we regret the Henchard who was proud, fiery, driven by imperious desires, uncaring of consequences, ruthlessly honest, but destructive of himself and others around him if they could not stand up to him, or escape? Or do we feel it is right, or a cause for gladness, that he is humbled, socialized, taught to respect and consider the lives and needs of the community if he would gain his own ends, that he becomes devious, indirect, but potentially a productive member of the social organism, a proper relation for the proper Elizabeth-Jane?

It is not an easy opposition to resolve, and it is clearly possible to hold both views at the same time, as perhaps Hardy did. In the event the question is not sustained for long, for the final object of Henchard's desire to love is removed from him by the return of Newson, and all possibility of his socialization ends; all that remains is death.

His last words are in his will, which ends:

> & that no man remember me.
> To this I put my name.
>
> Michael Henchard.

For most of his life Michael Henchard's ambitious and passionate nature has sought the power of wealth and status – to make a name in the world. The name he ultimately achieves is Mayor of the town of Casterbridge. This name, to be known thus throughout the region, provides him at last with a space for his ambition to fill; but as he enjoys it, he finds it is not enough. It is deeply ironic, if not tragic, that his pursuit of the well-beloved reduces him at last to his bare name and an attendant, though futile, injunction that the name itself be allowed to subside into oblivion. Despite Henchard's will it is certain that Casterbridge will remember him; to have been Mayor is to have left several indelible marks in the records of the town.

So far I have only explored the first element of Hardy's early title, but it is also important that Henchard and Farfrae are mayors of *Casterbridge*. There is, though, already an extensive critical discussion of Casterbridge, to which I do not wish to add very much.[4]

Though the narrator spends a substantial number of words evoking the town and its inhabitants for us, the impression we derive from his account is by no means homogeneous. The narrator of any Hardy novel is a complex organism, and in this instance he speaks with (at least) three separate accents. The physical detail of the town derives from the Dorchester experienced by the schoolboy

Thomas Hardy, walking in every day from Bockhampton in the 1840s and 50s, very much in the same way as Egdon Heath in *The Return of the Native* is the recreation of the vision of the same boy who played on Puddletown Heath in the days before he went to school – the distortions of observable reality are of the same kind in either case.

Analysis of Casterbridge is sometimes in the voice of that boy grown up and living in the town, intimately re-experiencing it, and sometimes in the voice of the cosmopolitan author from the metropole, revisiting the home town from which he has risen, patronizing it by building a *pied-à-terre* on its outskirts.

Casterbridge is sometimes seen as an extension of the country-side. The functions of the town are thoroughly ruralized, and '[b]ees and butterflies in the cornfields at the top of the town who desired to get to the meads at the bottom . . . flew straight down the High Street without any consciousness that they were traversing strange latitudes' (p. 58). It is the countryside concentrated, as if it were a group of rural parishes compressed into a narrower space, 'shepherds in an intramural squeeze' as the narrator describes the inhabitants of the suburb of Durnover (p. 92); the professional class that makes up the Town Council are the equivalent of the landed gentry, the village craftsmen represented by the shopkeepers (who sell agriculturally useful goods) and tradesmen (who deal in agricultural produce and perform agricultural services), the peasantry by the patrons of Peter's Finger. But there are distinctions as well as similarities.

Architecturally and historically the antiquity of Casterbridge as an urban community is carefully established, its close clutter of shops and dwellings and public buildings physically opposes the scattered countryside, sharply divided from the surrounding fields by the dark square of avenues that encloses it. Though all activity in the town is designed to serve the ends of the farmer and the surrounding rural parishes – markets, fairs, bulls and butterflies – yet still the gathering below the bow window of the Kings Arms hotel, carrying unsatisfactory loaves of bread, shouting through the window at the mayor, has a distinctly urban feel to it. For all its agricultural interdependence, Casterbridge is the home of essentially urban people. The professionals – doctors, lawyers, teachers – need the base of population to flourish. The bustle of life observed by the idle rich (Lucetta) is very different from the prospect from a manor-house window; at the other end of the social spectrum the dwellers of Mixen Lane – a fragment of the town notably outside the neat enclosing framework of hedges – are recognizably slum-dwellers.[5]

It is also true, however, that Casterbridge is contrasted with what we might think of as cities; it is not enough simply to consider town and country oppositions in Hardy. Casterbridge is urban without doubt, but it has a kind of intermediate existence which contrasts radically with metropoles; the context of comparison is partly size, partly economic function, and partly human behaviour:

> The yeomen, farmers, dairymen, and townsfolk, who came to transact business in these ancient streets, spoke in other ways than by articulation. Not to hear the words of your interlocutor in metropolitan centres is to know nothing of his meaning. Here the face, the arms, the hat, the stick, the body throughout spoke equally with the tongue. (pp. 61–2)

The responses and interactions that Hardy describes are essentially rural, having nothing of characteristic metropolitan inwardness. It is a matter of expressiveness, of energy, vitality, of living your meaning, which in cities has become overlaid with the middle-class restraints of polite custom and behaviour, or the working class restraints of secrecy and indirection. Henchard attempts a similar process when he tries to enforce standard speech on Elizabeth-Jane – the upper-middle class of the rural town aping the middle-class of the metropole. The narrator makes the direct functional comparison of rural with manufacturing towns. The latter 'are as foreign bodies set down, like boulders on a plain, in a green world with which they have nothing in common' (p. 62), a description that parallels the earlier description of Casterbridge: 'it stood as an indistinct mass behind a dense stockade of limes and chestnuts, set in the midst of miles of rotund down and concave field.' The essential urban similarity is in the 'mathematical line' (p. 29) separating town and country; the essential difference is the harmony in which the town of Casterbridge lives with its surrounding fields and downs, the symbiosis between the two.

It is a further complicating element in the reader's experience of Casterbridge that the narrator, or at least one of the narrative voices, that of the metropolitan sophisticate, is predictably pat-ronizing about the place, talking of 'the venerable contrivances and confusions which delighted the eye by their quaintness, and

in a measure reasonableness, in this rare old market town . . .
(p. 62)

It is thus hard to pin down in a single definition Hardy's imaginative recreation of Dorchester, and perhaps its ambiguity is essential:
both urban and rural, more urban than rural, yet so far from what
most readers in 1886 as well as the present would immediately
represent to themselves as urban, that it seems at once rural again.
Henchard is the least urbane of men, and only in such a shiftingly
envisioned place could he plausibly be mayor.

Casterbridge, however, and its inhabitants are quite sufficiently
urban to provide in concentrated form material for a sharp insight
into economic oppression, a community at war with itself, the
first that Hardy consciously offers in his novels. While Henchard
presides over a banquet at the best hotel, at which guests were
'sniffing and grunting over their plates like sows nuzzling for
acorns' (p. 35), the poor in the streets finger inedible bread. The
same night Christopher Coney says to Farfrae 'we be bruckle folk
here – the best o' us hardly honest sometimes what with hard
winters, and so many mouths to fill, and Goda'mighty sending
his little taties so terrible small to fill 'em with' (p. 53), and in the
morning Henchard urges the Scotsman to 'a solid staunch tuck-in'
on pigeon-pie and home-brewed ale, at which his plate is heaped
'to a prodigal fulness'. With characteristic irony Hardy notes that
in Peter's Finger ex-poachers and ex-gamekeepers, equally victims
of arbitrary rural class-power, swap stories of their bloody fights
conducted over the rights of a few men to keep food away from
those who need it. The condition of life, seen from the perspective of
Mixen Lane, is one of perpetual economic struggle or collapse, and
from this essentially urban point of view the novel might further be
read as a tale of class revenge.

'I do like to see the trimming pulled off such Christmas candles'
(p. 267). Thus Nance Mockridge on Lucetta at the high-point of her
life – wealthy, married to the Mayor of Casterbridge, in the public
eye at a civic ceremony as the first lady of the town and all the
surrounding countryside. The skimmity-ride, anticipation of which
stimulates Nance's remark, is Jopp's personal revenge on Lucetta
for not helping him to a place, but for Nance Mockridge and others
like her it represents the levelling of Lucetta to Mixen Lane, the vivid
demonstration to the Casterbridge world and to Lucetta herself that
she is no different from the white-aproned women in the doorways
of the Lane. It is an unintentional product of the event that it reduces

Lucetta further, to the ultimate condition of all humanity; and the revelation the ride embodies ensures that (unlike Henchard, the man with whom she is coupled in the ride) she is rapidly forgotten by all after her death, and particularly by her husband.

The revenge of Mrs Goodenough the furmity-seller is equally powerful and, directed against the function and the man at the centre of the novel, has wider ramifications. The immediate situation – Henchard the ex-mayor, the magistrate, sitting in the court's 'big chair', still retaining position, authority, the appearance of wealth, Mrs Goodenough standing before him, seedy, vulgar, penniless – offers so strong a contrast, that when she reveals Henchard's wife-selling and proclaims that he is morally unfit to judge her, the reader, who has always known of the wife-sale, still feels a sense of shock at the revelation. This is perhaps the central moment of the novel, the moment when the tragic hero is confronted with the consequences of his own moral flaw, the moment when the mayor understands that his power and his name will disappear. It is appropriate that it comes for the furmity-seller as a triumphant moment of class-revenge, but it is also appropriate in that Mrs Goodenough, more sharply than other characters, perceives the equality of all human beings in their weaknesses. As she talks to Susan of past days, she says:

> nobody could go, without having a dish of Mrs Goodenough's furmity. I knew the clergy's taste, the dandy-gent's taste; I knew the town's taste, the country's taste, I even knew the taste of the coarse shameless females. (p. 24)

Her litany of customers spans in a concentrated form the range of society; none was exempt from her own illicit trade, all are rendered alike in her account, the vicar with the prostitute.[6]

This reconnection of Mrs Goodenough and Michael Henchard contains, on reflection, more than the revenge of the underclass on the ruling class. The furmity-seller is Henchard's nemesis, but she is also his replicator in several ways.

Neither is a native of the area. The grain-based food she sells is not altogether what it seems, it has a hidden agenda, which Henchard's 'perverseness' finds out swiftly; the grain we hear Mayor Henchard has sold was similarly not what it seemed – the bread from his growed wheat is held to be 'unprincipled', as one might say the laced furmity is 'unprincipled'. When Susan returns to Weydon eighteen years after her sale to Newson, she finds Mrs Goodenough 'an old woman haggard, wrinkled, and almost in rags . . . once thriving, cleanly, white-aproned and chinking with money – now tentless, dirty, owning no tables and benches' (p. 23). The reader is offered no account of her decline, but her 'steeped' aspect in court at Casterbridge a year later, and the drunk and disorderly charge brought against her there, suggest that a partial cause at least might have been the too ready consumption of her profits. On the other hand the secret of her illicit dealing was bound to be found out at some time by someone in authority, by undercover excise officers, for example. The deleterious influence of alcohol and secrets on Henchard's career is evident.

Mrs Goodenough has a different, though hardly reliable, explanation of why she has come down in the world: 'Lord's my life – the world's no memory; straightforward dealings don't bring profit – 'tis the sly and the underhand that get on in these times' (pp. 23–4). The irony of this account is matched by the irony of Henchard and Jopp's manifestly improbable suggestion that Farfrae uses witchcraft to succeed in business, a suggestion followed swiftly by Henchard's visit to Conjuror Fall (pp. 184–6).

The furmity-seller, when interrogated by Susan at Weydon, faithfully recovers from her memory Henchard's instruction of seventeen years before to tell any woman who asked for him that he had gone to Casterbridge, when there was no inducement for her to do so, save common humanity.[7] It is similarly one of the deeply saving graces of Henchard that, amidst the multitude of wrong things he does, there is the startling and instinctive doing of the morally right thing.

Thus, when Mrs Goodenough and Henchard are brought face to face again in the court at Dorchester, Hardy has carefully prepared the reader to accept, almost before she announces it, equality between mayor and prisoner (in more than their common humanity), and further prepared the reader for Henchard's rapid disintegration. In part perhaps Hardy's motive for reintroducing her is the basic strategy which suggests that two similar careers establish a higher degree of mimetic verisimilitude than one, that the replication indicates a truth about the human condition; but in fact such replication can be taken much further in analysis of the novel.

None of the major characters in the novel is a native of Casterbridge or even of South Wessex. Save for a vague unstressed interlude while Dr Chalkfield is mayor, the chief citizens of the

town are foreigners, and their wives are foreigners. All enter the
novel with barely enough money to survive upon, and all at some
time achieve or marry wealth and power. From the current point of
view in the novel we may say that Lucetta was brought down by
class-warfare, as was Henchard, and (possibly) the furmity-woman.
All of which leads to the question: Is there any reason to think that
Farfrae will not be similarly reduced? Does the fiercely repetitive
nature of the plot more or less force us to the conclusion that Farfrae
too will be driven to a fall by the underclass of Casterbridge, and
Elizabeth-Jane with him? Well, I would like to postpone considering
this question until later, since there are other issues raised by the
extended title of the novel that have first to be taken into account.

For the first edition of the novel, it will be remembered, Hardy
augmented the title to read: *The Mayor of Casterbridge: the Life and
Death of a Man of Character*, adding two further elements that provoke discussion. There is a fairly straightforward though superficial
reason available for the introduction of 'Life and Death'. The stress
in the earlier simpler title on the office rather than the individual
left the way open for perverse readings of the novel that would
give as much consideration to Farfrae as to Henchard, or even
more perverse, that might argue that Farfrae, the surviving mayor
at the end of the novel, is the true centre of the narrative. I have
no wish to explore these possibilities, though it is easy enough to
imagine how an argument might be framed, setting aside in the
process only the whole tonal structure of the novel. It was perhaps
in part to dissociate himself from any such possible reading that
Hardy developed the more elaborate title, pinning the name Mayor
firmly to the name Michael Henchard.

The effect of introducing the phrase 'Life and Death' goes, however, beyond that proposed in such an explanation. It raises two
questions: first, if Hardy wishes thus to stress Henchard's life in the
novel, why are twenty years of his brief maturity passed over; and
second, what in the novel suggests that Henchard's death should be
held thus in balance with his life?

An answer to the first question can be reached by reconsidering
Henchard as mayor from a slightly different point of view. When
Susan and Elizabeth-Jane see him through the window of the King's
Arms, Henchard has reached a crucial moment in the development
of his life. Aged forty, he has fulfilled the prediction he made of
himself to the company in Mrs Goodenough's tent at Weydon: 'I'd
challenge England to beat me in the fodder business; and if I were

a free man again I'd be worth a thousand pound before I'd done
o't' (p. 10).[8] He is wealthy; and more, he is the first citizen of his
chosen town. The progress of his life for the last nineteen years is
summarized by his success, and Solomon Longways provides the
essentials for the reader (and Elizabeth-Jane); first that he is lonely,
and then that he is

> the powerfullest member of the town-council, and quite a prin-
> cipal man in the country round besides. Never a big dealing in
> wheat, barley, oats, hay, roots, and such-like but Henchard's got a
> hand in it. Ay, and he'll go into other things, too; and that's where
> he makes his mistake. He worked his way up from nothing when
> 'a came here; and now he's a pillar of the town. Not but what he's
> been shaken a little to-year about this bad corn he has supplied in
> his contracts'. (p. 37)

Farfrae, passing the hotel, hears Henchard defy anyone to make the
bad corn good again, and cannot resist entering Henchard's life.

Henchard has achieved all the material goals his imagination can
suggest to him, and he knows they are not enough; he is alone,
'stately and vertical, silently thinking' (p. 40), while his fellow
diners melt into drunken bonhomie. The whole of his life since
rejecting Susan, even including his misty affair with Lucetta in
Jersey, has been merely a preparation for the moment in which
he meets Farfrae and conceives a passionate love at first sight for
him. The personal has re-entered his life, and his crisis begins, the
conflict between his twin desires the course of which has already
been sketched. Hardy implies, perhaps, in his expanded title, that
Henchard's significant life, which was suspended when he failed to
find Susan and Elizabeth-Jane, resumed only when he drew Farfrae
into it.

The result is the inexorable and distinctly rapid process towards
death, more than one death. He dies as a man of wealth and power,
as mayor, long before he dies bodily. Once he is bankrupted and
all that he possessed is auctioned, 'there was quite a sympathetic
reaction in the town, which till then for some time past had done
nothing but condemn him' (p. 220). Henchard's life as a public
man is ended, framed for the townsfolk to examine. 'Now that
Henchard's whole career was pictured distinctly to his neighbours,
and they could see how admirably he had used his one talent of
energy to create a position of affluence out of absolutely nothing

– which was really all he could show when he came to the town as a journeyman hay-trusser with his wimble and knife in his basket – they wondered, and regretted his fall' (like the chorus in a classical tragedy). He seeks bodily death through suicide, but is metaphorically and painfully reborn for a brief life as a man for whom love is all-in-all; but the object of his love is withdrawn, and finally naked of desires, even of the desire for nourishment, taking all responsibility for all his actions into himself, he wastes away, and dies indeed.

This death is as strong evidence as one could wish to show how Hardy strained at the boundaries of realist fiction. The closest parallel is with Heathcliff, though the agent of Henchard's death is no spirit once human, but, perhaps, 'the coming universal wish not to live' (*Jude the Obscure*, p. 355). The death at an early age, through self-neglect and mental self-torture, of Louis Trevelyan (in Trollope's *He Knew He Was Right* [1869]) is a good example of how a fully realist novelist handles a similar situation. Henchard dies when he does because that is when he must die, because the imaginative logic of the narrative demands it; we only do not question his death, because we know it is right.

And then, finally, there is in the title the phrase that has remained crucial for very many interpreters of the novel: 'a man of character'. My attempt to understand what such a description of Henchard implies turns on a passage from John Stuart Mill's *On Liberty*. There is a certain amount of external evidence that Hardy knew the piece well, for he wrote on 20 May 1906 to *The Times* (the occasion was the centenary of Mill's birth) of his hearing Mill speak in 1865, identifying him as 'the author of the treatise *On Liberty* (which we students of that date knew almost by heart)' (*Life and Works* p. 355). In these days we are not so familiar with *On Liberty*, and in order to establish the connection between Hardy's creation and Mill's analysis, substantial quotation from the third chapter, *Of Individuality*, is not redundant, if read with Henchard's character in mind.

Mill is concerned to show that contemporary society is mistakenly distrustful of extraordinary individuals who have unique talents in various directions; in these lines he discusses the significance of the person who possesses powerful desires and impulses:

> To a certain extent it is admitted, that our understanding should be our own: but there is not the same willingness to admit that

our desires and impulses should be our own likewise; or that to possess impulses of our own, and of any strength, is anything but a peril and a snare. Yet desires and impulses are as much a part of a perfect human being, as beliefs and restraints: and strong impulses are only perilous when not properly balanced; when one set of aims and inclinations is developed into strength, while others, which ought to coexist with them, remain weak and inactive. It is not because men's desires are strong that they act ill; it is because their consciences are weak. There is no natural connexion between strong impulses and a weak conscience. The natural connexion is the other way. To say that one person's desires and feelings are stronger and more various than those of another, is merely to say that he has more of the raw material of human nature, and is therefore capable, perhaps of more evil, but certainly of more good.

The man of strong desires and impulses, Mill says, is potentially a greatly good man, so long as there is a balance in him between his desires and impulses and his conscience. This is a way of formulating the essence of much tragedy, for we may suppose that it is rare for any individual to hold within them this essential balance. More often, like most of Shakespeare's tragic figures, the intensity of desire and the power of its impulsive expression is at crucial moments uncontrolled by the conscience acting through the will. And so it is with Henchard. Amongst them the narrator and the other characters draw frequent attention to Henchard's deeply impulsive nature, put in service of his powerful ambition and his underlying desire to love. At the same time events demonstrate that at crucial moments in his life his conscience proves inadequate to the task of controlling his impulses. At first it seems like some diminishment of this condemnation that when he sells his wife, when he directs the commination psalm at Farfrae, when he interrupts the royal visit to Casterbridge, when he all but kills Farfrae in the hay-loft, he does so under the influence of alcohol, the effect of which is to put his conscience to sleep. But this is only the postponement of responsibility, for he deliberately drinks in order to to dull his conscience, in order to allow his impulses to have free rein. And to make clear what Henchard is capable of, his final destructive impulsive act, when he tells Newson that his daughter is dead, is performed when he is perfectly sober.

Nevertheless readers have always recognized that Henchard has

a greater potential, a fuller humanity than anyone else in the novel.
It is in part his tragedy that his potential is not fulfilled. The
identification of Mill's account with Henchard is reinforced in the
continuation of the paragraph from *On Liberty*:

> Strong impulses are but another name for energy. Energy may
> be turned to bad uses; but more good may always be made
> of an energetic nature, than of an indolent and impassive one.
> Those who have most natural feeling, are always those whose
> cultivated feelings may be made the strongest. The same strong
> susceptibilities which make the personal impulses vivid and
> powerful, are also the source from whence are generated the
> most passionate love of virtue, and the sternest self-control. It
> is through the cultivation of these, that society both does its duty
> and protects its interests: not by rejecting the stuff of which heroes
> are made, because it knows not how to make them.

It is Henchard's extraordinary energy which allows him to sur-
mount the prejudices of the ruling society of Casterbridge and com-
pels them to elect him mayor, and, as Mill reiterates the supremacy
of the energetic nature when combined with 'the most passionate
love of virtue, and the sternest self-control', we recognize again the
potential within Henchard that is essentially unfulfilled.[9]
    Immediately Mill defines what he means by 'character', and here
is the source for the final element in Hardy's title:

> A person whose desires and impulses are his own – are the
> expression of his own nature, as it has been developed and
> modified by his own culture – is said to have a character. One
> whose desires and impulses are not his own, has no character, no
> more than a steam-engine has a character. If, in addition to being
> his own, his impulses are strong, and are under the government
> of a strong will, he has an energetic character.

The remainder of the passage from *On Liberty* that I wish to quote
turns from the definition of the potential Carlylean hero to a brief
account of why contemporary society finds it hard to accept such
individuals:

> Whoever thinks that individuality of desires and impulses should
> not be encouraged to unfold itself, must maintain that society has

no need of strong natures – is not the better for containing many persons who have much character – and that a high general average of energy is not desirable.

In some early states of society, these forces might be, and were, too much ahead of the power which society then possessed of disciplining and controlling them. There has been a time when the element of spontaneity and individuality was in excess, and the social principle had a hard struggle with it. The difficulty then was, to induce men of strong bodies or minds to pay obedience to any rules which required them to control their impulses. To overcome this difficulty, law and discipline, like the Popes struggling against the Emperors, asserted a power over the whole man, claiming to control his life in order to control his character – which society had not found any other sufficient means of binding. But society has now fairly got the better of individuality; and the danger which threatens human nature is not the excess, but the deficiency, of personal impulses and preferences.

Thus, if we follow Mill, we can say that Henchard is a man of energetic character, but one dangerous to society because the strength of his impulse to power and of his desire to love is at crucial moments in his life not matched by the strength of his conscience operating through his will to prevent such impulses and desires infringing on the rights of others. Mill recognizes that society is wrong (and ultimately deprives itself of potential for growth) to outlaw people of individual energy (and in fact the town council of Casterbridge does not initially do so with Henchard, but rather harnesses his energy – without however caring particularly for the individual who possesses it).

At the same time, however, Mill accepts that society has a right to protect itself when the operation of such energy limits the potential of others for growth. 'The means of development which the individual loses by being prevented from gratifying his inclinations to the injury of others, are chiefly obtained at the expense of the development of other people.' This point raises serious questions for the reader of *The Mayor of Casterbridge*; Farfrae and his wife Elizabeth-Jane are the most prominent and the most punctiliously proper representatives of society in the novel, and they reject Henchard, abandon him, outlaw and ultimately condemn him to death.[10] Following Mill, they are right to do so, for even if he has expiated the crime of selling his wife, he has sinned again in telling Newson his daughter is dead. However it seems clear from the hostility the narrator displays towards Farfrae at the end of the novel, and the coolness that seems the keynote of Elizabeth-Jane's nature, that Hardy and his narrator do not intend the reader to take Mill's position. There is no equivocation about Henchard's act of denial – it is wrong; but the narrator ensures that the reader understands why the impulse to lie is so powerful for Henchard in a way neither of his judges does. Farfrae is incapable of distinguishing the man from the function, seeing him only as a day-labourer – he judges largely by the surface, and when he sees something deeper, he says: 'with a man of passions such as his there is no safeguard for conduct' (p. 242), forcing us to judge between passions and conduct, warmth and cold, anarchy and disruptiveness and moral conformity to conventions of behaviour – the range or the limits of human potential. Elizabeth-Jane is sympathetic, kind, loving even, but she has so little passionateness herself that it is impossible for her to comprehend her step-father. Even Newson, who is not bothered by the 'trick' once he has become reunited with his daughter, and treats the matter as a practical joke, is wrong in this instance.[11] It is no joke, but rather the desperate instinctive grasping of a passionate man for his last chance of happiness in a society that has little sympathy or understanding for the passionate and the energetic.

If we are inclined to forgive or even to approve Henchard's lie to Newson, then we are parting company with Mill, and becoming ourselves revolutionaries against Victorian society. This is Hardy's ultimate critique – or maybe his amplification – of Mill's ideas on a man of character. A social theorist cannot deal in individual cases, and Hardy's application of Mill's ideas reveals Hardy's fundamental discontent with a society that can abandon a man such as Henchard to death. But we cannot rest content with such a conclusion, for at the same time Hardy shows that the strength and energy that drives Henchard to success drives him equally rapidly to defeat, and the working out of this sequence suggests that Victorian society is not unique in penalizing powerful energies and desires, that the nature of human existence anywhere in the world and at any time ensures that the controlled and the equable alone prosper.

This is a familiar proposition in Hardy criticism. Though the success of the mediocre is seldom found in so naked a form as it is in *The Mayor of Casterbridge* – perhaps Gabriel Oak's triumph in *Far From the Madding Crowd* is the only comparably powerful statement of the idea – from Sergeant Troy to Jude Fawley and Sue Bridehead Hardy's novels offer a series of individuals who try in some way to fight social convention and the nature of human existence, and are destroyed in the conflict.

The Life and Death of the Mayor of Casterbridge: A Story of a Man of Character is permeated with confusing and conflicting accounts of why things happen in the world the way they do. If Henchard is 'a man of character', then the place to begin an investigation of these accounts would seem to be with the notion that character is fate, even though the context in which the issue is raised in its definitive form concerns Farfrae rather than Henchard:

> Whether it was that his northern energy was an overmastering force among the easy-going Wessex worthies, or whether it was sheer luck, the fact remained that whatever he touched he prospered in . . . . But most probably luck had little to do with it. Character is Fate, said Novalis, and Farfrae's character was just the reverse of Henchard's. (p. 115)

There is little doubt that this is one of the theses the novel tends to validate. When (to refer to an example that also relates to Farfrae) Lucetta says 'Donald's genius would have enabled him to get a footing anywhere, without anybody's help!' (p. 266) we accept that she is right, despite the narrator's subsequent doubts; we have no trouble in imagining him (had he turned Henchard's original offer down) the mayor of some Canadian grain-belt town. His character would ensure a similar fate.

There are, however, certain unsettling features within this apparently authoritative passage. For instance, it is not unreasonable for the narrator to stress Farfrae's 'northern energy' as the character trait responsible for his success, but he then confuses the issue by saying that Farfrae was in character precisely Henchard's opposite. This is confusing since the reader cannot help but recall the narrator's previous assertion that it was Henchard's exceptional energy which had brought *him* success. How acute, we are led to ask, is the narrator as a judge of character? Another troubling detail is that most commentators suggest (intertextually) that Hardy's allusion to Novalis's idea cannot be read without reference to George Eliot's

prior use of it in *The Mill on the Floss*, where Eliot's narrator calls
the notion that character is destiny one of Novalis's 'questionable
aphorisms' (Book VI, Chapter 6), and proceeds to suggest that
circumstance is equally powerful in shaping our ends.

Up to a point, however, it is demonstrable that the natures of
the major figures in the novel shape their own lives and those of
others. But the greatest problem at the heart of the proposition that
character is fate is its apparent exclusivity; it tends to limit to one the
range of meanings of the name 'fate', a limitation which is strongly
at odds with other formulations in the novel, and with the form of
the narrative itself. On the one hand there is the notion of a personal
fate – what happens to a person; on the other, there is abstract fate
– a force that causes things to happen to all people. Novalis seems
to have had the personal sense in mind: our future is what it is
because we are the people we are. Ultimately his neat aphorism
has insufficient potential for the analysis conducted by the narrative
voices (or by the characters themselves), and there is a plethora of
references in the novel to concepts like Providence, fortune and
destiny, which exclude human agency altogether.

It is inevitable in any approximately realistic interpretation of
Victorian society that some characters should attribute events to
divine intervention. When Farfrae finally gives in to Henchard's
impulsive, compulsive desire for him to stay in Casterbridge and
become his manager it is because he is convinced that their encounter is 'Providence! Should anyone go against it?' (pp. 64–5). There is
a conventional Christian overtone to the word 'Providence'; and his
religious (if not Christian) understanding of causation is made clear
in a parallel phrasing at a similar moment of decision (his acceptance
of the mayoralty of Casterbridge). Farfrae says to Lucetta (who had
hoped they would leave Casterbridge): 'See now how it's ourselves
that are ruled by the powers above us! We plan this, but we do
that . . . ' (p. 243). The question is, how far do we accept Farfrae's
approach to life, here or elsewhere?

That Hardy was attempting in the novel to draw a distinction
between a religious understanding of a causative force and a secu-
lar one is suggested by two further passages from the novel: on
p. 179 the narrator, considering the consequences for Lucetta and
Elizabeth-Jane of the newly-fledged attraction between the former
and Farfrae, says of Lucetta that she 'with native lightness of heart
took kindly to what fate offered', and of Elizabeth-Jane that she
'wondered what unwished for thing Heaven might send her in place

of [Farfrae]'. The tenuously religious Lucetta receives contentedly the chances that neutral 'fate' presents her with, but the deeply religious Elizabeth-Jane ponders on the agency of the explicitly Christian 'Heaven'.

A similar distinction is perceptible in a paragraph on p. 88 when the narrator says of Elizabeth-Jane that she retained a 'fear of the coulter of destiny despite fair promise', while reporting in the same paragraph that she says to herself (in interior monologue) that she will not be gay because it 'would be tempting Providence to hurl mother and me down, and afflict us again as he used to do'. Though 'he' is not capitalized, Elizabeth-Jane's identification of Providence with God seems to be implied, while the narrator uses the neutral 'destiny'.

Farfrae and his wife Elizabeth-Jane are the only characters to attribute agency to 'Providence' or 'Heaven', and though they do not invoke God directly this may well only be because they consider it unlucky or ungenteel or vaguely blasphemous so to do. By the end of the novel they have become representatives for the reader of all dominant social norms, and one of these, one indeed of the most important, is an observance of religious conventions. There seems to be some doubt, then, about a divine version of the causality of events.

Henchard himself is contradictory in this area as in many: he is the only major character to invoke God by name; he is a churchwarden; and yet there is no sense at all of him as a man who sets any store by Christianity or Christian observance.[12] For a brief time after he is saved from killing himself by the appearance of his effigy at the place he had chosen for his suicide, he wonders if his preservation is miraculous. The narrator comments: 'The sense of the supernatural was strong in this unhappy man, and he turned away as one might have done in the actual presence of an appalling miracle' (p. 297). Even when he sees that there is a natural explanation for the appearance of his image in the pool, he says 'Who is such a reprobate as I! And yet it seems that even I be in Somebody's hand!' (p. 299). It is just possible to imagine at this moment that Henchard has at last seen the light, will become born again, and thus finally integrated into society. On the next page, however, the narrator comments: 'the emotional conviction that he was in Somebody's hand began to die out of Henchard as time slowly removed into distance the event which had given that feeling birth', and at once we recognize how characteristic it is (character being [personal] fate) that his belief in a benificent divine providence should be purely transitory.

When Henchard decides to forswear strong drink, he does it before God, in a church, head on a Bible; but he does so not out of religious conviction, but because the imagery and associations of the place and objects and ritual are appropriately solemn and portentous, and suit his current frame of mind. The narrator of Larkin's 'Church-Going' shares some of these apprehensions.

Henchard is impulsive, and his capacity for feeling is very great; for the most part he is unconcerned with supernatural agency, but at moments when emotions of some description are intensely roused in him, he turns outside himself. When, for instance, he discovers that Elizabeth-Jane is not his child the narrator analyses his response:

> His lip twitched, and he seemed to compress his frame, as if to bear better. His usual habit was not to consider whether destiny were hard upon him or not – the shape of his ideas in cases of affliction being simply a moody 'I am to suffer I perceive,' – 'This much scourging, then, is for me.' But now through his passionate head there stormed this thought – that the blasting disclosure was what he deserved . . . . Henchard, like all his kind, was superstitious, and he could not help thinking that the concatenation of events this evening had produced was the scheme of some sinister intelligence bent upon punishing him. Yet they had developed naturally. (pp. 126–7)

In this passage, as in the 'character is fate' passage, there is evidence of radical ambiguity. The narrator's account is that because the pain Henchard feels is sharper than usual, sharper than he can easily contain, he turns outside himself, speculating that the force ordering events in the world, neutral destiny in this instance, (the existence of which he has apparently always implicitly accepted) has for once judged him, and personally intervened with a punishment to match the crime of wife-selling. The narrator, however, dismisses Henchard's 'sinister intelligence' as the overwrought emotionalism of an unintellectual and superstitious man, and points out the traceable sequence of cause and effect that had brought him to this moment. George Eliot would have been proud of her disciple, and the reader is encouraged to feel thoroughly superior to Henchard. But there are (at least) two narrative voices speaking to us in the novel on this issue, voices that might be characterized as 'rationalist/realist' – the voice just attended to, that finds a logical antecedent cause in the past of human action for every present event – and 'determinist/immanent will' – the voice that uses in many places 'destiny', 'fate' and other such words to indicate a force that makes things happen quite independent of human agency.

Consider, for example the following: 'Ever since the evening of his wife's arrival with her daughter there had been something in the air which had changed his luck. That dinner at the King's Arms with his friends had been Henchard's Austerlitz: he had had his successes since, but his course had not been upward' (p. 135). Only twenty pages earlier the (a) narrator had denied that luck had anything to do with Farfrae's success.[13]

Or again this, where the (a) narrator says that access to music might have rendered Henchard less comfortless in his despair, 'for with Henchard music was of regal power . . . . But hard fate had ordained that he should be unable to call up this Divine spirit in his need' (p. 296). It isn't altogether clear why music should be unavailable to him; even if he can't play himself, there is music in Mixen Lane or he can go to hear church-music. But the point is that this narrator specifically invokes 'hard fate' whose ordinance has prevented the man from gaining relief. How is this different from Henchard's 'sinister intelligence'?

Or lastly, this: 'Poor Elizabeth-Jane, little thinking what her malignant star had done to blast the budding attentions she had won from Donald Farfrae, was glad to hear . . . ' (p. 166). There is a perfectly adequate sequence of cause and effect in the previous chapters to account for the growth of attraction between Lucetta and Farfrae, and yet we are told here that such a rational explanation is illusory , and that Elizabeth-Jane's personal 'malignant star' had in fact caused it all.

Since the narrative voice is fundamentally contradictory, not anyway a homogeneous thing, the reader is left free to choose one or all of these methods of accounting for the way things turn out. When Elizabeth-Jane watches by her mother's death-bed we are shown 'the subtle-souled girl asking herself why she was born, why sitting in a room, and blinking at the candle; why things around her had taken the shape they wore in preference to every other possible shape; why they stared at her so helplessly, as if waiting for the touch of some wand that should release them from terrestrial constraint; what that chaos called consciousness, which spun in her at this moment like a top, tended to, and began in' (p. 119).

There is no answer, and the narrator's silence in face of these direct questions is perhaps the most eloquent commentary of all on the issue. But there is the temptation for the critic of the novel to draw back one step further towards the creative fount, and consider the role of the Thomas Hardy who is the inscriber of the chaotic consciousness/es that 'guide' the reader through the fiction. In this novel the veil of realism over the fiction is stretched very thin in some places, particularly those that have to do with the way things happen. It might be said with some justice that it is T Hardy novelist who is fate. It is he who ensures that for Henchard and for others at the moment of intensest hope there comes crashing destruction of hope. This instrumentality of the author is closely tied up with another aspect of causality, a view that might be expressed by 'secrets are fate'.

It is possible to argue that the really disabling element in life is to have secrets; that much of the evil that occurs in this novel, and in others by Hardy – *Tess of the d'Urbervilles*, or *The Return of the Native* for instance – occurs because secrets have not been told (thus leading one to take a dim view of the ending of *Under the Greenwood Tree*).

> Had the incident [Henchard's selling his wife] been well-known of old and always, it might by this time have grown to be lightly regarded, as the rather tall wild oat, but well-nigh the single one, of a young man with whom the steady and mature (if somewhat headstrong) burgher of to-day had scarcely a point in common. But the act having lain as dead and buried ever since, the interspace of years was unperceived; and the black spot of his youth wore the aspect of a recent crime. (p. 218)

At any moment in Henchard's career in Casterbridge the revelation of this secret would have been a setback, but coming as it does at the time of his greatest financial difficulty, it prevents the possible extension of his credit through the influence of his good name, and rapidly accellerates proceedings against him for bankruptcy.

If Lucetta's secret liaison with Henchard had always been known, then there would have been no skimmity-ride, and she would not have died (though also she might not have married Farfrae). Henchard warns Lucetta that Farfrae 'is sure to find out something of the matter, sooner or later', offering advice that he cannot follow himself.

The discovery of Susan's secret would have hurt Henchard at any time; but it is so grotesquely painful as to be deliberate, not just as a fictional device for effect, but as a direct statement from the novelist about the nature of existence, that immediately after opening of himself 'without reluctance and without fear' to Elizabeth-Jane as his daughter, Henchard opens a letter which reduces all the anticipation, love, hope to a ruin of ashes. He finds she is not his daughter.

Henchard keeps to himself his knowledge of Newson's return. The narrator notes of Henchard that 'a great change had come over him with regard to [Elizabeth-Jane], and he was developing the dream of a future lit by her filial presence, as though that way alone could happiness lie' (p. 290). In the next sentence Newson returns to destroy the dream – as the narrator memorably says, 'Henchard's face and eyes seemed to die.' Secrets, Hardy says throughout his fiction, are destructive; but here as elsewhere it is not the fact of the secret's revelation that is so striking – if Newson is alive, then there is every reason why he should exert himself to find Susan and his daughter; it is the timing of the revelation at the moment calculated to cause the deepest anguish that reveals nakedly the malice of the author. Here, one might say, is Henchard's 'sinister intelligence'. Hardy simply destroys the illusion of mimesis, removes his novel from the conventions of Victorian realism, and announces that the novelist is fate.

Study of his work, particularly of the last novels, *The Dynasts* and the poetry, suggests though that there is for Hardy a deeper realism involved in his manipulation, in that he is thus only reflecting the ill-managed plan of causation in the world. What does it ultimately matter who or what is responsible for what happens; Elizabeth-Jane's questions need no answer; it is the pain or the pleasure that results which is important.

As the man of character leaves Casterbridge as fully bereft of all things as when he had arrived there, the narrator summarizes for us his thoughts:

> He experienced not only the bitterness of a man who finds, in looking back on an ambitious course, that what he has sacrificed in sentiment was worth as much as what he has gained in substance; but the superadded bitterness of seeing his very recantation nullified. He had been sorry for all this long ago; but his attempts to replace ambition by love had been as fully

foiled as his ambition itself. His wronged wife had foiled them by a fraud so grandly simple as to be almost a virtue.

It was an odd sequence that out of this tampering with the social law [presumably the same social law that the narrator of *Tess* says Tess has been made to break] came that flower of nature Elizabeth. Part of his wish to wash his hands of life arose from his perception of its contrarious inconsistencies – of nature's jaunty readiness to support unorthodox social principles. (p. 319)

The first paragraph neatly catches the essence of Henchard's life; but the second is rather strange. It suggests that Henchard wants to die in part because the social law is not always supported by nature. But when has Henchard ever felt that conformity with society's orthodoxy was the only virtue in life? Perhaps what the narrator intends here is to say that Henchard shares the basic human wish to have life predictable, to have appropriate effect follow the cause; when it doesn't, when we seem sport for the gods (or nature), then life isn't worth living?

On the next page there is a further portentous narratorial commentary:

Externally there was nothing to hinder his making another start on the upward slope, and by his new lights achieving higher things than his soul in its half-formed state had been able to accomplish. But the ingenious machinery contrived by the gods for reducing human possibilities of amelioration to a minimum – which arranges that wisdom to do shall come *pari passu* with the departure of zest for doing – stood in the way of all that. He had no wish to make an arena, a second time, of a world that had become a mere painted scene to him. (320)

This passage bears a family resemblance to that at the end of *Tess of the d'Urbervilles* in which the narrator talks of the President of the Immortals at play with Tess, and it is relatively easy to set aside the mechanical machinery of the gods as proceeding from the frustrations of a cynical narrative voice. If the gods really rule the world, then any claim that character is fate is nonsense, and life and free-will an illusion. But by this time we know, despite the tone, that the voice making this statement represents only one aspect of authority in the novel, which is so fragmented as to be no authority at all.

There are other questions raised by the passage. What, for instance, are Henchard's new lights? Self-restraint; humility; socialization? And what 'higher' things might he be able to accomplish? Presumably higher in a moral sense, more directly beneficial to his fellow humans? And are we to believe that the series of events recounted in the novel has proved the world a vale of soul-making for Henchard? Apparently so, but this account seems to describe quite another man from the one we see trussing hay and wishing for death. The image of Henchard's past life conducted in an arena, full of conflicts with wild beasts and gladiators, taking up the whole Roman background to the narrative, is more appropriate.

The Mayor died a long while ago in the Casterbridge arena; Michael Henchard dies in a hut in the heart of Egdon Heath, the natural environment above all untamable by man. Like Eustacia Vye he dies because there is no longer any reason he can see to live, or because Hardy can see no reason for him to live; because ambition has dissipated and love comes to ashes and there is nothing else. Unaccommodated man is destroyed by vacancy within and by the elements without.

The last word in the novel is with Elizabeth-Jane:

> Her experience had been of the kind to teach her, rightly or wrongly, that the doubtful honour of a brief transit through a sorry world hardly called for effusiveness . . . her strong sense that neither she nor any human being deserved less than was given, did not blind her to the fact that there were others receiving less who had deserved much more. (p. 334)

The question raised by this summary is who or what gives to humans less or more? If character is fate, then Elizabeth-Jane's understanding is sharply awry. It is most likely that she would credit the Anglican Providence with agency, but the narrator who is interpreting her thoughts would more probably have some neutral concept like the Immanent Will in mind. The reader is at liberty to feel that Hardy has so manipulated the lives of his characters that to go beyond the idea that the writer is destiny serves no purpose.

6

Tess of the d'Urbervilles

Tess of the d'Urbervilles is so direct in its appeal and unambiguous in its story line that all commentary seems redundant. It is the story of an exceptionally gifted peasant girl of decayed aristocratic stock who is betrayed by two men: one is rich and sensuous, the seducer of her body and, for a while, her emotions; by him she has a child which dies in infancy. The other is the intellectual, freethinking son of a clergyman, whom she loves with her whole being, and who abandons her when he hears, immediately after their marriage, of her earlier violation. Subsequently the husband comes to understand his moral and intellectual arrogance, and searches for the girl, only to find that the extreme poverty of her family has driven her back to the other man. So strong is the girl's love for her husband and so powerful her disgust at what the other man has forced her to become, that she kills the other man. Husband and wife, united but on the run from the police, spend a few days of loving reconciliation together before the girl is arrested, tried, sentenced to death for murder, and executed.

This plot is not particularly original in its framework, and in the end it cannot by itself account for the novel's power. Two other elements in its creation have a significant role to play: one is that *Tess of the d'Urbervilles* marks a climax of Hardy's exploration of the integration of characters with their environment, the other is the passionate commitment to the central character with which the novel is written. This combination offers the most deeply moving reading experience that I know.

Perhaps this is all that should be said about the novel – but the temptation to go further, to explore some of the implications of such a summary, is too strong, and in keeping with an underlying pattern of this volume, I want to concentrate upon the first, the most easily assimilable face presented by the novel to the reader – though one that many readers do not notice: the title-page. It reads:

TESS OF THE / D'URBERVILLES / A PURE WOMAN / FAITHFULLY PRESENTED BY / THOMAS HARDY / ' . . . Poor wounded name! My bosom as a bed Shall lodge thee.' – W. SHAKESPEARE.

The first word of the title-page is the most important in the novel. It often happened that novelists in the eighteenth and nineteenth centuries chose the name of the central character of their book to do duty as the title, partly because the novel from its origins was very much concerned with the presentation of character and the author often wished to direct the reader's attention from the beginning to the appropriate personality. It was, though, also the case that the circulating libraries, all-powerful reflectors of taste during the second half of the nineteenth century, found a most ready market for novels simply titled for the central character. Perhaps this was because such a title seemed to the average reader to suggest a straightforward biographical fiction without too much subtle complication. It may also be suspected that by 1890 the laziness born of habit played a part in the continuation of the practice. It is not, however, a practice that Hardy ever followed in its simple form, and here and in his next novel *Jude the Obscure* it is as if he used the convention only to qualify it with ambiguities.

Tess Durbeyfield is undoubtedly the source from which the energy of the novel springs, and it seems inevitable that the book should have been named for her. What seems much less inevitable is the immediate sequel on the title-page. In what sense, we may ask, is it the most important thing that we know or learn about Tess that she is a direct inheritor of the great and once powerful family of d'Urberville? Why, in what he knew would become the novel's universally accepted name, should Hardy draw our attention first to that aspect of her history?

Here is an answer. Tess is an exceptional woman, a Durbeyfield by social status, but a d'Urberville of the spirit. Hardy wanted to be certain as we begin reading that we should be sensitive to the ironies involved in her birth. Hardy's attitude to noble families was ambivalent. In this novel, in *The Hand of Ethelberta*, in *A Group of Noble Dames*, and presumably above all in his never-published first novel *The Poor Man and the Lady*, Hardy shows that he understands the arrogance and brutality, even the vulgarity of the aristocracy and gentry. On the other hand Hardy himself was delighted to be on friendly terms with Lords and Ladies, and was equally aware of the opportunities for refinement of mind and spirit offered, however inequitably, by the aristocratic life. One distinction in general terms that Hardy seems to have made, both in fiction and in life, is between the women and the men of the aristocracy. The pattern of upper-class life, he implies, is such that the women do tend to be refined in spirit, while the men tend to be bathed in blood-sports and violent behaviour. Whether we agree with him is a different matter.

Hence Tess, without the nurture, inherits nobility of nature from her knightly ancestors. Alec Stoke-d'Urberville, whose money-lender father has attached the decayed name to his own, inherits with his father's wealth the power and sensual brutality that go with the medieval robber baron's name. He employs this violent power on Tess and Hardy notes that the ironic 'justice' thus involved may be good enough for Jehovah in his eye for an eye, tooth for a tooth frame of mind, but is hardly satisfactory in a humane society – a comment designed to provoke in the contemporary reader the question: What sort of society, then, are we living in?

Tess also inherits the pride traditionally associated with noble families, and on the clash between her pride and her social and economic position much of the process of her tragedy depends. Angel Clare can call her 'the belated seedling of an effete aristocracy' when he is building up a case against her to support his instinct to abandon her, but her pride does not allow her to respond to the phrase's manifest inappropriateness even as an insult. She strikes Alec d'Urberville with a heavy leather glove just as her medieval forbears would have wielded in anger a mailed fist. She in the end exacts her own form of justice on Alec. She has the strength, pride and fineness of spirit that Hardy associates with the superior gentry, the passion and the violence.

On the other hand she is born into the family of a poor rural tradesman, into a group of 'waiters upon Providence', and she inherits many of their social attitudes, including their fatalism. Her beauty comes from her mother of no name, not from her father – remember the horrible d'Urberville portraits at Wellbridge Manor – as does her intimacy, conscious and unconscious, with nature. Thus she is simple Tess Durbeyfield , but she is 'of the d'Urbervilles' as well, and the combination creates the rare passionate proud sensitive open strong beautiful girl/woman who supports the novel. It also creates the many tensions in her character that lead her to the gallows. The most obvious are those between humility and pride, and between innocence and sensuality; but Hardy also makes it clear that there is also conflict within Tess between acquired conventional belief and instinctive independence of mind, and between ignorance and education. It might be said that ultimately the tension within her character is one between obedience and rebellion.[1]

We are next informed by the title-page that Tess of the d'Urbervilles is 'a pure woman'. This is the phrase that caused so much uproar when the first edition of the novel was first published. The contemporary reviewers almost to a woman concentrated their attention upon Tess's purity, using in their polemics the terms of ethics and religion, and it seems certain that Hardy appended the description to the title-page of the first edition (it did not appear on the manuscript or the serial versions), as a challenge to the standards of contemporary readers. It is, by the way, one of the paradoxes of Hardy's nature that in his fiction he often in this way, under the power of his creative activity, challenged conventional moral or religious or social attitudes, and just as often was shocked and hurt when he provoked thereby an outraged response from people holding these conventional views. In this instance, at any rate, the provocation offered by 'pure' was so great that very few commentators, Victorian or more recent, seem to have considered that Hardy almost certainly also had in mind an alternative meaning of the word. Though some would hold it to be unimportant whether Hardy consciously made use of the ambiguity inherent in the word 'pure', it is hard to imagine that the poet, the meticulous reviser always looking for the precise phrasing of his ideas, should not have intended the reader of his title page to consider Tess also, or even primarily, as essential woman, wholly woman, as pure woman.

Thus again Hardy establishes duality through these alternative versions of the character who is at once Tess Durbeyfield and Theresa of the d'Urbervilles: she is also to be seen as an emblem of purity on the one hand and as an emblem of the quintessential female on the other. And as we read further into the title-page the source of this duality becomes clearer.

The pure woman Tess of the d'Urbervilles is to be 'faithfully presented' to the reader 'by Thomas Hardy'. At first sight this seems a straightforward attempt at verisimilitude, Hardy suggesting to the reader that what follows is an accurate retelling of a true (to use another word from the same arsenal as 'pure', ready to go off in the user's face like a rusty rifle) story. And there are moments in the novel when it seems that this indeed must have been the case:

Then their sister . . . poured forth from the bottom of her heart the thanksgiving that follows, uttering it boldly and triumphantly, in the stopt-diapason note which her voice acquired when her heart was in her speech, and which will never be forgotten by those who knew her. (p. 99)

The vivid impression left by the last words of this sentence is that the narrator was certainly one of those who knew Tess.

This interpretation of 'faithfully presented by Thomas Hardy' seems a valid one. Hardy wrote in letters to friends concerning the first editions of all his novels from *Two on a Tower* (1882) onwards variations on the lament that what he had finally achieved was a poor and limited version of the conception of the story that he had developed before he began writing. It seems to me wholly probable that Hardy remained more faithful to the original idea that he had of Tess's story than to that of any other. It is reasonable to argue, taking into account all the compromises and alterations to this first idea which he was forced into by serial editors, and which he felt constrained to make by his perception of the bland blankness of his middle-class readership, that still the essence was preserved, still he had honoured his original commitment to the girl, to the image of the girl he had before a word of the draft manuscript was written. To argue that in fact Hardy on the title page of Tess is announcing that he has been faithful to a vision that held for him some essential truth.

But it also seems to me a limited interpretation of the words 'faithfully presented by Thomas Hardy', particularly when the experience of many re-readings of the novel is brought to bear on them. Here is a dramatized and highly fictional version of what I think the title-page implies. A man, who has been called Thomas Hardy (a fragment of that Thomas Hardy to whom I have been referring so far as the novel's author), has a true vision of a girl, a girl whose qualities move him almost to fall in love with his vision, in the manner of the legendary sculptor Pygmalion who fell in love with his own sculpture. This Hardy lets the girl enter his imagination and, possessing a fertile inventiveness, he gives her a life – a past, present and future. He writes down this character and her history, and inscribes on the first page of the manuscript a quotation from Shakespeare's 'Two Gentlemen of Verona' that to his mind catches vividly the role he has played in his relationship with the girl whose story he has imagined:

Poor wounded name! My bosom as a bed / Shall lodge thee.

He was her protector, defender, comforter, lover – but one who ultimately failed in all those roles, since in the end he could not prevent her from dying, nor the vision of her departing from him as he wrote the last words. Nevertheless he will lodge her name in his bosom, and he will write her name at the top of his manuscript; he will follow the name with the description 'pure woman'. And he has the consolatory satisfaction of having imagined himself into his fiction. He is Angel Clare. As this character he loves, rejects, and finally protects, defends, comforts and more fully loves the girl. Less willingly he admits that he is also Alec d'Urberville who lusts for the girl and uses her, but before the close of his imaginings the girl has killed this aspect of himself, though at the cost of her own life – one of the reasons why Thomas Hardy will lodge Tess's name in his bosom with love.

At first this manuscript remains locked in the most secret place known to this Thomas Hardy. But after a period of reflection he wants to let it free, to let others experience the intensity and beauty of his vision. And so he gives it to a very close relative who also happens to go by the name of Thomas Hardy. This second Thomas Hardy, rather than a visionary and fertile creator, is a cultivated gentleman, a critic of art and life, a local historian, something of a philosopher – indeed he combines so many accomplishments that his acquaintances sometimes wonder that one man can compass so much, and are unsurprised when one of his interests clashes with another and apparent contradictions result. This latter Thomas Hardy is moved by the narrative he reads, and suggests that it should have a wider audience. He is also sure that it will not do as it is, that it will not attract the attention of the middle and upper-class book-buying or book-borrowing public; and so, with the full assent of his relative the first Thomas Hardy, he proceeds to edit the girl and her life. To the original manuscript he adds many touches: references to poetry, painting, sculpture; passages of philosophical summary of sometimes conflicting import; fragments of local history, social history; snatches of religious theory; but most significantly his experience as a man of the world drives him to place the girl in a broad social context and to wrap her story with an argument about her purity, using as his key the phrase 'pure woman' that he found on the first page of the manuscript, adding to it only an indefinite article.

It is this second Thomas Hardy also who marks his own part in the preparation of the text for publication by adding to the title-page a note of his faithful presentation of the girl and her story, sincerely believing that he has been faithful to the first Thomas's vision, quite unable to see that his additions have thoroughly altered the nature of the imagined narrative. Thus there are two voices that mingle in the version of the vision that finally reached the public. The latter of these narrative voices has several different tones at its command; and yet, because Thomas Hardy the gentleman-critic, for all his versatility, is sensitive and is very close to Thomas Hardy the imaginative creator, we only rarely sense a disharmony between the two, as we take in Tess and Turner and theology all on a page together.

That account of the novel's creation is a fantasy. There is no evidence in the British Library manuscript of the novel to suggest that it was composed in such a fashion. But metaphorically the account represents one facet of something central to that composite being we are happy to call Thomas Hardy the novelist. It can be shown in small things as well as large. The ambiguous attitude to witchcraft in The *Return of the Native* is a tiny example. Throughout most of the novel the reader is invited to share Clym Yeobright's dismissal of witchcraft as superstitious ignorance: for instance, when he hears that in church Susan Nonsuch has stuck a pin into the arm of Eustacia Vye because she believes her to be a witch, he asks his mother whether now she will accept that the heathdwellers stand in want of his plan of education. And yet towards the end of the novel we see Susan make a wax model of Eustacia, thrust it through with more pins, and melt it in her fire; within minutes Eustacia is dead. What are we to believe? If we follow Hardy, or Hardy's narrators, then we believe both with mutually contradictory but equally vital aspects of our self; intellectually we accept that witchcraft is an outmoded superstition with no relevance to our modern lives, but emotionally we pay tribute to the power that the concept has over us.

So it is too with the issue of Christianity; Hardy was quite capable of loving the Bible and the Prayer-book and the Hymnal, of caring for churches not just as architectural designs, but as conductors of something of value, of entering fully into the beauty of the services; and yet at the same time denouncing utterly the Christian Churches as institutions, and declaring that they represent and mediate a bankrupt creed that has outworn its usefulness in this world.

It sounds perhaps as if Hardy was an artist at the old game of having your cake and eating it, but that is much too simple. It is rather that he was able to rest in uncertainties, mysteries, doubts, without any irritable reaching after fact and reason, that he is a negatively capable writer (in Keats's phrase), who didn't feel uncomfortable allowing apparently conflicting tendencies to coexist within him (indeed he probably had no alternative, so deeply ingrained does this habit of mind seem to be), but rather found them fruitful in his writing. His often repeated assertion that there was no coherent philosophy to be found in his writing, but rather a series of seemings, is characteristic of this negative capability, as too is the fact that these seemings are sometimes contradictory, even within the same text.

The separateness of Hardy's intellectual and emotional response to small and large issues, the two Thomas Hardys as I have tried to characterize them in my dramatized fantasy, does not often produce contradiction in *Tess of the d'Urbervilles*, but it does produce a specially fertile mixture of sympathy and argument, of understanding of the characters from the inside and from the outside. The double fiction of the writer embodied in the narrative voice of the novel – 'Thomas Hardy' the envisioner of Tess and 'Thomas Hardy' the sometimes bitter and sententious gentleman-critic – offers the reader two hardly separable, intertwined views of her life and of the other lives that help to shape it, voices that make the fabric of the novel the rich material it is.

Thus the title page offers much evidence about how we should read the novel. The dual focus on Tess as peasant and aristocrat; the dual focus on Tess as woman and martyr; the dual existence of the narrative, mediated between two voices; the revealing epigraph.

Now here is a reasonably uncontroversial statement that I want to test by the light of the title-page: it is the unconscious conflict within Tess between nature and society that provides the main dynamic force that drives the novel. What I want to suggest is that this conflict derives directly from the opposing insights of the two 'Thomas Hardys' whose voices conduct the fiction.

To the creator Hardy Tess is a leopard at a pause, a field mushroom, a pink rose, a sap-filled tree, a wounded pheasant; and more than this. Tess in vital growth is the Froom Valley, Tess in arid emotional starvation is Flintcomb-Ash; Tess receiving the age-old violation her ancestors had dealt is the ancient Chase, Tess suffering the consequences of her violation is Wellbridge Manor; Tess as a kept woman is the splendid but seedy fairy town Sandbourne, Tess as a briefly fulfilled woman is the real fairy palace Bramshurst Court, shut up for years but now momentarily released and filled with love. For this primary Hardy, Tess is a fragment of the natural world, naturally seeking the proper environment for the moments of her life. She is purely and naturally a woman, desiring understanding and satisfaction, meeting male violation of her body and mind, and coping with it, barely, so painful is it; taking in the end a violent remedy out of nature, and finding relief and joy in a momentary union. It is only at the very last that the second Hardy takes over entirely, with more painful results.

To Hardy the gentleman-critic (and I have nothing pejorative in mind in this description – on the contrary, without his voice the novel would be immeasurably the poorer), Tess is an example of the destructive effect of society's pressures and conventions upon a nature naturally pure and unstained; Tess is an issue. He will not allow her to think only as her nature would suggest that she should; he will not allow her to be simply a peasant, existing in a primitive society of harmony with the rest of the world in its pleasure and its pain. Instead Tess has to be educated in the ways of Victorian society, read in English as well as Dorset, conditioned from an early age by the ethical teachings of the church. It is his voice, for instance, that spells out for us the irony in the situation at the end of chapter XIII. He argues that Tess, wandering in the woods near her home, has been falsely conditioned by English society, as embodied in school and church, to feel herself outcast, by reason of her sexual violation and pregnancy, from the 'purity' of the natural world around her, as well as from that society. In a true view, though, this voice contends, Tess would be seen as thoroughly in harmony with the creatures around her, and (as he suggests in a different place), her experience with Alec d'Urberville in Cranborne Chase would be seen as part of her education rather than as a sin. This is the kind of thing I have in mind when I say that one Thomas Hardy has 'presented' the vision of the other Thomas Hardy. As Hardy the creator embodies Tess in simile so the critic Hardy surrounds her with hedges of argument and allusion; to use a comparison from Wordsworth, as the primary Hardy enacts a 'Tintern Abbey' view of nature, so Hardy the critic lashes the 'Immortality Ode' view of life.

Of course Tess is not the only character in her novel, though between them Tess and the world around her leave precious little space for anyone else to grow in. Nevertheless the dual voices can also be seen at work where Tess's two lovers are concerned.

Alec d'Urberville, most people agree, is little more than a cardboard cutout, two-dimensional rapist and bounder. Originally though, the primary Hardy had it that Alec's conversion to Evangelism after Tess's departure from his life and his mother's death was quite genuine, answering to some emotional need or weakness in him. The second Hardy, respecting the primary creation, accepted this version of the character's life. But when the book was published, critics and friends suggested (from their viewpoint near the summit of conventional opinion), that a meaningful conversion in such a man was highly improbable, and perhaps even blasphemous. The gentleman-critic Hardy eventually decided to make changes to Alec's conversion, but I do not think he did so for the reasons that were urged. It was not that he could no longer believe that Alec was capable of experiencing a genuine religious conversion – or of being unconverted by Tess's power over him – but it was rather that he recognized belatedly that the conversion and its sequel, if it is genuine, heartfelt, forces the reader to think about Alec's character in a way that just isn't available to him in the rest of the novel. His conversion as it originally stood makes Alec for a moment interesting, and I think that Hardy the gentleman-critic accepted that the creator Hardy had in this case raised expectations that he simply hadn't space enough, or energy to fulfil at most other places where Alec is involved in Tess's story. It was a gradual, and perhaps painful process, but Alec's conversion was reduced in sincerity through alterations in successive texts until it reached what we read now, something at the level of a music-hall joke.[2]

The critic Hardy had a much greater problem with the other important male character, Angel Clare. Put simply, Angel has to be capable of inspiring the deepest love in Tess, and at the same time capable of ruthlessly rejecting her when he learns that she has had a child by another man; and finally he has to be capable of growth to a stage where he can reject his rejection, unlearn his unlove. The amount of revision to details of the characterisation of Angel made in several successive stages is really quite large, evidence of the concern of the composite Thomas Hardy. It is reasonable as a generalisation to suggest that what happens in these revisions is that the emotional and intellectual intensity of Angel's love for Tess is increased, and its physical expression is diminished.

The effect is as if the primary creating Hardy was not specially interested in making Angel consistent in his behaviour, since Tess was all his concern, but that subsequently the critic Hardy began in his 'editing' of the narrative to see the need for a clearer definition of the kind of man Angel could be, or ought to be, and undertook in detail some of these changes. To take only one example, the description of Angel when he appears at Talbothays, it is clear that he was one man in the first manuscript readings, and another when the book was published. At first he had a tender voice, eloquent eyes, and a humorous turn to his too delicate mouth; in the later version we see him with an appreciative voice, fixed abstracted eyes, and a firm close of the lower lip. As representative features they indicate considerably differing personalities, and this kind of rethinking is evident wherever Angel appears.

In the end though, however delicate and subtle the revisions to Angel's character, there is no way that the reader can feel sympathetic to Angel during the second half of the novel. Indeed, so intense is our concentration upon Tess, directed there by the equal intensity of the primary Hardy, that we have trouble even in understanding Angel; and understanding is the most we can hope for. The following chapter is one attempt at such an understanding.

Comparisons have often been made between *Tess of the d'Urbervilles* and Hardy's last novel *Jude the Obscure* (1895), and debate has in recent years run back and forth concerning which should be considered Hardy's finest work in fiction. If the two novels are looked at in terms of the structure of the character-relations in the narrative, roughly the terms in which I have been viewing Tess, it has often been suggested that when Hardy followed *Tess of the d'Urbervilles* with *Jude the Obscure* he inverted the narrative line of the earlier novel, and explored the effect of two women, one aggressively physical (Arabella Donn) and one uncertainly spiritual (Sue Bridehead), on one man ultimately destroyed by the tensions within his nature (Jude Fawley). I have always felt, though, that Jude is too weak a creation, both in terms of Hardy's imaginative investment, and in the dramatisation of his personal dilemmas, to sustain the burden of the comparison; and I would go further, and suggest that it is more satisfying to turn back to *The Mayor of Casterbridge*, for a point of reference.

As my earlier discussion of the novel attempts to show, and as many others have pointed out, Michael Henchard is alone at the centre of the novel, and like Tess he attracts our attention and sympathy to the virtual exclusion of Farfrae, Lucetta or even Elizabeth-Jane, all of whom struggle to make any impression on the reader. It seems as a conclusion not unreasonable to suggest that Hardy is at his very best as a novelist when he allows himself to concentrate his considerable imaginative power on a single character, and it is characteristic of all his writing that the novel in which that character is a woman marks the height of his achievement in fiction.

7

Angel Clare's Story

[Note. If the reader should require more introduction to this narrative than the above title, it may be said I had the privilege recently of examining the papers of the James family of Marnhull, and that amongst them found the following document, now published with the consent of the family. There was no date attached, but internal evidence suggests that it must have been composed in 1915 or 1916. The writer, Mr Michael James, was born in 1858, and died in 1928.]

I've read Mr Hardy's account. In fact I've read each version, as he has tinkered with it. How could I not, since I was so deeply involved. And I would have let his account rest, but that as I come closer to death, I worry that my grandchildren, and their children, may sometime read Mr Hardy's powerful and disturbing book, and I will not be alive to tell them how it seemed to me. So in the end I've decided to write it down for them. Mr Hardy is a fair, even a generous man, and he has a sympathetic imagination, but it was Tess he knew, not me; it was her story he was telling. And though he was in court, and heard my testimony, and faithfully embodies some of my thoughts and feelings in his account, I do have something more to say, though only this rotten fever, and the consciousness of my mortality and his book's apparent immortality, have persuaded me to write. Perhaps it would have been simpler if I had let him interview me back in 1889; but it was too painful then, and I was too angry.

Where should I begin? Well, one of the things that seems most important now is the class business. I think, since I came back from Brazil, I have been as nearly free of a consciousness of class as an Englishman can be, but when I first went to Talbothays, I had only got as far as an indifference to the forms and observances of the society I grew up in. When I began to learn agriculture by staying for a while and working on various kinds of farms, I felt towards the workers mostly a good-humoured condescension.

At Talbothays things were rather different, in that some of the labourers lived in. But still at first I kept myself to myself, and hardly noticed the special arrangements that were made for me, to keep me from too intimate contact with the workfolk, thought nothing of the curtseying and the pulling of the forelock and the sirring. My whole life had been conducted thus far with such an accompaniment, directed at my parents when I was younger, of course, but accorded to me as soon as I began to look like a man. It was like the air I breathed.

When I arrived at Talbothays I thought myself a radical, a rebel. I had rejected the religious faith of my father some years before; now I was rejecting the sterile narrow intellectual life of my brothers, returning (in the sense that some of my ancestors, certainly, were agriculturists) to the dynasties-outlasting process of getting food for man's body. Ploughing, or shearing, or milking, I thought, no-one would have power to tell me how to think or what to believe – there would be intellectual liberty. And I was right, I still think, in a limited way, so long as I could be master of my own land, and could associate only with those who respected my freedom; it might have worked in Australia, or South Africa. But never in England. Of course I hoped to make money as well, but it was the ideal of freedom and idea of return, of working to fulfil mankind's most basic need, that drew me to it. Romantic, of course, sentimental, even, though I think I have in late years made something real out of the half-practical idealism.

I have just re-read what Mr Hardy wrote about my life before Tess arrived at Talbothays. It still seems odd to see myself called Angel, but I suppose he had his ironic purpose. Can you imagine my father and mother calling a child of theirs Angel? But Mr Hardy probably would have made it Jesus if we were in the custom of using the name, as the Spanish are. But, aside from the tendency to make me speak like my father, which I think I had got out of the habit of doing by the time I left school, I cannot really disagree with the image of me he presents as rising out of the past. (I noticed, by the way, that in the manuscript of his account of these events which Mr Hardy gave to the British Museum a few years ago, and which I went up to town specially to look at before I set to writing this – what – explanation, he said at first that I loomed out of the past. There is an ominous quality in 'loom' which he must have regretted forgoing in favour of the much more positive, even organic 'rise'. But I suppose too much prefiguring of the disaster, even if addressed to the readers' subconscious, was inadvisable.) I suppose my mouth is small, though who is to say that a woman's mouth shall be small and a man's large? My whole frame is spare, though farming had, even then, toughened it (lifting Marian across that flooded road was nevertheless as hard work as I ever hope to have). And if there was something vague and nebulous about my expression, my body was hard and full of life. Mr Hardy implies that my life was somehow a failure, because people had said that I might do anything if I tried, and I ended up farming. All I can say is that it has been enough for me, however unexpected or backward a step it might have seemed to others. In this I feel a kinship with a man who figures in another of Mr Hardy's Wessex chronicles, whom he there calls Clym Yeobright, and whom my father knew.

He got most of the material about my quarrels with my father from Cuthbert. I learned later that Mr Hardy's friend Horace Moule had been Cuthbert's tutor for a short while, and that Moule introduced the two at Cambridge in the seventies. I must say that when I read the account as it appeared in the *Graphic*, besides being astonished, it did bring the scenes back to me very vividly. One or two details were wrong, though, and I wrote to him about them. Foolish, no doubt, and it would have been better to let the whole business alone. Almost everyone outside Dorset thought the serial purely a work of fiction, and those nearer home who remembered the business knew how much of it was indeed fiction. And having written once, I found myself writing again and again. Sometimes he paid attention, sometimes not. That was his prerogative, of course.

Anyway, I remembered quoting father's beloved *Hebrews* at him, just for the sake of the cheap thrill of seeing his face as I did so. That upset him more than anything, almost, and I regretted it the moment I said it. I was pleased Mr Hardy included it in the book when it came out in three volumes, though he left the reader to sense the cruelty of the gesture. I was much more pleased with another change that he made at my suggestion. Father asked why he should provide me with a University education if it was not to be used for the honour and glory of God, and Cuthbert must have told Mr Hardy that my answer was 'that I may put it to other uses'. Cuthbert is all right, and liberal up to a point, but I suspect he had blocked out my real reply: 'that it may be used for the honour and glory of man'. I think that if there is a grace that I possessed as a young man underlying all that I did, or tried – a grace that might have saved me from the horror of my life – it was an idealistic and disinterested love of my fellow humans. Sadly this theoretic commitment remained largely theoretic, until it was too late.

When Mr Hardy talks of my 'reading human nature' in the dining-room at Talbothays, he says no more than the truth. I did not share their lives, I observed them, tried to interpret them. (You should know, by the way, that he originally suggested that the arrangement by which I had a separate table from the other dairypeople was my own idea because I was too snobbish to eat with them. I put him right on that too, and in the book version he correctly attributed the notion to the dairyman's wife. Being not so far above the dairymaids in class, she was very strict in keeping the gap as wide as possible, and I couldn't disrupt her well-meaning arrangement. It did allow me to read when I felt like it, but still, I would willingly have shared the table with the others.) Mr Hardy has collapsed my experience on several farms into this one, of course. By the time I reached the Froom Valley I had already found by experience what I knew by reason (which is no real knowledge), that individuality is as richly discriminated amongst the rural workfolk as in my own class. But still my experience was with the eyes and ears only, not with the whole self. That was to come, of course. If I did feel delight, it was that of an observer, a connoisseur of characters; I had only ditched one set of clichés for another.

He's right though, to say that the ache of modernism, the unrest of contemporary society, had vanished as soon as I had become well accustomed to working with my body instead of my mind. There were muscles I never knew I had; I discovered a depth of stamina in myself, after long nights of lambing, that I had quite unsuspected from my walking holidays with my brothers. Strolls really, they were, to the accompaniment of Felix's arid dogma. It seems hardly possible even now that I had nearly danced with Tess years before we met at Talbothays. If I had chosen her then . . . but no, that's ridiculous. Even if she had stood out as a stunning beauty, which she didn't, it still would have been one dance and then off. Mr Hardy makes too much of it, I do believe. No conceivable mechanism could have brought us together then; I lived twenty or more miles away, in a different class. I suppose when he laments that d'Urberville took her and I didn't, he implies that humanity should have evolved by now an efficient erotic labelling characteristic, so that when suited couples meet they recognize each other at once, and all unsuitable mates are repelled, whatever the aesthetic or sexual charge in the individual physical form. Such a development would certainly give novelists less to write about. But in life as it is, how could I have known that one of this mass of white-dressed women, old and young, the whole village-full pretty much, would turn out to be the one I should choose to marry? We have to deal with the world as it is; why waste time wishing it could be as it never will be?

I had seen a lot of Dorset and the surrounding counties on these walking vacations, and I would have said I knew the countryside pretty well. But it wasn't until I began tramping the downs above Bridport with the shepherd and his dogs, day and night, in fair weather and foul, that I began to feel the world as well as see it, not just to discriminate between plants, which I had been able to do from childhood, but to understand something of the place of each in the organization of nature, and of man. Mr Hardy, poetical but accurate, says that I made close acquaintance with 'the seasons in their moods, morning and evening, night and noon, winds in their different tempers, trees, waters and mists, shades and silences, and the voices of inanimate things.' It is true that I had only known these things before as a background to what seemed more important, but no-one brought up in a small Dorset town like Beaminster could be ignorant of them entirely, or ever ignore them. It was a sharpening of the senses, particularly of hearing. I had always had a good ear for birdsongs, but when, one night, I caught myself distinguishing a fir from an elm by the sound of the wind passing through it, I knew that I had advanced to a new level of sympathetic perception. And this was an important change, I think, one that helped on the second and greater change. Though the world was richer and more various than once I thought it, I had hardly yet learned the first thing about the conscious beings who populated it.

I moved on from Bridport to Talbothays in April, and Tess arrived that May. Just as I failed to pick her out at Marnhull (though how was it a failure), so too I remarked that the table was fuller by one than before, but no more. Mr Hardy says that I was always more aware of the general nature of what was about me than of the individual details, linking his suggestion, I suppose, to his sense that I seemed habitually preoccupied and vague. That might have been true before I took up farming, and Cuthbert may well have given him the hint; but it was certainly no longer true concerning the natural world, and if it was true concerning the people around me, it was much less so. Tess, whom I now think of as having been the most lovely woman I have ever known, never stood out in a crowd. She didn't push herself forward, and though her form was perfectly proportioned she was no more than average in height, and neither her hair nor her colouring was particularly striking. It was her mouth and her eyes that set her apart from all others to my mind, and, of course, her voice. Mr Hardy uses all those musical analogies; I noticed, reading through his manuscript last year, that he wrote at first that it seemed 'soft', and then changed it to 'fluty'. He says somewhere else that the deeper note when she was particularly moved was remembered by everyone who knew her vibrating like the stopt-diapason note on a cathedral organ, or something like that. He has an ear for such things. But even if I hadn't noticed the quality of her voice, what she said would have attracted my attention; how could it not – a milkmaid describing in homely terms an intense mystical extasis?

However, it is with my response to her words, and the idea behind them, and my awareness of her presence at the table that this account of our life together begins to differ from Mr Hardy's. You can tell from the manuscript in the British Museum that he thought hard about how I must have reacted. At first he wrote that I said to myself: 'What a superb daughter of Nature that milkmaid is', but the adjective wasn't right. He tried 'true', but that wouldn't do, and then 'genuine', before returning (it must have been reluctantly) to 'superb'. He knew that wasn't what he needed, and eventually he settled for 'fresh and virginal' in the cheap book edition (where much of what I particularly object to first got into his story), which in the first element comes close to something of what I felt, but the second is way off the mark. I can see he couldn't resist the irony, and that he wanted to lay hints for his readers of the particular kind of pernicious folly I would perpetrate against Tess, but her untouched quality, what Sir Willoughby Patterne in Meredith's *The Egoist* thought of in his vile self-occupation as the bloom on the plum, was the last thing on my mind. She had just talked of feeling her soul separate from her body, in such a way as to make me feel it happen along with her. Of course Crick was too practically-minded to understand, but I was not considering the young woman's apparent virginity, but rather wondering at such a quality of sensibility in such a place, and then, as I caught her glance, remembering her eyes from somewhere in my past, somewhere pleasant.

I have similar reservations about Mr Hardy's description of my thoughts regarding the conversation I had with Tess after she had been drawn to my harp-playing. He makes me sound much more abstracted than I really was. It was her almost pantheistic sense of the trees and streams that caught my fancy, not so much the personification of the future. Mr Hardy seems to forget how fully my recent outdoor experiences had prepared me to sympathize with such a view. On the other hand, I don't think he stresses enough the feeling I have now, that I *ought* to have been able to sense that her imaginative representation of the future as a series of threatening days, fierce and cruel implied some disaster, or series of bitter hardships in her past. That I ought to have recognized that her desire to know why the sun shines on the just and the unjust alike, expressed with such passion, addressed some rooted misery in her life. But I had not yet learned to interpret humans as I had learned to interpret nature, and I was partly misled by her freshness. No excuse, though.

Tess, it seems, thought me poetic. Perhaps it wasn't just facts and ideas she absorbed from me. I don't know. But 'poetic' describes perfectly the inward intensity of my sense of her. For a while I was amazed at myself, on a level with a dairymaid. But that passed, passed long before she told me she was a d'Urberville.

It was, I think now, through my new understanding of nature that Tess entered my heart and my soul that summer. I found I knew more names of things – birds, plants, insects – but she knew more about how it was with them, what their particular essence might be. I could explain, label; she, with a word, or a phrase, made them live in my imagination. I taught her facts, and ideas (more fool I), not just about nature, but history and philosophy; she introduced me to life. And slowly, quite unconsciously I think, to herself, my first human. I was seduced by the beauty and the richness and the vitality of the landscape we walked through, and eventually I advanced through the environment to her; learned, as Mr Hardy so acutely puts it, to call her Tess instead of Demeter, while growing to believe at the same time that she really was what she seemed at times, the epitome of my ideal of womanhood. At first, to me, it *was* a very Forest of Arden kind of existence, a kind of pleasant pastoral condescenscion in which she found tongues in trees and I sermons in stones. We seemed as all rural lovers must seem, like Adam and Eve alone in paradise, without, that summer, even Adam's penalty. But after a while, I think after I had been home, I was no longer conscious of the gap between my social position and my life on the farm. I think the gap diminished as my fascination at learning Tess grew to love for her, driven on by sex but different from it.

When I had her in my arms in the flooded lane, oh then I knew what wanting a beloved woman was. Of course I knew about sex; I'd sown my wild oats, that time in London, when I thought I was in love for one day and night. But her false hair, her coarse skin, her artificial laughter, her tears produced at will – above all what in the end I intuitively felt, her desperation – gave me the strength to break free. Then I was all contempt and disgust, at myself and at her: now I think I understand her need, and I am ashamed, a little, at the cruelty of my words to her that dawn. Though they were true, and I longed to be free of her, still they must have cut, for her tears then were I think not false.

But the bearing of Tess in my arms, against my breast, moved through me like wave after wave, involuntarily. I would have kissed her then, I bent to, but a memory of that past experience suddenly chilled my lips, and I could no more kiss her than I could have flown with her. Mr Hardy says 'suspension at this point was desirable'. Well I did feel as cold as his words imply, but it was from a violent conflict of feeling rather than rational calculation. [I will say nothing about the vile invention of a wheelbarrow Mr Hardy was forced into for the *Graphic*; of course I wrote to him about it, and he told me that his editor wouldn't allow such intimate physical contact. Anyway he changed it in the book version.]

On the other hand he catches much better than I could the way the world conspired to intensify desire:

> Amid the oozing fatness and warm ferments of the Var Vale, at a season when the rush of juices could almost be heard below the hiss of fertilization, it was impossible that the most fanciful love should not grow passionate.

This is precisely how it seemed, the audible erotic charge. Mr Hardy seems to enact in his imaginative senses – perhaps in his physical senses for all I know – George Eliot's famous image in which she talks of the intolerable burden it would be to hear the grass grow, the squirrel's heart beat; except that he senses these things with sympathy, even joy sometimes, not always as a pain. And when he talks of an influence from the sky that came to me like an annunciation, well it did feel like a divine inspiration, an arrow from Eros. I was very disappointed when he changed 'annunciation' to 'excitation' in his recent Wessex edition; perhaps the Christian overtones of the word were too powerful for him, when what he wanted to stress was the sexual nature of what he imagined me feeling. Why I didn't kiss her then I don't know; it was obvious she wanted me to at that moment. I suppose Mr Hardy is right; just pure chivalry, or an overscrupulous conscience. There are times when a kiss is the only right thing, and it was then. I suppose it was an outcrop of my Pauline upbringing, still not far beneath the surface anywhere in my life; and it didn't, in the end make much difference, for the kiss came. And there was still, as I have often mentioned, the class business, which I hadn't yet fully set aside as irrelevant to anything important in life.

There was another detail I suggested to Mr Hardy that he remove from the *Graphic* which bears on my class-instincts. He said that, several hours after my declaration of love, I was thinking that 'feeling had indeed smothered judgement that day', and I'm sure I was, amongst many other things, concerned about the class difference between us; wondering, in a preliminary way, whether we had any future together. But he continued his imaginative recreation of my thought with 'What end, or ground, or reason, was there to show for his inconsiderate declaration?' I am sure I thought nothing of the sort; 'unconsidered declaration' might have been all right, but as for 'reason', what reason is there ever behind such moments, and though I had then, and still have a bias towards the rational in philosophy and life, you would have to be a cold fish indeed to premeditate such an embrace as that. I did think, I must have thought about possible ends, but as for 'ground', what I had felt myself, and felt in her was ground enough; putting it into words was a formality. Anyway, I'm glad to say he took that sentence out altogether.

I discovered something even more interesting about Mr Hardy's account of the aftermath of that decisive moment only when I got a look at his manuscript. Immediately after reporting these thoughts of mine, his narrator you will find, whatever version you read, discriminated between our responses to the embrace, saying that Tess 'seemed stilled, almost alarmed, at what had occurred' and of me that 'the novelty, unpremeditation, mastery of circumstance disquieted him – palpitating contemplative being that he was. He could hardly realize their true relations to each other as yet . . . ' What I learned from the manuscript was that at first he had us share these responses, writing 'the two had kept apart, fevered, almost alarmed at what had occurred. The novelty, the unpremeditation, the dominating force disquieted them, palpitating bundles of nerves as both of them were. They could not realize their true relations to each other as yet . . . ' I think this must have been the impression that he got from Tess herself, but after a while he found it necessary to his purpose to see her as more passive, me more as authoritative. In the change I am made to seem concerned about my lack of control over the situation, where originally we were both disconcerted by the strength of the passion we had revealed to each other; I know I was, and I think she was, and the change diminishes a reader's sense of the power of what had happened to us. I am also made contemplative as well as palpitating, an adjective I don't on the whole quarrel with, but at that time of supreme emotional confusion contemplation was far from possible, and indeed Mr Hardy makes this clear in the almost surreal vision he invents for me of the fabric of the dairyhouse alive with sexuality:

> The aged and lichened brick gables breathed forth 'come!' The windows smiled, the door coaxed and beckoned, the creeper blushed confederacy. A personality within it was so far-reaching in her influence as to spread into and make the bricks, mortar, and whole overhanging sky throb with a burning sensibility.

I can't think that I would ever propose to myself so poetic a fantasy, but it catches well the overpowering emotional intensity we were both experiencing that evening. Contemplation, indeed!

All the existential thoughts about Tess which he gives me are a fair, compressed version of what went through my mind over two or three days. I wasn't sure that marriage would be good either for me or for her, and since in our culture it is the convention for the man to ask the woman this particular question, I felt, at least for a time, that I had to think for both of us. And of course I couldn't make up my mind. It wasn't that I was particularly worried about marrying Tess; but I *was* worried about marrying a dairymaid. Perhaps if I became a farmer, the difference in class would be immaterial, but there would still be a host of assumptions we could not share once we got down to living together, habits of mind, ways of living that were masked at present by the novelty of our situation, and by our mutual passion. Would these differences get in the way of that comradeship that alone will sustain a marriage? I thought all this and more, but, as Mr

Hardy writes, I was driven towards her by every heave of my pulse.

So to get a breathing-space, I went home for a few days. The conclusion was foregone; I think I knew even before I left that there would be nothing at Beaminster rectory that would stop me doing what the whole of my being was on fire to do. And Mr Hardy correctly says that I felt more than ever alienated from my family that time. These are his words – I would not have used such rhetoric, but they are accurate:

> Latterly he had seen only Life, felt only the great passionate pulse of existence, unwarped, uncontorted, untrammelled by those creeds which futilely attempt to check what wisdom would be content to regulate.

The impress of this 'pulse' went deep into my own life; how superficial my brothers seemed, how sadly narrow my father. It is amazing how flexible Mr Hardy's prose is, for in the simplicity of what he says of my love for Tess as I proposed her as wife to my father and mother, he catches precisely the deepest, overwhelming, single thought that echoed under all my waking hours at home: 'It was for herself that he loved Tess; her soul, her heart, her substance'.

What a mixture of pleasure and pain it is to relive those months when I courted Tess. Oh how I did love her, how I wanted her, how deeply I felt completed only when I was with her: 'the ardour of his affection [was] so palpable that she seemed to flinch under it like a plant in too burning a sun.' Yes; oh, yes, indeed, that is how I felt, and Tess only seemed to flinch, being caught up in our shared heat. Of course I poured iced water on it all by asking her to marry me as soon almost as I saw her again. But how was I to suspect her secret? The next weeks were amazing to me. I suppose a fragment of my surprise at her refusal was the class thing; it would, I think, even now be hard for a liberated, emancipated male of the middle class not to feel slightly surprised that a milkmaid had refused his offer of marriage. But mostly it was because I knew, as well as I knew anything, that she had felt the way I had felt before I went to Beaminster. Without the key, without knowledge of her secret, how could I have been expected to interpret her apparently contrasting attitudes to me and to marriage with me. I was hopeless, I fully admit, utterly ignorant of the lives and thoughts and emotions of my fellow men and women. But I had begun to learn, to understand this individual, to care for her in more than a theoretical way. Perhaps I should have guessed something deep and important was wrong; perhaps many other people would have done so; I can't tell. But I am sure that full comprehension of Tess was barred to me by her possession of a secret whose existence I had no wit or instinct to discern, let alone to guess at its nature. I have learned to abhor and detest secrets; they have a ghastly taint of death about them, a flavour of mortality.

It sounds so facile, so foolish now, that I replied to her cry that she would tell me all about herself and her experiences:

> Your experiences, dear; yes, certainly; any number . . . . My Tess has, no doubt, almost as many experiences as that wild convolvulus out there on the garden hedge, that opened itself this morning for the first time.

It sounds condescending too, with an assumption that because she was a peasant she couldn't have had any real experiences. Again, in part (I believe a small part) it was; but much more it was a response to her innocence of habit and thought, her rich unsophistication, her wondering curiosity about everything, her freedom from many of the social constraints with which I was so familiar. She seemed untwisted by life, despite her sometimes melancholy or bitter perceptions; she seemed to live as if there were nothing to do but live all out, if you see what I mean. The people I knew best all lived behind artificial masks of restraint. How could Nature allow someone with her experience to remain free of all outward or inward signs of it?

I said to myself, countless times, 'she loves me, she likes the idea of marrying me, why won't she do it? Why, why? She says she isn't good enough for me, and I tell her that our class difference is an irrelevance, but she persists'. How slippery language is. When I thought she meant 'good' in social terms, she meant morally good. Should I have worked that out, suspected something? Even now I think not. I would have had to be a different man; someone like d'Urberville might have done so, perhaps. Loving Tess was like loving the world around me made human; Mr Hardy understood that; he felt the same way. Kissing Tess was like kissing Nature incarnate. And this isn't an idealization, an abstraction. At first it was, Demeter and all that, but not once we had embraced; all metaphors about her, all ways of describing her, experiencing her were from nature. I suppose I might have thought of the natural laws of procreation. But it was the human, the soul, that made her more than nature, and prevented insight of that kind.

I didn't impose on her; I restrained myself, though it was hard, I even avoided her to a degree, tried to talk to her, to set aside my physical need for her. It seemed fair, since she was so distressed. Mr Hardy makes it seem ridiculously formal:

> Their condition of domiciliary comradeship put her, as the woman, to such disadvantage by its enforced intercourse, that he felt it unfair to exercise any pressure of blandishment, which he might have honestly employed had she been better able to avoid him.

This is the language of the bad journalist, or the court reporter; and of course it reflects on me, as if the stiff overwriting reflected my thought pattern. But then, by this time he is clearer about his purpose in describing our relationship. And yet he still cannot altogether suppress the truth of how it was, because Tess told it to him:

> Clare persistently wooed her in undertones like that of the purling milk – at the cow's side, at skimmings, at buttermakings, at cheesemakings, among broody poultry, and among farrowing pigs . . .

My love was another element of nature, my nature reaching out to hers; that is how she felt it. She told me so near the end, and she must have told him. As she must have told him that she grew to believe my love would cherish and defend her, under any conditions, changes, charges, revelations. I probably would have said as much and more if she had asked.

Oh, if only she had told me her secret then, if only she had had the courage to tell me on the way back from Wool, then when I was passionately seeking her, everything would have been different. I don't know what I would have said, or done. I am not the same man now, and I find it hard fully to become the inexperienced impassioned loving prig I was then. But all the alternatives are better than what happened. I might have rejected her out of hand as I did months later, passed the rest of the journey in shocked silence, and left Talbothays the next day. But I don't think that is the most likely. I would have been shocked, but don't forget, Tess had not committed herself to me; we had never even kissed lip to lip. She was a mystery to me; the mystery would have been explained. If I had not at once gone away; if I had stayed at the farm, thinking how this changed matters, I think there is a fifty-fifty chance that I might have learned from nature, I might have continued to learn from what I knew of the world about me that what Tess had told me was no more than a part of the functioning of that world. Simply the onward action of the cart, the return to Talbothays, the reentry into that familiar society, the need to keep her secret before the others, might all have helped me to retain my new experience, and keep suppressed my father's pernicious dogma. And then the heightened desire of the unattained; it is so much stronger than the desire for the obtained, of a different kind, single-minded. That might have helped too. Of course it would have been better still if it had been always known, a kind of very tall wild oat of the kind that middle-class young women are not allowed, but rural girls can live down, since country customs are less strict. If I had got to know her before I was told about it, and I saw how much as a matter of course the others took it, then it surely would not have meant much to me. I don't know. I am afraid that the man I was then would not have married her even if her Sorrow had been generally known and forgotten as unimportant. But even if I had abandoned Tess and the farm at once, how much less harm would have come to her than eventually did!

The first time I knew about the letter Tess's mother sent her was when I read it in Mr Hardy's book. Even at the last Tess didn't tell me of it. Perhaps she thought as I do now, that she should have followed her mother's advice, and kept the secret for ever. We would have moved away from Dorset soon enough after our marriage, and the odds against my ever discovering it from any outside source would have been very slim. And then, later, if it had come out, especially if we were in some frontier region of America, or in the outback in Australia, it would have seemed irrelevant beside our present joy in life together. But at the same time, I recognize that it would have taken a conscious act of will of great strength not to tell me when she did, her nature being what it was, the circumstances being what they were. But still, having married me with the secret intact, I am sure she should not have told me of it so soon after. This is not an attempt at self-exculpation; merely the judgement of a sixty-year-old man who has gained some wisdom through experience, though of course as always too late for it to be much good in my own life.

That kiss she gave me, instead of her secret, on the way back from Wool: it still takes only a slight act of imagination to feel her lips and her hands, and her body against mine. It was an initiation for me, and I feel it more sharply now, I do believe than I did even at the time. And perhaps, again I can't be sure, it was a moment of passage from one state to another; it was a commitment on her part, but my life with her after it was different too. I had attained to my desire, and instead of anxiety and persuasion, it was togetherness, and anticipation of marriage, planning; indeed I was at first rather disconcerted by the openness of our togetherness, until again I saw that it was accepted as natural by everyone around us. And yet another class-convention fell away from me. After all, we loved one another, we were to be married some time, it was our greatest joy to be together; it would, I now saw, have been illogical to hide our joy behind conventional middleclass modesty, reserve, restraint. Even more it seemed as if I was the comrade not just of Tess, though I wanted no more, but also of the river, the meadows, the birds, the trees, the breezes, the radiant sky. You have no idea how intoxicating it was.

At the same time though, Mr Hardy intensified his distortion of me, and I think some sensitive readers of his account have understood that this was so. He wrote of Tess's worship of me:

> There was hardly a touch of earth in her love for Clare. To her sublime trustfulness he was all that goodness could be, knew all that a guide, philosopher, and friend should know. She thought every line in the contour of his person the perfection of masculine beauty; his soul the soul of a saint; his intellect that of a seer. The wisdom of her love for him, as love, sustained her dignity; she seemed to be wearing a crown. The compassion of his love for her, as she saw it, made her lift up her heart to him in devotion. He would sometimes catch her large worshipful eyes, that had no bottom to them, looking at him from their depths, as if she saw something immortal before her.

Perhaps Tess did feel something like this, but I was quite unaware of it in such terms, terms that make it utterly impossible for any man to live up to. I felt it as love, only, a passionate desire for my company, which I returned. I knew more than she did, I'd thought about life as an idea and a problem, where she had felt it; I could talk about it in historical or widely comparative terms, and she longed to listen and question. That was flattering I suppose, but if I thought about it at all, it was that I had something she wanted, and I gave it to her. Mr Hardy made it seem a one-way process of worship, particularly when he gave his version of my nature:

> She had not known that men could be so disinterested, chival-rous, protective, in their love for women as he. Angel Clare was far from all she thought him in this respect; absurdly far, indeed; but he was in truth more spiritual than animal; he had himself well in hand, and was singularly free from grossness. Though not cold-natured he was rather bright than hot; less Byronic than Shelleyan. He could love desperately, but with a love more especially inclined to the imaginative and ethereal; it was a fastidious emotion which could jealously guard the loved one against his very self.

Some of this is true, but is not particular to me, but to men of my class and upbringing. We were taught to honour the women we loved, to treat them as easily breakable dolls, to keep from them all sexual knowledge until it was essential for procreation. Of course no man ever really treated the woman he loved body and soul with the extremes of respect and reserve that such a teaching enjoins, but the spirit of restraint and respect is engrained against the sexual drive, and holds it in suspension until that great social dam, marriage, is breached in a series of vows. I accept fully the literary comparison, and I have reasonable self-control (though even Mr Hardy's account of my growing love for Tess had already provided several examples of its total failure). If by saying I 'was singularly free from grossness' he means that I didn't try to fling her in the nearest bed of rushes; or even that I didn't try to persuade her to carnal knowledge, then he's right. But what man short of a sensual savage will molest a woman, especially one he loves, or even use words or emotional blackmail towards such an end? Either Mr Hardy has a very low estimate of his sex, or else he was trying to suggest that I was obsessively pure and fastidious. It is right that I was still more spiritual than animal, but since my time at Bridport and now here at Talbothays that was changing, and Tess's love, her intimate connection in my heart with the country we roamed through, with the farm and its work, were rapidly stimulating to growth my latent instincts, so that self-control was more in request than ever before in my life. But again the impression Mr Hardy gives here is exaggerated. I think back to that first time when I saw Tess and didn't dance with her. I had had no sexual experiences at all, or even romantic ones to speak of, and yet I was eager to dance, my instinct was to join with some of those girls in that most intense sensual experience. Spirituality, as I take it Mr Hardy means it, would have sent me scurrying along after Cuthbert and Felix, surely, with my nose in their book.

I have gathered a certain amount of evidence from my reading of the different versions of Mr Hardy's account to show that he knew that he was gradually distorting what he really understood about me. For instance when he records Tess's sense that I was 'disinterested, chivalrous, protective' in my love for her, he comments, in the text that everyone reads nowadays that I was 'far from all that she thought [me] in this respect; absurdly far, indeed'. But at one time he put it this way, that I was 'not all she thought [me] in that respect'. Much simpler; and without that tendentious 'absurdly', which diminishes not just my protection of her, but her love for me through its exaggeration. Then he added to the manuscript as an afterthought that phrase about my singular freedom from grossness, and at the same time changed a suggestion that I 'could love intensely' to one that I 'could love desperately'. 'Desperate' has overtones quite alien to the nature of my love for Tess, but 'intense' is certainly accurate. But that wasn't enough. When the first edition came out, I was quite shocked to find that he had changed his estimate of the nature of my love. From saying that it 'inclined to the solicitous and cherishing mood', which I would have contested anyway, he altered the passage to say that my love 'inclined to the imaginative and ethereal'. Now to my ear and eye that seems just nonsense. How could one love Tess even desperately, and not have a solid grasp of the real woman, her lips, her hair, her body, want and need all of that. Of course I had an idea of what she was as well, but what lover does not have an image of the beloved to keep with him when she is not there. I suppose it might have been imaginative, in that I figured the future as well as reflected on the present. But there was, I promise you, nothing of the ethereal in my image of her. But Mr Hardy needed to feel that there was, for his own purpose, I suppose. He must have forgotten what he had written earlier: 'It was for herself that he loved Tess; her soul, her heart, her substance'. That's how it was, and I suppose I might have written to Mr Hardy to protest. But it would have been useless I imagine, since he went even further when the book was put out in the cheap edition the following year, adding the adjective 'fastidious' to his analysis of my kind of loving.

Mr Hardy describes Tess's love for me with such loving intensity, and says nothing of how I felt to be walking with her, my arm round her waist, her head on my shoulder, her body pressed against mine, our hearts and minds so in harmony with each other and the landscape. It was a pure joy, I think the only pure joy I have ever experienced in my life. She was so fully interested in all things, longing to swallow the whole world of knowledge and thought from my lips, as it were. And I gave her what I could, and thought with my young man's intellectual confidence (arrogance perhaps I should have said), that it was the truth. Well, some of it was a truth. And in return, when she saw I was really interested, she told me legends and stories she had heard at home, and sang me songs her mother sang, and filled my days with happiness, with her gentle loving gaiety.

But still, she was a puzzle to me at times, when she would insist on not being good enough for me. As I've said already, I mistook her meaning. When I said:

> Distinction does not consist in the facile use of a contemptible set of conventions, but in being numbered among those who are true, and honest, and just, and pure, and lovely, and of good report – as you are, my Tess.

When I said that I was thinking still of the class difference. No wonder she got more upset, thinking as she did, that she was not honest, or pure, or of good report, or just to me. And at this remote distance I have to say that though I know she was pure in all senses that have any value in the human sense, her handling of her secret was not just to me. Anything would have been better than what she did with it.

Well, we got married. Perhaps I did rush things on a bit, but I'm sure that it was not because I was miffed at my parents for getting in the way of my 'true destiny' as Mr Hardy quite unwarrantably added in his manuscript. At least his original sources didn't give him the basis for such a reckless speculation. It makes it sound as if my heart hadn't come to be in farming at all. But such a speculation was part of his developed purpose in, shall I say, transforming what happened after our marriage.

One of the aspects of Mr Hardy's writing that has always puzzled me is revealed particularly intensely during the pages of his book that lead up to our wedding. He is, as I have already said, imaginatively sympathetic to a fine degree in his filling of the personalities of others, and the great strength of his half-fictions, half-biographies is in the interaction of humans with each other and with blind and senseless circumstance. And yet he can't help introducing into his account of Tess and me, as into many other narratives, a whole host of superstitiously ominous details, which taken cumulatively would seem clearly to imply that disaster was around the corner; they are set like markers for anyone to see that the marriage shouldn't happen. And yet Mr Hardy doesn't believe in them himself, really. As you read the book, from the moment when Tess reminded me that I did not dance with her on the green, and he adds what I do not remember her saying (perhaps she thought it, though) 'O I hope that is of no ill-omen for us now!' – from that moment there comes a string of omens: Tess's fancy about the dress I bought her, the miscarried letter, the cock crowing three times in the afternoon (pure fabrication), and above all the terrible, useless d'Urberville stuff, most of which he invented. For instance, the church wasn't nearly as far off as he implies – after all, Tess and the others were walking the three miles to it when I carried them across the flooded road – and I hired an ordinary fly for the journey. Even worse – if truth is better – was his alteration of the inn at Wool at which we spent the first days of our married life to the old manor house with those dreadful d'Urberville portraits – which are real enough, I have since seen them and can hardly be surprised at Mr Hardy's desire to incorporate them somehow. The house had earlier given her an occasion, you will remember, to evade telling me her secret – but it was in fact inhabited in 1884.

I can at least in part understand Mr Hardy's fascination with ominous warnings: they increase the readers' involvement with events, and allow them to feel superior to us who ignored or didn't notice them. It is also true that Tess shared the tendency of all countryfolk towards superstitious belief and fatalism, though as I was learning her nature and absorbing fragments of it, so she was of mine, and in some moods she would have recognized superstition for what it was. Perhaps I mustn't forget that Mr Hardy is a countryman too, however overlaid with urbanity, and perhaps part of him did believe in them, as part certainly rejected them.

I find it much harder to cope, however, with his emphasis on Tess's noble ancestry. She *was* a lineal descendant of the d'Urbervilles. But so what; why should it be true, as he implies, that her temper and her pride, the two qualities she possessed that did her more harm than all the rest of her put together (if you exclude her beauty), be genetically acquired from her remote noble ancestors? Why not acquired as a reaction to her immediate family? Well, of course it is debatable, but it is irritating when Mr Hardy even makes me provide him with some of the fuel for his class-speculations by inventing for me a thought that my family would like her better if they knew she was a d'Urberville. Of course anyone who knew my mother and father would realize that that would have been a foolish idea. No-one had less reverence for mere social status than they, though it is true that such information might have brought Felix and Cuthbert home to look at her. They would have stayed, once they looked, but not because she was a d'Urberville. I certainly never had such a preposterous notion. And the whole d'Urberville business adds to the doomed sense of our relationship. He even presents a motion on my part of reconciliation towards Tess on the first unhappy night of our marriage as being prevented by a sight of those unpleasant d'Urberville portraits.

But of course much of what Mr Hardy describes happening during the days after our wedding was his invention – some of it inevitable, since he decided to place us in the manor-house – but some of it explicable only in terms of the way he chose (or had) to see our respective roles in those events. I think it would be simplest if I give my version, at least in outline, of what we said and did during those dreadful days.

It was, in essence, really very simple. I told her about the woman in London, and she told me about Alec d'Urberville. I should have seen how they were, as Tess said, the same thing. When they happened we were both young, sexually innocent, even ignorant, seized by a powerful force we didn't understand, responding to it at first instinctively, then when reason and conscience became active again, running away as fast as we could. I ran quicker, and was the crueller; she stayed longer, weeks instead of days: and I can remember how that fact weighed with me more heavily than it should perhaps have done. But I found to my dismay that I hadn't shed completely – or even at all, deep down, when tested like this – the class and moral prejudices of my upbringing. I felt, even though my brain repudiated the feeling, that this sexual experience was bad on the part of a man, but a venial sin only, whereas it was a sign of utter depravity in a woman, a cardinal, almost the cardinal sin.

But this unwarrantable feeling would not have been enough alone to provoke my reaction; there was on this score a running battle between my feelings and my reason, which might have been decided either way. It is at least possible that I had for long enough consciously rejected the teachings of my father's religion and the society which enshrined its teachings in its fabric of convention to overcome the early rooted, engrained feeling.

There were however two other factors. The first was the child. I found that it was one thing to accept, even intellectually, that my wife had known another man, partially under duress, and quite another to accept that she had had his child. I have noticed that Mr Hardy in his other works is acutely sensitive to the feelings of some of his male characters about paternity, and I know that in his last piece of fictional biography he has a character declare that in a rational society the question of paternity should be a question for the mother alone, and that all the children of a society should be the general care of the whole society. But in this respect he is forgetting his Darwin; the urge of the male to propagate his own genes is strong even in sophisticated civilized English society. And there are further aspects of this drive; I at least found it impossible to believe that I should not be the father of my wife's first child. That it had died helped, but did not mend the matter. Perhaps if I had been totally uneducated, and had grown up in daily unavoidable awareness of the miscellaneous sexuality of most of nature, I might have taken this too, in the end. I don't think that anyone in England with my background would have accepted easily the idea of the baby.

But time might have dulled the hurt, almost sense of betrayal I, however irrationally, felt. What turned the scales against Tess was something that I have even yet not learned to accept in myself, so trivial does it seem now, and so significant did it then become. It is what I now think of as the Malvolio response. I saw myself as a dupe, a gull, a cuckold even; and my reaction was Malvolio's: 'I'll be revenged on the pack of you!'

Mr Hardy has a very terrible scene of quiet horror, in which calmly and by a kind of rational suppression of emotion I controlled our future by saying that she was not the woman I loved, but another in her shape. Everything that follows in his book stems logically, frighteningly logically, from that initial scene. And it is all false, damnably false. We quarrelled violently and at some length. I accused her of deliberately deceiving me, of making a fool of me, of wanting to cover her sin with my name, of pretending passion for me, of using the tricks she'd learned from him to seduce me, all sorts of horrors, I can't now, thirty years away, recall the precise words, or all of them, but it doesn't matter. And the heat of my words was fuelled, not diminished, by my memory of that woman in London, who *did* have such an end, and used well tried erotic devices in her attempt to attain it. Those jewels Tess was wearing – if even they had not been there, perhaps the resemblance would not have been so acute, and I might not so have lost control.

Mr Hardy has Tess remain passive under my coldness; I think perhaps he is right, perhaps if I had been as icy and implacable as he says, standing simply on the letter of my inherited socio-religious dogma about the relationship between sexual intercourse and true marriage, she might have remained stunned; she was ever slow to temper. But when a certain nerve in her was touched she would burst out with violence. Think of her reactions to d'Urberville as Mr Hardy reports them, 'My God, I could knock you out of the gig!', or striking him in the face with her glove so that his mouth bled. Well, she didn't strike me, though it might have been better if she had.

At first she tried to explain how she had, time and again, attempted to get up the courage to tell me, how she had even written me a letter about it, but I wouldn't listen, didn't believe her story about the letter, and she was pained by that, and then I accused her of not really loving me, of using feminine arts to get me to marry, coming on and then retreating, just to get me inflamed, and other pernicious stuff like that. Looking back, I think she was on the verge of breaking down then, weeping, and she began to plead with me to see how much she loved me truly, moved towards me with her arms wide; but, remembering that first passionate kiss she gave me on the way home from Wool, I asked her whether her fancy man had taught her how to use her lips, and that turned her abruptly away, and began a brief dialogue in which we traded further insults. It all sounds too coarse and degraded to be true, but that's how it was. She was deeply insulted by what I accused her of; I was deeply hurt by what I saw as her deliberate deceit. Well, of course it ended from exhaustion, as all storms do, and there we were on opposite sides of the room, weary and frightened. If we hadn't been frightened, I think we might have simply fallen into each others' arms. But fear kept us apart. After a while, she said in a quiet voice that I couldn't interpret, that she would go home the next day if I wished

it. I thought for a moment, and it seemed best; I couldn't face her
or myself. It was late and she went to the bedroom, and slept or
not until morning. I watched the night through on the sofa in our
sitting-room, trying to think, but to no purpose. In the morning it
still seemed parting was all that was possible. She gave no word of
love, nor did I; it was all practical arrangements. How foolish it all
was, how stupid, how avoidable. She told me later that for her part
I seemed now too far above her, too remote a gentleman, no longer
the man she had loved, who treated her as his equal. And that was
right; I was filled with the bitterness and sorrow of being ousted by
a shadowy other from the position I thought I had held, in social
terms, in relation to Tess, and with anger at being so duped; I could
not see her as simply Tess. She was the one who had made me feel
like this, and I had to get away.

She went by train, a roundabout route; I hired a horse. And
that was that. We parted as strangers to each other, which in real
terms, for the day, we were. If we had had another day together, if
some chance had kept us together, this alienation must have been
destroyed. At Talbothays I had learned to love Tess as a force of
my being, and that force had only been temporarily submerged in
contrary emotion. Mr Hardy does not overvalue the 'hard logical
deposit' in my nature, but he does overestimate the permanence and
the power of the re-appearance of the prejudices of my upbringing,
when he calls me 'the slave to custom and conventionality' (though
I accept I had – and have – limitations in plenty). It was a transitory
response to pain, and my love for Tess, which, after all, was rational
as well as sexual, would have reasserted itself in time under such
circumstances. But we parted, as I have said, as virtual strangers,
and the image of us as separate was fixed in my consciousness.
I did not, after all, know her, understand her; how could I have
loved her? It must have been an illusion. This thought-process I
found irrefutable, but if only our continuance at the inn had been
as long as Mr Hardy makes us stay at the manor, time, contiguity,
observation and reason would have made me see the illogicality
of rejecting so rational a love for an accident of that nature I had
learned to know so well. It must have been so.

And so Mr Hardy distorts my nature here, and (if any reader
apart from myself would find it possible to read the novel from
my point of view) in fact contradicts his own account of me and
my love (or at least his original account of it; later versions, as
I have already pointed out, force me more into the mould he

needs; but nothing, I should have thought, could make the man the ardour of whose passion caused Tess to flinch, into the man who can so coldly and dispassionately send her packing). It is all this business of making Tess out to be a pure woman. Anyone could see that she was pure, but he wants to stress the point by making me despicable. He wants to pin the blame for this separation mostly on me, and partly on society, and perhaps a fragment on Tess for not using sex to get me back (though no-one reading the book would remember that in the grossness of my guilt as he expresses it). Do not misunderstand me; I am not seeking to evade guilt or responsibility. I was older, supposedly wiser, supposedly free of class and moral conventionalities; I should have been able to cope with the humiliation. I couldn't. Perhaps I shouldn't have felt it. But the blaze of our marriage in a couple of hours was not all my doing; as we loved, we quarrelled and we parted – together. How can I tell now what the right words from her then might have done, as much as the right words from me. Mine should have been 'I forgive you; I love you.' But at that time I didn't. What might hers have been? I can't imagine. To quote Mr Ford's new novel, 'This is the saddest story'.

Several times after this I thought to go to her; I suppose her pride forbade her coming to me. But I didn't, and I think it was through fear of finding her still the woman I didn't know. By then I had reflected long on our courtship, and in reflection our love always seemed real. But then that frightful scene in the inn was more recent, and more potent. And there were the facts. Her lover and her baby. I didn't mind them so much as I had; I could see that they didn't make her a different woman of themselves. But those few hours of our married life together were still singed into my consciousness, and the dreadful sense of loss and treachery and abandonment, and fear. And she was not beside me to give the lie to these memories with her mere presence. So I didn't go to Marlott. And I went to Brazil instead. So much can depend on a single impetus to anger and bitterness. It is true, I think, that if I hadn't gone abroad so soon after our separation, I could not have kept away from her.

Mr Hardy makes the worst out of that incident with Izz Huett, though it was bad enough. He realized before the cheap edition came out that he had overdone it, and went a little way to making me seem less heartlessly self-centred and callous. I think Tess never heard the story from Izz herself, but only from Marian, and it is wrong in some particulars, most importantly that I actually asked

Izz to go to Brazil with me, which I didn't; I can't understand how Mr Hardy could invent the notion and think that it squared with the character he had created, let alone with what he knew of me. There was, though, so much love for me shining out of her dark eyes, so much hope when she heard Tess and I had quarrelled, that I did kiss her, which was nearly as bad, since I then left her at home in tears. Her kiss was, yes, longing, even despairing. But it wasn't passion incarnate like Tess's. Her honesty regarding Tess's love for me was one of the purest and noblest acts I have experienced. Deeply shaming.

What remains of my life with and without Tess is substantially indicated by Mr Hardy. Through a strange combination of fear, pride and acceptance of social convention in Tess (Mr Hardy added Tess's growing conviction that d'Urberville was alone her husband to the cheap edition of his book), the poverty of her family, the urgent pressure of d'Urberville (Mr Hardy also added to the cheap edition d'Urberville's line about his knowing men and being certain I would never return), my intolerable absence, and blind circumstance, she went back to the man who had seduced, raped her, I don't know which. How could it be rape if she stayed for weeks afterwards? He didn't use force. I think she must have had some pleasure in their lovemaking, both then and later in Bournemouth. But I'm wandering. She went with him to that rather down at heel resort.

Meanwhile in Brazil I had plenty of time for reflection, and I hadn't been there long when I saw what a huge mistake I had made; how unwise and unkind I had been, how, as Mr Hardy puts it, 'the beauty or ugliness of a character lay not only in its achievements, but in its aims and impulses; its true history lay not among things done, but among things willed.' Disease and bad weather kept me an intolerable time away from the coast. I was lunatic to go to Brazil in the first place, so I can't lay any blame on circumstance for retaining me once I was there. But if I had achieved a return when I willed it, none of the tragic things would have happened. It is easy to say such things with hindsight, but I *knew* that evil would come of the delays, so great was my desire to be home. And when I got her letter, so full of submission and love, that merely intensified the desire further. But I could have averted it all by not leaving in the first place. I know.

I was impressed by the stranger Mr Hardy mentions as having influenced me, but I had no need of another to tell me I had acted wrongly, and, as I have tried to suggest, my feeling of revulsion about Tess's sexual experience was never the logical stumbling block to our reunion. Such revulsion was temporary, based on personal jealousy as much as moral conviction, and had already long dissipated – though an image of her, bitterly defending herself against my attack, still remained to make me anxious and uncertain about how such a reunion could be accomplished – until the arrival of her letter, that is. You will want to know why I didn't write to her then; well, I was near Rio, and any letter would not have travelled much faster than I could; and I had no reason to suspect that a day or two might make any difference.

I returned to find her angry note, much more in tune with our day of married life together, and so I delayed again. Then I sought her out, found her at Bournemouth, that 'Mediterranean lounging-place on the English Channel' as Mr Hardy so aptly calls it.

It seems so hard that I was too late. I think I knew it really the first second I saw her. The clothes she was wearing: they were a man's choice, I instinctively felt, and they were not just rich, but decadent too – her gown was lemon yellow, as Mr Hardy originally wrote, the very colour of nineties decadence. He changed it to grey-white for the first edition, I suppose as part of the purity campaign (as if such a campaign were needed to make the point!) She seemed like another woman again than the one I had loved; her voice, her eyes were other. Only her hair was the same. There was no point of contact between the form I saw before me and my memory of her, even in the wedding-dress I had bought for her. It was like a nightmare we were sharing, and I remember the sensation came over me so strongly as I was reading the first edition of Mr Hardy's work that I wrote to him reflecting on it. As a result he added that paragraph which both expresses the truth of my perception and helps to make the case he was after:

> But he could not get on. Speech was as inexpressive as silence. But he had a vague consciousness of one thing, though it was not clear to him till later; that his original Tess had spiritually ceased to recognize the body before him as hers – allowing it to drift, like a corpse upon the current, in a direction dissociated from its living will.

It works for him because it means that he is free to regard the stabbing of d'Urberville as an act of the directionless body, and it reflect the sense of total disjunction I had, the hopelessness of relating this figure to anything I had known.

I still find this brief exchange more personally painful than our earlier quarrel. The flare-up on our wedding-day could only have been avoided if we had been different people; but this meeting on the doorstep of the Herons could have been prevented if all sorts of chance circumstances had not occurred to enforce it.

There are some things about Mr Hardy's narration I have never worked out, and there is a case in point here:

> They stood, fixed, their baffled hearts looking out of their eyes with a joylessness pitiful to see. Both seemed to implore something to shelter them from reality.

It seems as if he had been there, observing us; I mean he phrases it as if it were so. I know from the way that he has imagined my thoughts that he has a vivid and acute imaginative sympathy (when not driven by other purposes), but this is something different. He asserts what neither of us knew, or could express, and yet I feel it must have been as he says it was. I could almost accuse him of being in the bushes, spying on us with a telescope.

Well, Tess killed Alec. It is so easy to overlook moments when Mr Hardy's Immanent Will randomly provides joy rather than pain: Tess, by fortunate chance, overtook me. I might easily have been miles away in some quite other direction if I had not chosen to go back to my hotel, or I might have caught an earlier train, or any other of the numerous possibilites might have occurred. It wasn't perhaps a chance in a thousand that Tess found me, but it was certainly against the odds. I had some trouble in believing that she had in sober earnest done what she said (Mr Hardy, of course, has to assume that I put her violence down to her d'Urberville blood, but that is a fixation of his, not mine). Mr Hardy catches very well in Tess's dialogue the half madness, half self-detachment that impressed me so vividly, along with the overwhelming flood of love she poured on me. She had no consciousness, I think, that she had committed murder; what she had done was to erase the man and his power from her life, to leave it empty for me to fill. And oh, I filled it, as she filled mine. My moral sense was suspended under the pressure of our need for each other, or became transformed, so that the only imperative was what would keep us together for now and for ever.

For a few days at Moyles Court we knew the ecstacy of passionately mutual love. A cliché of pulp-romance, perhaps, but real to me, none the less, and to Tess: 'within was affection, union, error forgiven: outside was the inexorable'. My error, not hers. This was our marriage, and, though it is possible that, had chance permitted us to escape to somewhere beyond the reach of the British police, we might have lived contentedly and fruitfully together for many years, I now agree with Tess, that the chances were at least equal that in some situation of commonplace marital disagreement, I would in anger have turned on her with a reminder of d'Urberville, and that probably would have ended our content. So complete and interinvolved were our confidences then, however, that I could not imagine such a possibility; Tess was clearer-sighted than I, and I think it was because her love for me had even less of self than mine for her.

It was inevitable that sooner or later someone would have found us; it is the second law of thermodynamics, if not divine judgement, that dictates that mankind cannot live in paradise on more than temporary terms. If we had left earlier, our chances of escape altogether would have been much better; but Tess willed it otherwise, and as I have said, I think now that she was right. She would have stayed until the police came, but I, unable to bear the thought of losing what I had found, hurried us away north in a desperate hope of evasion. That the end came at Stonehenge assisted the dramatic power of the narrative as it was told in court, and Mr Hardy found in it more material for his serious reflections; but for me, all I wished was that there was somewhere for us to hide.

Of course in the way Mr Hardy has designed the narrative, my refusal to hold out to Tess the comfort of a meeting after death seems final and harsh, as if even then the logical deposit in my nature that he talks about when we were at Wool barred my love for her. In a way he's right; however self-consuming my love for her was, it couldn't eat away everything, and I couldn't tell the illusion-saving lie, the sort of lie Mr Conrad's Marlow told to Kurtz's Intended. That just shows how great her love was beside mine. But it is also true that we talked of these things again and again in Winchester gaol; I tried for a while to make her see that to plead guilty to murder was suicide, but eventually she helped me to believe in her certainty that death was the only way to keep love alive, though I could not share it. And then we spoke about death, and her belief in spirits, until again I accepted, and still believe, that I might be wrong, and that the rejection of the Christian heaven and hell doesn't mean that there are not other supernatural possibilities. I still don't think anything will happen to my body or my consciousness after I die save dissolution; but Tess's deep-rooted, instinctual belief has allowed me to live in uncertainty. Though reason says no, the fact that Tess was right in one prediction, my love for her *has* remained intact, inviolate, undiminished across the years, (less in the foreground of my daily living, of course, but always there), this fact lends to my residual uncertainty a quality of hope that it might be so, that Tess might have been right about an existence after death too.

Thus it is that now I can't regret Tess's death. It comes to us all, and it came to her while our love was still thorough and unbroken, intensified even by our grief at parting. Her only regret was that I couldn't bear to let her go, even though I respected her will in the matter. When I walked away from the gaol that morning, hand in hand with Liza-Lu, I wanted to die too. It was only Tess's charge that I care for her sister that kept me going; I don't think I could have killed myself deliberately, but a man can lose a will to live, just as an animal can, and then disease or accident will soon take him. But I kept a hold on life for Lu's (and Tess's) sake, and she has since repaid me many fold. I think Tess, wiser than me to the end, knew how it would be, and planned my survival. It might have been cruelty, and so it seemed at first, but now it is another cause I have to love her.

So the question is not 'why did Tess die?' It is rather 'why was Tess in a position that made it seem right to her to die?' And to that there is only a complex and unsatisfactory answer.

Mostly I feel 'Who is to blame except me? I cannot cast responsibility onto others.' And I have tried to express as fully as possible how I am to blame. But occasionally I think back through her life, and consider other claims. Her mother and father, for instance: they gave her life without asking her if she wanted it; but so do all men and women, in marriage and out of it. Her father gave her some drops of noble blood, and some might say with Mr Hardy, though I cannot, that her pride and her quick temper derived from this genetic inheritance, and that ideas above her station drove and led her into the situation that began the trouble.

Her mother was more dangerous really; she gave Tess beauty and inconsequentiality. Wherever Tess got her instinct for virtue it was not from her parents. Tess was a mystery to her mother. If Tess had been only a little more like her mother, and had refrained from telling me of her Sorrow, at least until we had children of our own, all might have been well. But I can't hide behind that thought either.

That man, d'Urberville; her victim as she was once his? Well, if there had been no violation there would have been no separation and no killing. Yes he too was guilty, he must share the responsibility. But seeing with eyes that have been scourged with suffering and death, I can say from my heart that what d'Urberville did to her was venal compared with what I did. As I have cause to know, she survived his body and his child intact, grown, rich in mind and spirit, and in the end there remained from the experience as evil only the residue of guilt induced by the conventions of this pernicious constricting Hebraistic society we all passively acquiesce in. Afterwards he just blackmailed her, got at her through her family, for whom she was ever provider. I was gone for ever. How could she resist his money; what did her body matter beside their need; how could such a caring conscience let her family starve and go houseless. And once she had made the bargain, she would keep it.

Then there is Life; Mr Hardy's Immanent Will, the force that stirs and urges everything. He can't seem to make up his mind whether this force is neutral, simply randomly causing, or whether it is malicious – in effect whether it is unconscious or conscious. In *The Dynasts* he says it might be evolving consciousness, and perhaps if that is so, what happened to Tess might be seen as one of its stumbling attempts at conscious control, like the early fumbling attempts of the ancestors of the primates to oppose the thumb to the fingers. One might argue that all the flaws and virtues of our natures were as nothing compared with the random or designed chances that threw Tess into contact with d'Urberville and me at those exact times, that caused certain critical events, like the death of Prince, or the letter under the carpet, or the attack of cholera just when I was on the point of return from Brazil. The 'President of the Immortals' view of Tess's history. But I don't believe it, any more than Mr Hardy does, really. He loved Tess perhaps as much as I did, and his anger betrays him here; much better if he had directed it in that last paragraph at my folly.

Perhaps a dispassionate judge now might say that it is all mixed, that we all contributed to Tess's joy and to her misery, as did chance, as did that remoter force, society (though it is hard to see what joy social constructs ever provided for her). And further, that some of what happened happened because she was the woman she was. But I am not a dispassionate judge, and at the last all I can feel is that if I had been wiser; if my love had been as self-consuming as Tess's; if even I could have kept always in mind my father's charity; then Tess and I would be flourishing still, together.

Note: In response to enquiries the author may state that the note at the beginning of this chapter was introduced solely to provide for the narrative an air of verisimilitude.

8

Sex, Marriage and the Decline of Traditional Community in *Jude the Obscure*

In working out his last novel *Jude the Obscure* Hardy discovered that the characters and their interaction provoked a more intense and thorough account of two aspects of human relationships than he had first anticipated (to judge by his letters to the editor of *Harper's Magazine*). The more powerfully embodied of these explorations is what came increasingly to seem for Hardy the novelist the most pressing concern for *fin-de-siècle* mankind (whom, with hindsight, we may imagine as just beginning to surface from the long pre-Freudian dream) – the sexual natures of men and women. The more aggressively argued issue is the directly related one of marriage. Underlying these is Hardy's original notion for the novel, an account of the struggle of an isolated, intellectually ambitious workman caught in the final decay of the traditional rural community.

From the moment when the two Cythereas embrace in his first novel *Desperate Remedies* Hardy seems to have been driven, consciously and subconsciously, to explore sexuality. It is perhaps the most powerful impulse in him as a novelist, and it forces him continually into tension caused by three conflicting pressures: what he wanted to show, what he thought it was acceptable to his audience and the circulating libraries to show, and what his bosses the magazine editors would allow him to show. The resulting text of any of his novels is in this respect almost always an uneasy compromise. But no-one now reading for the first time the account in *Far From the Madding Crowd* (1874) of Sergeant Troy's sword play with Bathsheba Everdene in the hollow fringed with ferns can mistake Hardy's intentions; it seems hard to imagine that his first Victorian audience could either. With some exceptions (*The Trumpet-Major, The Major of Casterbridge*) each successive novel approaches more closely an open account of the place of sexual imperatives in human relations, until by *Jude the Obscure* Hardy has reached the conclusion that most of the actions that shape our lives have their root in this force for pleasure and pain – which it is thus urgent that we examine and attempt to understand.

Jude Fawley grows up lonely, innocent, chaste, apparently unaware of his sexuality, or of anyone else's. When Arabella Donn flings a pig's penis at him it is as if a dam has been breached in his nature. At this charged moment Hardy emphasises the randomness of sexual attraction – Jude's will has no power in the matter. (Hardy might have repeated here the notion that he raises in *Tess of the d'Urbervilles*, and which permeates his poetry, that it is an ill-arranged world in which the wrong sexual partners meet while the most appropriate mate exists unconsciously elsewhere). Thus Arabella

> saw that he had singled her out from the three as a woman is singled out in such case, for no reasoned purpose of further acquaintance, but in common-place obedience to conjunctive orders from headuarters, unconsciously received by unfortunate men when the last intention of their lives is to be occupied with the feminine. (p. 36)[1]

The remarkable indirection of Hardy's diction in this passage is an element in his strategic distancing of sexual urgencies from the sensitive Victorian reader, and so pervasive is this strategy that the novel becomes often dense with paraphrase, hint and metaphor. There are some details, however, that Hardy will not veil in rhetoric, and this is particularly so when Arabella is involved. Even in the *Harper's Monthly Magazine* serialized version she speaks of her desire for Jude to her friend Anny 'in a curiously low, fierce tone of latent passionateness':

> I want him to marry me. I must have him. I can't do without him. He's the sort of man I long for. I shall go mad if I can't give myself to him altogether! I felt I should when I first saw him!

Hardy substantially revised her words and the description of her voice in speaking them, altering 'fierce' to 'hungry', 'passionateness' to 'sensuousness', and 'I want him to marry me' to 'I want him to have me; to marry me', but the amended passage (p. 47) is scarcely more frank than the original. Hardy must have felt he was taking something of a risk presenting his magazine audience with such evidence in a woman of powerful sexual needs. The easy way out for his readers would have been to see Arabella as whore, in temperament if not yet in actuality; and later in the novel Hardy provides hints that she may indeed have become one.[2] But Hardy also gives a subtle gloss on such easy readings: when Jude, disillusioned with the University, having drink taken, wanders into a public hall in Christminster, where a promenade concert is in progress, the narrator comments that the hall is 'full of shop youths and girls, soldiers, apprentices, boys of eleven smoking cigarettes, and light women of the more respectable and amateur sort' (p. 121). Remembering the phrase of the carter whose description of Christminster is Jude's first awakening to the place – 'Not but there's wenches in the streets o' nights' – the easy interpretation of 'light women' is simply 'prostitutes', but the next paragraph poignantly transforms such a response: 'The spirit of Sue seemed to hover round him and prevent his flirting and drinking with the frolicsome girls who made advances – wistful to gain a little joy.' The pleasure of sexual contact is what the girls want, and what Jude might be in a mood to offer, were he not romantically attached to his ideal of Sue. The notion that sex is a joy – even the notion that sex might be a joy, even for 'light' women, quite independent of love or marriage! Oh Mr Hardy, what stone is there left to turn in your prurient imagination?

Arabella succeeds in tricking Jude into marrying her, but finds that life with him is not as satisfying as she had hoped, and with perfect self-centredness and sublime indifference to accepted social practice she abandons him and emigrates with her family to Australia. Her sole legacy to Jude is his aroused sexuality – 'a fresh and wild pleasure' (p. 39). It is as a contrast to his experience with Arabella that Jude creates for himself such an ideal image of his cousin Sue Bridehead.

When Sue and Jude begin to be friends, the primary aspect of her personality that conditions the kind of relationship she has in mind is her deep and paradoxical desire to keep aloof, to remain intact, independent, unobligated. She had managed to sustain such a desire in the face of the threats and arguments of the leader-writer she had lived with in London, because she didn't love him, and because he was not 'a sensual savage'.[3] She expects to be able to operate the same control, expects to be able to remain unpenetrated in her comradeship with Jude; but she is so preoccupied with herself in relation to him that she does not notice what Arabella and her friends see at once – that Jude is a man who once awakened to its power and sweetness will need and enjoy sex. On the other hand, she is quite happy to talk about it. If Arabella is open about her sexual desires, Sue is only marginally less explicit in discussing her sexual fears when she and Jude finally begin to live together.

Jude imagines that he and Sue will be lovers on their first night together, and so he books only one room at the Temperance Inn at Aldbrickham. Sue's response when she hears this is to look at Jude, bend her head, and say that she didn't mean that they should be lovers, though she had been afraid that he might. Jude's assumption is based primarily (and not unreasonably) on the passionate kiss that he and Sue have recently shared for the first time:

> They had quickly run back, and met, and embracing most un-premeditatedly, kissed close and long. When they parted for good it was with flushed cheeks on her side, and a beating heart on his. (p. 227)

Hardy believed that a first kiss, passionate, on the mouth, shared between people in love, said not only 'I love you', but 'I want to make love to you' as well. Social training, inhibitions, taboos might prevent such a consummation at once, or even soon; but the kiss Tess gives Angel in the waggon riding home from Wellbridge is saying I am yours body and soul, as is Dick and Fancy's at the Ship Inn, Troy and Bathsheba's among the ferns, Giles and Grace's in her garden, and Sue and Jude's here. They are declarations not just of love, but of willingness, desire for that further physical union of one with the other. (And it is important to remember that Tess never – so far as we know – kisses Alec.) How then can Sue (were she a consistent person) go to live with Jude after such a kiss and not expect to share her room with him? Though the fact that she has left her husband does not necessarily give him a justification for assuming she will do so, the kiss does. In the discussion that ensues he accuses her of being incapable of real love, by which he means that surrender of the self in an ideal community of two that he so romantically imagines. Her answer is:

> My liking for you is not as some women's perhaps. But it is a delight in being with you, of a supremely delicate kind, and I don't want to go further and risk it by – an attempt to intensify it! I quite realized that, as woman with man, it was a risk to come. But, as *me* with *you*, I resolved to trust you to set my wishes above your gratification. (p. 252)

Hardy's carefully placed dash after 'risk it by' indicates that had she not been prevented by socialization she would have continued with something like 'a gross physical assault', or 'by suffering a sexual invasion of which I am dreadfully afraid, and which I have no apparent instinctive need for, even though I do love you.' She seems also to have forgotten her prescription about 'sensual savages' unless she is already seeing Jude in that role, or unless she is having second thoughts about what a 'sensual savage' might be. However it is, she correctly (for the time) believes that she can safely put the burden of her continuing virginity on Jude's chivalrousness.

Jude (not surprisingly, considering T. Hardy novelist's palpable design) begins to see himself as a replicator of Sue's leader-writer, something he describes as 'a torturing destiny'. Then he wonders if she refuses to make love with him because in the end, despite her 'affectation of independent views' she is 'enslaved to a social code'. She denies this, acknowledging, however, that often she doesn't have the courage of her convictions. This exchange penetrates to the heart of another recurrent feature of the novel, the paradox that Sue's 'scintillating' radical intellect is combined with a marked tendency towards conventional behaviour and expression.

It is a further ironic arrangement of T. Hardy novelist that, as a result of Sue's desire not only to be but to be seen to be virginal, when she and Jude get at a late hour to Aldbrickham they go to a seedy hotel called the George, wherein the room that Sue takes is the very one in which Jude had once before spent a night making love with Arabella after her return from Australia. Through a nicely malicious maidservant Sue discovers this detail, and attacks Jude with it. The ensuing dialogue is Hardy at his best, exploring their widely opposed attitudes to sexual need:

'O it was treacherous of you to have her again! *I* jumped out of the window!'

'But Sue, she was, after all, my legal wife, if not –' Slipping down on her knees Sue buried her face in the bed and wept.

'I never knew such an unreasonable – such a dog-in-the-manger feeling,' said Jude. 'I am not to approach you, nor anybody else!'

'O don't you understand my feeling! Why don't you! Why are you so gross! I jumped out of the window!'

'Jumped out of the window?'

'I can't explain!' (p. 255)

Here Sue echoes Grace Fitzpiers exclaiming to Felice Charmond of her husband Edred: 'He's had you' (*The Woodlanders*, p. 184), and the sexual implication is clear – perhaps, in her jealousy, the clearest that Sue ever makes. Jude, however, finds it hard to be direct: for his 'approach' the reader, Victorian surely as well as modern, must understand 'make love with'. What Jude can't comprehend is what Sue herself genuinely finds impossible to explain, that Sue's self-centred fear of losing her perfect intact self in a sexual encounter, her physical fear of being torn open, the physical repulsion she feels from her husband Richard, and her consciousness of not loving him, drove her to jump out of a window rather than face the possibility of his making love to her. Sue's use of the word 'gross' to describe Jude's sexual nature becomes self-revealing by the end of the novel.[4] She continues:

'I – I thought you cared for nobody – desired nobody in the world but me at that time – and ever since!' continued Sue.

'It is true. I did not, and don't now!' said Jude, as distressed as she.

'But you must have thought much of her! Or –'

'No – I need not – you don't understand me either – women never do! Why should you get into such a tantrum about nothing?'

Sue can't understand that Jude is easily aroused sexually, that he likes sex, that Arabella is probably quite good at it, that he hadn't had any for quite a while. The implication is that for Jude insistent sexual desire can be felt independently of the agglomeration of emotions called love; and in saying that women never do understand this, he is generalizing about a psycho-physiological difference between men and women. Opinion will be divided about the validity of this generalization. Later in the novel Sue says that women could live in love without sex, but 'men can't because they – won't. An average woman is in this superior to an average man – that she never instigates, only responds' (p. 372). This more aggressive generalization seems to have less to recommend it, to be no more than Victorian cliché: the novel, for instance, may instruct us to despise Arabella, but it does not also ask us to consider her exceptional.

Indeed we might say that sexually Jude and Arabella have much in common, while egotistically Sue and Arabella have much in common. It is, for instance, in the passage under consideration, utterly characteristic of Sue that she can't let things rest in Jude's acquiescence that they should not be lovers, but takes pleasure in teasing him. She goes back to her discovery that Arabella and Jude had slept in the room she now occupies:

> Looking up from the quilt she pouted provokingly: 'If it hadn't been for that, perhaps I would have gone on to the Temperance Hotel, after all, as you proposed; for I was beginning to think I did belong to you!'
> 'O, it is of no consequence!' said Jude distantly. (p. 256)

In 'distantly,' Hardy catches precisely the mixture of frustration and pique and suspicion in Jude's mind at this moment. Sue is throughout the novel an epicure of emotions, and this is one of a succession of cruel little games she plays with Jude.[5]

In the end, six months or so later, Sue gives way to Jude's sexual desire, primarily through her continuing jealousy of Arabella, but also because Jude for once is driven to express his sexual frustration openly. Arabella comes to Jude and Sue because she is in some kind of trouble, and asks him to walk with her to discuss it. Jude prepares to go, but Sue is distracted:

> 'But she's not your wife! . . .   And I –'
> 'And you are not either, dear, yet,' said Jude.
> ' . . . Please, please stay at home, Jude, and not go to her, now she's not your wife any more than I!'
> 'Well, she is, rather more than you, come to that,' he said taking his hat determinedly. 'I've wanted you to be, and

I've waited with the patience of Job, and I don't see that I've got anything by my self-denial. I shall certainly give her something, and hear what it is she is so anxious to tell me. No man could do less.' (p. 278)

There is emphasis here on the social and religious perception that sexual union is the essence of marriage; certainly the convention is convenient for Jude's purposes, as it is on several occasions for Arabella's. It is quite illogical for him to expect, or even to hope that his sexual self-denial would slowly erode Sue's own wish that it be prolonged, but logic is not often one of Jude's strengths. No compromise is possible over virginity. Sue reads a strong hint beneath Jude's last sentences that if things turn out that way he will again make love with Arabella, and she becomes more desperate in her jealousy, hysterically accusing him of being about to abandon her, which is nonsense:

'I have nobody but you, Jude, and you are deserting me! I didn't know you were like this – I can't bear it, I can't! If she were yours it would be different!'

'Or if you were.'

'Very well then – if I must I must. Since you will have it so, I agree! I will be. Only I didn't mean to! . . . I do love you. I ought to have known you would conquer in the long run, living like this.' (p. 280)

The crucial difference from her previous attempt at making a community of two on her own terms is that she loves Jude where she did not love the leader-writer. It is the crack in her self-made armour, the crack through which Jude here 'conquers' her. The subsequent question, debated in the novel and by critics outside it, is whether Jude has thus blackmailed Sue into sexual submission, whether he has 'coerced' her? Who is right – Jude who comes to believe towards the end of the novel, as Sue begins to abandon him, that he should not have forced himself sexually upon her, or Jude who accepts at this point her reluctant agreement to make love with him?

The related question the reader has also to resolve in the context of the novel is whether sex is an animal drive to be suppressed, whether it is 'gross' as Sue says, whether it is the assertion of male power over the female in the antithesis of community; or, on the other hand, whether, as Jude feels, it is a physical expression of community, of the deepest fellow-feeling available to humans? For Jude the loving relation is incomplete without physical union. Seen in this light his early restraint is superhuman, saintly, mortification of the flesh as much as the sort that Sue proposes to herself at the end of the book.

How is it possible to reconcile these views? Through love? Temporarily perhaps. But Hardy suggests there is no available permanent reconciliation. From *Under the Greenwood Tree* to *Jude the Obscure* he proclaims that one given of life is war between the sexes. The only change over his fictional lifetime is that he becomes more able to dramatize both sides of this war; in *Under the Greenwood Tree* or *Far from the Madding Crowd* it is really only the male point of view which gets identified and discussed. By *Tess of the d'Urbervilles* and *Jude the Obscure* the perspective is more evenly balanced:

> Here the two sexes had met for loving, hating, coupling, parting, had waited, had suffered for each other; had triumphed over each other, cursed each other in jealousy, blessed each other in forgiveness. (p. 121)

> Under the hedge which divided the field from a distant plantation girls had given themselves to lovers who would not turn their heads to look at them by the next harvest, and in that ancient cornfield many a man had made love-promises to a woman at whose voice he had trembled by the next seed-time after fulfilling them in the church adjoining. (p. 9)

In these quotations Hardy further implies an equality in the war, but in *Jude the Obscure* (and in *Tess of the d'Urbervilles*) there is a tendency to suggest also that on the whole women lose the war. They lose it because they are physically weaker and because they have to bear children (for example, the description of the girls asleep at the training college, pp. 145–6), they lose it because the terrain on which the battle is fought is a society constructed by men within which they thus have an advantage (for example, Phillotson's account of the 'honourable' response of a man to a wife's desire for freedom, p. 241), they lose it because they are taught weakness and subterfuge (as in Jude's plea to Sue for honesty, pp. 272–3), they lose it because they are not taught logic or expected to have courage (see Jude's reaction to Sue's conversion to Christianity, pp. 370, 422). This is Hardy's theoretical, rational, idealist position, however, and like many other such positions in the novel it is in part subverted by what actually happens. Sue is able to assume a position of power in relation to her leader-writer precisely because she can count on the conventional gentlemanly responses to 'pure' women, and she tries the same approach with Jude, only to be betrayed by emotions in herself over which she has no control – love and jealousy. Arabella similarly counts on the conventional attitudes of Victorian society to ensure that her particular trick with Jude will work in her favour (though Sarah and Anny make clear, in the provisos they add in suggesting the stratagem to her, that you have to be sure of your man as 'romancing, straightfor'ard, honest' [p. 47] before you try it. It is perhaps an open question whether Arabella augments their advice by only pretending to be pregnant).

In a further carefully-laid irony T. Hardy has Arabella remind Phillotson of the socially established rights and powers of a husband through the Mosaic pronouncement on the subordinacy of women to men:

'Then shall the man be guiltless; but the woman shall bear her iniquity.' Damn rough on us women; but we must grin and put up wi' it! Haw haw! (p. 335)

This, as her laugh implies, rather than expressing her humility, is in effect the opening of her campaign to get Jude back again, in which campaign she uses social conventions about women to the full to gain her end. Phillotson's answer, 'I have never known much of womankind', is thoroughly appropriate. Arabella wins all the wars between herself and men that she engages in, and if some readers are prompted to reflect dismissively upon the means of her victory, enabled by the narrator to consider her coarse, vulgar, animally sub-human even, they have as a corrective only to reflect on the way that Sue (whom it is hard to think of as vulgar or coarse, or animalistic) ultimately wins her battle with Jude.

There is just one moment in the novel in which a fully achieved harmonious community created by sexual love between man and woman is seen as possible; the irony is that it is given to us in Sue's voice:

We went about loving each other too much – indulging ourselves to utter selfishness with each other! We said – do you remember? – that we would make a virtue of joy. I said it was Nature's intention, Nature's law and *raison d'être* that we should be joyful in what instincts she afforded us – instincts which civilization had taken upon itself to thwart. What dreadful things I said! And now Fate has given us this stab in the back for being such fools as to take Nature at her word! (p. 357)

From this brief summary of the two and a half years Sue and Jude spend together having children it seems that Sue became a convert to sex, that she achieved through union with Jude that joy (the word becomes in this novel a shorthand for sexual satisfaction) which the sad girls at Christminster were seeking. It is hard in the light of Sue's remembrance, to credit Hardy's by now famous claim in a letter to Gosse:

> though [Sue] has children, her intimacies with Jude have never been more than occasional, even while they were living together. (*Letters* 2.99)

And though Jude for a time feels guilty for opening to Sue what Arabella opened to him, at their last meeting it is Sue's own repressed sexual desire for Jude that is the final note of their relationship. She confesses to Mrs Edlin this last meeting with Jude in Marygreen church, and uses the word that has come in the novel to be a standard euphemism for 'sexually': 'Jude has been here this afternoon, and I find I still love him – O, grossly! I cannot tell you more' (p. 415). This alarming recognition that she still wants to make love with Jude is powerful enough to drive her to the ultimate sacrifice of herself to the letter of the religious law, the consummation of her marriage with a man who is physically repugnant to her and whom she does not love. The reader's recognition not just of her spiritual but also of her sexual love for Jude renders this outcome even more intensely vile to contemplate.

Sue's behaviour in the last chapters constitutes the harshest indictment in the novel of marriage as explicitly ordained by the Christian church, but throughout the action both narrator and characters seek to explore the inhumanities of the institution. Hardy suggests that the cruelty in the social practices we have evolved as conscious humans to cope with the destructive power of sexual instincts is that, instead of educating the young and strengthening the power of their reason to control or channel those instincts,

contemporary social practice was to limit their indiscriminate application by pretending for as long as possible in the growth of the
individual to maturity that they don't exist, and when no longer
possible to punish by exclusion transgressors of certain established
rules. Arabella knows these rules, and how to use or ignore them
when it will be to her advantage to do so, but she has no concern
with their intrinsic validity. Sue knows the rules, and though she
rejects their validity, she remains bound and broken by them, the
intellectual idealist tragedy. Jude is bound to Sue by love, and thus
he too is broken by the rules, even though he is prepared himself to
take a more pragmatic view their application. The narrator in this
as on other moral and philosophical issues is very close to Sue's
position – a source of much paradoxical tension in the novel.

Despite the measured and gently aggrieved tone of Hardy's 1912
postscript to the novel's preface, and the careful disclaimer at the
opening of the fifth chapter of Part Fifth, there is no doubt that as he
wrote the novel he was angrily bitter about marriage, and that the
strength of his emotions forced that bitterness unmediatedly onto
the page in several demonstrable ways.

The most blatant of these is the continual but quite false assertion
that marriage destroys not just love, but affectionate fellow-feeling,
loving-kindness between the partners to it – that blows and curses
are the true note of marriage. Here, for better or worse, we have
the hand of T. Hardy novelist again. It is no coincidence that each
couple Sue and Jude encounter during their abortive attempts at
marriage is more sordidly ill-assorted than the last. It is naked
authorial cynicism which invents the consciousness of the landlord
who suspects Arabella and Jude are not married because he sees
them kiss and is only convinced that they are 'respectable' when he
hears Arabella fling a shoe at Jude's head (p. 406). It is a distortion
of experience when the narrator says that Cartlett and Arabella 'left
the tent . . . in the antipathetic recriminatory mood of the average
husband and wife of Christendom' (p. 311).

It is another criticism of the disproportionate violence of Hardy's
feelings about the destructiveness of marriage that it leads him to
give to the characters, particularly to Jude and Sue, dialogue which
suggests a real local deafness for the rhythms and vocabulary of
speech on this particular subject:

Wifedom has not yet assimilated and digested you in its vast
maw as an atom which has no further individuality. (p. 197)

A reviewer of the first edition commented on this horror, and Hardy revised 'assimilated' to 'squashed up', which only makes things worse. At least the earlier version has a kind of ghastly integrity of tone.

By such excesses of authorial intervention as fate, by such wild improbabilities in dialogue, Hardy may be held to undermine his intention through overdetermined stridency. It may however also be that he calculated that only by so over-enforcing his argument that marriage is a social mechanism for the destruction of love and the happiness of loving partners could he get the majority of his readers, convention-bound, to pay attention.

More insidious because more subtle is the assumption by the narrator of theoretical positions concerning marriage that are unsustainable in practice. For example, at the wedding of Arabella and Jude we have the first account of what marriage is:

> And so, standing before the aforesaid officiator, the two swore that at every other time of their lives till death took them, they would assuredly believe, feel, and desire precisely as they had believed, felt, and desired during the few preceding weeks. What was as remarkable as the undertaking itself was the fact that nobody seemed at all surprised at what they swore. (p. 56)

The narrator here is simply using a form of words, as if he were an outsider to Victorian England, or indeed to western culture altogether. How should anyone, save a few people who thought like Hardy or Sue, have been surprised? It is the kind of comment Hardy might earlier in his career have prefaced with something like 'a reflective foreigner might have found remarkable the fact that . . . ' No-one involved in the ceremony, not even the parson, would have thought that Arabella and Jude were swearing exactly what the narrator says they are; for the sake of forcing the issue, he anticipates Sue and assumes a literalist position. Pragmatic interpretation of the marriage vows would see them as a prop to social duty: providing a framework for keeping the family together and maintaining the decent semblance of love, and unity. Jude reflects on his first marriage to Arabella:

> Their lives were ruined, he thought; ruined by the fundamental error of their matrimonial union: that of having based a permanent contract on a temporary feeling which had no necessary

connection with affinities that alone render a life-long comradeship tolerable. (p. 69)

The use of 'affinities' and 'comradeship' here is carefully managed
so that, at least on a second reading of the novel, the words will help
to make the connection with what Jude believes marriage with Sue
might be. However, after several attempts actually to marry her,
Jude says to Sue:

> The intention of the contract is good and right for many, no
> doubt; but in our case it may defeat its own ends because we
> are the queer sort of people we are – folk in whom domestic
> ties of a forced kind snuff out cordiality and spontaneousness.
> (pp. 300–301)

He accepts that a relationship outside marriage would suit him
and Sue better, but (searching for community, and recognizing the
significance of marriage within it) he refuses to condemn marriage
altogether. The implication of his suggestion, that Sue and he
are exceptional natures attempting to find a way to survive in a
culture which has turned decisively against the exceptional, seems
thoroughly justified. Sue on the other hand (with no notion of
community, and little fundamental concern with anything beyond
self) maintains in reply the absolutist position she shares with the
narrator:

> Sue still held that there was not much queer or exceptional in
> them: that all were so. 'Everybody is getting to feel as we do.
> We are a little beforehand, that's all. In fifty, a hundred, years
> the descendants of these two will act and feel worse than we.

Jude recognizes that society rarely demands precise, literal adherence to its ceremonies, unless they are challenged openly; all that is
needed is a little common-sense and flexibility. In the novel this
view is represented most fully by Mrs Edlin, a survivor, one might
say, from the village community of *Under the Greenwood Tree*:

> Nobody thought o' being afeared o' matrimony in my time, nor
> of much else but a cannon-ball or empty cupboard. Why when I
> and my poor man were married we thought no more o't than of
> a game o' dibs. (p. 302)

She thinks marriage should be taken easily, as it comes, as a festival. Don't think about it, just do it, make the best of it together. But she also recognizes, in three separate places, that this idea is out of date, that society has changed, and thus marriage has also changed. Her final, telling comment is that 'Weddings be funerals 'a b'lieve nowadays.'

At various times before the death of her children Sue claims that marriage is absolutely cruel; that it destroys individuality; that it is a trap set by a woman to get a man; that it is a 'sordid contract, based on material convenience in householding, rating and taxing, and the inheritance of land and money by children making it necessary that the male parent should be known' (p. 220); that it is a tragedy artificially manufactured for people who in a natural state would find relief in parting; that it is a barbarous custom binding them together; that it is a licence to love on the premises; that by compulsion it extinguishes love rather than promotes it. What underlies this sequence of views is her root concern with her individuality, her self, which she discovers by experience with Richard is compromised by a legally enforcable union with another.

Once the intellectual basis of her nature is turned by the murder of her children (as in 'The Withered Arm' Gertrude Lodge's blood is turned by touching a hanged man's neck) she rejects her former subversive attitudes towards marriage, but not the self-concern which generated them. As she has criticized marriage with primary attention to the ideal form of the institution envisaged in the letter of the ceremony, so she accepts the Christian view in its ideal literal form. Both intellectual acts are at bottom self-serving. Earlier she rejects marriage because she is afraid of what it implies, later she accepts the whole of the sacramental teaching concerning it because her physical and emotional fear has been turned into a greater fear for the safety of her own soul. As she can force the loving Jude into unnatural celibacy to preserve the intactness of her body, so she can force herself into sex with a man she loathes to rescue the intactness of her soul, in the process, as we see, abandoning even common humanity.

When Jude, thoroughly ill, near the end of the novel travels to Marygreen to see Sue one last time, she passionately kisses him but refuses to run away with him. She orders him to leave her, but as he goes she hears his desperate coughing 'and in a last instinct of human affection, even now unsubdued by her fetters, she sprang up to go and succour him. But she knelt down again, and stopped her ears with her hands till all possible sound of him had passed away' (p. 412). With this motion she finally abandons humanity, love, lovingkindness, caught in the fetters of a barren desire to save her soul. It is appropriate that in doing so she kneels at the east end of the new church at Marygreen, the church that at the beginning of the novel had symbolized the irreversible decline of the traditional rural community.

The effect of the betrayal by Sue of her own once deeply held critical attitudes to marriage is to reinforce their validity. The episodes of Sue's remarriage to Richard are still more harrowing than the revelation of the deaths of the children, because they constitute for her a torment to which we, as well as Arabella, can see no end until she dies.[6]

Marriage may be Hardy's most prominent target for attack in *Jude the Obscure*, but it does not seem to be the major concern of the novel's central consciousness. Jude would like to marry Sue, but it is not a particularly burning issue with him, as it is with Sue and the narrator. Jude is only in superficial ways Sue's 'counterpart', despite the narrator's insistence on their similarity. His search in the novel is that of the isolated man for a community that will accept him and help him to achieve his ambitions. Hardy had already charted in *Tess of the d'Urbervilles* the decline of traditional rural community; in *Jude the Obscure* he traces the consequences for the individual of this decline.

At the beginning of Chapter 51 of *Tess of the d'Urbervilles* Hardy takes the opportunity given by the forced removal of the Durbeyfield family from their cottage in Marlott to consider changes in the patterns of employment and settlement in South Wessex:

These annual migrations from farm to farm were on the increase here. When Tess's mother was a child the majority of the field-folk about Marlott had remained all their lives on one farm, which had been the home also of their fathers and grandfathers; but latterly the desire for yearly removal had risen to a high pitch. With the younger families it was a pleasant excitement which might possibly be an advantage. The Egypt of one family was the land of promise to the family who saw it from a distance; till by residence there it became in turn their Egypt also; and so they changed and changed.

However, all the mutations so increasingly discernible in village life did not originate entirely in the agricultural unrest. A depopulation was also going on. The village had formerly contained, side by side with the agricultural labourers, an interesting and better-informed class, ranking distinctly above the former – the class to which Tess's father and mother had belonged – and including the carpenter, the smith, the shoemaker, the huckster, together with nondescript workers other than farm-labourers; a set of people who owed a certain stability of aim and conduct to the fact of their being life-holders like Tess's father, or copyholders, or, occasionally, small freeholders. But as the long holdings fell in they were seldom again let to similar tenants, and were mostly pulled down, if not absolutely required by the farmer for his hands. Cottagers who were not directly employed on the land were looked upon with disfavour, and the banishment of some starved the trade of the others, who were thus obliged to follow. These families, who had formed the backbone of the village life in the past, who were the depositaries of the village traditions, had to seek refuge in the large centres; the process, humorously designated by statisticians as 'the tendency of the rural population towards the large towns', being really the tendency of water to flow uphill when forced by machinery.

This passage, adapted with interesting additions and variations from Hardy's 1883 essay 'The Dorsetshire Labourer', is his clearest fictional statement of the ongoing destruction in the eighteen-seventies and eighties of the self-supporting stable community that lies at the base of *Under the Greenwood Tree* or *Far From the Madding Crowd*. Perhaps the most significant change in *Tess of the d'Urbervilles* from 'The Dorsetshire Labourer' is the addition of the detail that the artisan village class 'were the depositaries of the village traditions'. We should interpret such traditions broadly, as traditional patterns of thought and behaviour as well as local historical and topographical lore. When this group was 'forced by machinery' to the large towns, it marked the end of village community as Hardy had understood and explored it in his first novels.

In *Tess of the d'Urbervilles* Hardy gives brief accounts of several villages – Marlott, Trantridge, Flintcomb-Ash amongst others – and despite the explicit statement of the irreversible decline of village culture, aspects of community survive. Marlott has been subject to the kind of agricultural change Hardy finds destructive, but nevertheless when Tess gathers enough courage to face the village after the birth of her child, she finds herself drawn into a sympathetic, healing community:

> Tess's female companions sang songs, and showed themselves very sympathetic and glad at her reappearance out of doors, though they could not refrain from mischievously throwing in a few verses of the ballad about the maid who went to the merry green wood and came back in a changed state. There are counterpoises and compensations in life; and the event which had made of her a social warning had also for the moment made her the most interesting personage in the village to many. Their friendliness won her still further away from herself, their lively spirits were contagious, and she became almost gay. (p. 97)

This is the last time in the novel Hardy is able to envisage a positive response to trouble by a village community. By the time Tess reaches Flintcomb-Ash community has undergone to the full the process of depopulation and deracination Hardy described in 'The Dorsetshire Labourer':

> There was no exaggeration in Marian's definition of Flintcomb-Ash farm as a starve-acre place. The single fat thing on the soil was Marian herself –, and she was an importation. Of the three classes of village, the village cared for by its lord, the village cared for by itself, and the village uncared for either by itself or by its lord – (in other words the village of a resident squire's tenantry, the village of free or copyholders, and the absentee-owner's village, farmed with the land) – this place Flintcomb-Ash was the third. (p. 277)

And yet Tess, Marian and Izz at Flintcomb-Ash maintain for a while that community of cooperation and friendship (and even tradition) which was so fully a part of life at Talbothays. Subsequently Tess returns to Marlott and with her family's removal from the village the novel finally abandons ideas of community; all that is left is the transitory holiday-resort population of Sandbourne. This gradual diminishment of community throws into sharp contrast the last ecstatic community of two celebrated by Tess and Angel at Bramshurst Court. For Hardy the relationship of man and woman, when based on sexual mutuality and loving-kindness, is the most basic of all communities. When that disintegrates too, all that remains, for one partner at least, is death.

If, seen from this particular angle, the richness that is *Tess of the d'Urbervilles* does chart imaginatively in Tess's wanderings through South and Upper Wessex the erosion of community, at the heart of *Jude the Obscure* is an exploration of how it is to live in a world where community is an empty word, in which rural traditions of behaviour, cooperation, interaction have vanished under pressure of new ideas, a new economy.

At the beginning of *Tess of the d'Urbervilles* there is the Marlott club-walking and subsequent dance, deliberately chosen and described by Hardy as emblems of stability and continuity in village life. We first see Tess in a band with most of the women of the village, parading with them, dancing with them in the established ritual; and then at home with her family, performing other communal rituals.

At the beginning of *Jude the Obscure* there is Marygreen, equally deliberately chosen by Hardy to represent the discontinuance of tradition, his description climaxing in the obliteration of the village gravestones:

> The site whereon so long had stood the ancient temple to the Christian divinities was not even recorded on the green and level grass-plot that had immemorially been the churchyard, the obliterated graves being commemorated by eighteenpenny cast-iron crosses warranted to last five years. (p. 6)

Our introduction to Jude is to an isolated individual unsupported by the continuity or the common interest of a community, either of village or of family:

> As you got older, and felt yourself to be at the centre of your time, and not at a point in its circumference, as you had felt when you were little, you were seized with a sort of shuddering, he perceived. All around you there seemed to be something glaring, garish, rattling, and the noises and glares hit upon the little cell called your life, and shook it, and warped it. (p. 13)

The narrator suggests that Jude's isolation is only in the common run of things:

Somebody might have come along that way who would have asked him his trouble, and might have cheered him by saying that his notions were further advanced than those of his grammarian. But nobody did come, because nobody does . . . (p. 27)

Unless, of course the novelist chooses to have them come; as for instance Farfrae comes to Henchard in his needs, or Gabriel Oak to Bathsheba Everdene's farm at the time of fire. However, the reader cannot quarrel with the general sentiment; it is only the absolute terms of the statement that give pause.

This isolated individual, parentless, rootless, thrown inward on his own resources, dreams of community. By chance and temperament (a familiar combination of forces in Hardy) Jude fixes on the scholarly and religious community of the university town of Christminster. The first account he hears of Christminster comes from a carter who has never been to the place, but who identifies the two communities that Jude will encounter when he reaches the city – the 'College life' and the 'wenches in the street'. The language is salted with dialect and homely expressions, and the carter's attitude to the university is that 'they raise pa'sons there like radishes in a bed . . . 'tis their business, like anybody else's' (p. 20). This attitude to the work of the university is an echo of tranter Dewy's attitude to Maybold and the church choir; what they do is their business, and no better or worse than what other artisans do. Jude, however, 'yearning in his heart' to find a community to attach himself to, wantonly idealizes the carter's account:

> 'It is what you may call a castle, manned by scholarship and religion.'
> After this figure he was silent a long while, till he added, 'It would just suit me.' (p. 21)

And this image (or illusion) of a future community sustains him through the loneliness of his preparation for it.

He is still isolated (despite his intervening marriage to Arabella) when he finally reaches the city he has so fully imagined, equipped with the learning which (if he has considered the matter at all) he must believe will be the key that will unlock the door of the 'castle, manned by scholarship and religion' with as little effort as he had anticipated as a child there would be in understanding Latin and Greek:

> Knowing not a human being here Jude began to be impressed
> with the isolation of his own personality, as with a self-spectre,
> the sensation being that of one who walked, but could not make
> himself seen or heard. (pp. 79–80)

Jude finds the two communities in Christminster that the carter
hinted at and everyone recognizes, the conventional town and gown
distinction; and yet he remains in the city as far from sharing
in either as when he entered it. In essence this is because the
university ignores him, looks straight through him (see p. 87 where
the students and dons 'saw through him as though through a pane
of glass at their familiars beyond'), and because his vision of the
university prevents him from sharing in the life of the town:

> For a moment there fell on Jude a true illumination; that here in
> the stone yard was a centre of effort as worthy as that dignified
> by the name of scholarly study within the noblest of the colleges.
> But he lost it under stress of his old idea. He would accept any
> employment which might be offered him on the strength of his
> late employer's recommendation; but he would accept it as a
> provisional thing only. This was his form of the modern vice of
> unrest. (p. 85)

For a moment it seems as if in the mason's yard there might still exist
a craft-community to which Jude could give allegiance, but the idea
fades as soon as it comes. The narrator says that Jude's refusal (or
inability) to explore the communal shelter from isolation that might
be offered in the stoneyard is part of the general social 'unrest' of
the late nineteenth century which also drives rural workfolk to seek
a change of farm every year. Jude cannot commit himself to his work
as a mason and what it might bring because his desire is not just for
any community, but for a community that will help him to fulfil his
social and intellectual ambitions. He imagines that if he could get
entry to the magical world of Christminster learning, he would be
enabled to 'look down on the world through [the college's] panes'
(p. 87).

The novel makes clear at several places that in his particular
dream Jude was part of a substantial new social movement: 'he
sometimes felt that by caring for books he was not escaping the
commonplace nor gaining rare ideas, every working-man being of
that taste now' (p. 66). When he reflects on the letter he has written

to the heads of colleges asking for advice, he wishes they had remained unwritten: 'It is just one of those intrusive, vulgar, pushing applications which are so common in these days' (p. 117). The whole matter is summarized by Jude in his sermon at Encaenia:

> It is a difficult question, my friends, for any young man – that question I had to grapple with, and which thousands are weighing at the present moment in these uprising times – whether to follow uncritically the track he finds himself in, without considering his aptness for it, or to consider what his aptness or bent may be, and re-shape his course accordingly. I tried to do the latter, and I failed. But I don't admit that my failure proved my view to be a wrong one, or that my success would have made it a right one; though that's how we appraise such attempts nowadays – I mean, not by their essential soundness, but by their accidental outcomes. (p. 344)

To return again to *Under the Greenwood Tree*, we may think of Jude as an ambitious young man in some ways similar to the innovative Dick Dewy, but belonging to a later generation. Dick moves from Mellstock with his new bride to open up a branch of his father's business, advancing yet remaining part of the traditional rural community. Jude has been cut off from what might survive of the culture of Mellstock in early childhood, and his ambitions take him much further still.

Eventually Jude realizes that the gates of the castle will not open at his touch, and even before its ivory towers politely repel the mild frontal attack constituted by his letter to the heads of colleges, Jude seems to himself as if (at last) awakening from the dream:

> He saw that his destiny lay not with these [colleges], but among the manual toilers in the shabby purlieu which he himself occupied, unrecognized as part of the city at all by its visitors and panegyrists; yet without whose denizens the hard readers could not read, nor the high thinkers live. (p. 119)

This insight (as with his recognition of the folly of his marriage to Arabella) leads him straight to drink, and in a further, alcohol-heightened illumination he observes at the central crossroads of the city, called here Fourways:

It had more history than the oldest college in the city. It was literally teeming, stratified, with the shades of human groups, who had met there for tragedy, comedy, farce, real enactments of the intensest kind. At Fourways men had stood and talked of Napoleon, the loss of America, the execution of King Charles, the burning of the Martyrs, the Crusades, the Norman Conquest, possibly of the arrival of Caesar.

He began to see that the town life was a book of humanity infinitely more palpitating, varied, and compendious, than the gown life. These struggling men and women before him were the reality of Christminster . . . (p. 121)

This, like his insight in the mason's yard, comes in the novel with the force of truth. It balances the spirits of the generations of craftsmen, shopkeepers, farmers, who kept the town alive through the centuries, against the academics, since the middle ages parasitical upon the town life, contributing to its economy as consumers, but to its felt life, nothing; the amplitude of experience embodied in the life of the town laid down in strata of experience over centuries, against the narrowness of the range of activities and experiences contained within the glass towers of learning. It is the full rich humanity of the town which is absent from the university. The university is a convenient emblem for entrenched power and privilege of all kinds, maintaining its position in a world which is changing so rapidly that its powers and privileges will soon seem to guard only dust and ashes.

Thus Christminster contains two communities, one remote from Jude and inaccessible to him, which is exclusive and apparently moribund, the other immediately present, accessible and apparently full of life. Yet this generalized vision fails to find any embodiment in the narrative. The only fragments of town life that Jude actually encounters are associated with public houses and music halls, and are a source of humiliation to him. If other of the 'palpitating, various' communites of urban Christminster are to be found, Jude does not find them.

Jude's insight into the value of the urban life of Christminster when compared with the University community makes a permanent impression upon the reader, but for Jude it is a passing thought. In part this is because he has read too many words and thought too deeply about what the University ought to mean, so that it has become an ideal which has penetrated his emotional being to the degree that no reasoned or inspired argument can exorcise it. In part, however, the perception possesses no enduring power with him because it is the product of alcohol.

A DIGRESSION ON THE EVILS (OR OTHERWISE) OF DRINK

Hardy is curiously ambivalent about drinking in his writing. It is impossible to forget that cider is one of his 'great things', along with love and dance, that the virtues of old mead are lovingly evoked in several novels and stories, that cider-making is one of the great festivals of his fictional and poetic year. But on the other hand we also remember Poorgrass so drunk he can't get Fanny and her baby to the churchyard in time to be buried, the rum-fuddled Henchard selling his wife, the Durbeyfield parents drinking away their family's livelihood. Another scene in *Tess of the d'Urbervilles* shows this ambivalence brilliantly. As the villagers of Trantridge go home after their dance, the narrator explains:

> the fresh night air was producing staggerings and serpentine courses among the men who had partaken too freely; some of the more careless women also were wandering in their gait . . . Yet however terrestrial and lumpy their appearance just now to the mean unglamoured eye, to themselves the case was different. They followed the road with a sensation that they were soaring along in a supporting medium, possessed of original and profound thoughts; themselves and surrounding nature forming an organism of which all the parts harmoniously and joyously interpenetrated each other. They were as sublime as the moon and stars above them; and the moon and stars were as ardent as they. (p. 69)

One might suspect irony in this account, but the language seems to discount that possibility. The narrator seems to distance himself from 'the mean unglamoured eye' of some other observer's objective vision, and to enter fully and enthusiastically into the truth of the alcoholic ecstacy. The mean eye would call it illusion, but the narrator describes an experience which is a perfect summary of one of the things his novelist achieves in *Tess of the d'Urbervilles* or *The Woodlanders*: the harmonious and joyous interpenetration of man and nature.

Rural labour is a hard life, as we will have cause to know before *Tess* is ended, and alcohol is a drug which provides temporary release into a 'supporting medium'. So too is dance; indeed without the preceding dance the Trantridge folk would not so have felt themselves in harmony with the world, freed from the grinding routines of their everyday life in the willed pleasure of voluntary movement, the exercise of their lived bodies.

However, another narratorial voice immediately undercuts this insight in the following paragraph by reminding us of the effects of drunkenness explored at the opening of the novel: 'Tess, however, had undergone such painful experiences of this kind in her father's house that the discovery of their condition spoilt the pleasure she was beginning to feel in the moonlight journey.'

Jude drinks to evade the reality of his nature, to drown the consciousness of his loss of a dream, an ideal, of his failures – the farce of his marriage, his abandonment of the university, his loss of Sue to Phillotson (twice); he drinks angrily and guiltily. 'Drinking was the regular, stereotyped resource of the despairing worthless' (pp. 70–71). It is always followed by remorse; it is an emblem of his weakness; it runs parallel with his instinctive desire for sexual satisfaction; there is nothing pleasing about it. Yet, as we have seen, it is under the influence of a few drinks that he has his moving and true vision of the essence of Christminster, and the Lamb and Flag where he drinks is not only sordid and unideal (which, in Hardy's presentation it certainly is), but it also possesses a vitality lacking elsewhere:

> the scene was altogether more brisk and gay. The faces of the barmaidens had risen in colour, each having a pink flush on her cheek; their manners were still more vivacious than before – more abandoned, more excited, more sensuous, and they expressed their sentiments and desires less euphemistically, laughing in a lackadaisical tone, without reserve. (pp. 189–90)

This is Arabella's world, and there is a frankness and a gaiety and life here that is worth having, to set against the drunkenness and the ignorance. It is the final scene of drunkenness in the novel, however, that turns the balance of Hardy's attitude. Arabella is an expert at inebriation, maintaining Jude at precisely the right level of intoxication so that he will go through another ceremony of marriage with her. The way that Arabella is able to keep Jude so drunk for so long is almost surreal; he seems to have no will of his own. Hardy can't allow Jude the degrading responsibility of choosing to re-marry Arabella, and her alchemical skill with the bottle deprives Jude of free will, makes her the equivalent of an inexorable First Cause.

After Jude leaves Christminster to follow his cousin Sue Bridehead to Melchester we lose sight of community, even of the kind of urban community which Jude is powerless to join in the university city. The various towns to which we are introduced – Melchester, Aldbrickham, Stoke Barehills, Kennetbridge, Alfredston, are given varying densities of existence in Hardy's presentation of them, but in none is there any sense of a community to which the central characters might belong. There are hints in the Working Men's Club to which Jude belongs in Aldbrickham, but it is introduced only so that we see how it rejects him. There may well be community available at Melchester also, but we do not see it. In order to continue the vivid contrast, already established in Christminster, between Jude's idealistic intentions and the reality of the world he designs to enter, Hardy has him move, now he wishes to be ordained, to the major ecclesiastical centre closest to Christminster. Presumably the cathedral clergy look right through Jude as the dons and undergraduates did in Christminster, but we are not even shown this much contact with them. As before, we see Jude reading by himself and working as a mason at restoring the decaying material fabric embodying the institution he wishes to be part of.

It is at Shaston, where Jude is only ever a visitor, that we have the strongest sense of the communal nature of the place. Though the novel takes place entirely in Wessex (with the exception, just, of Christminster), it has little of the wealth of local history, character or topographical description which characterize Hardy's other novels and stories, even those which are only partly or marginally set in Wessex. The most substantial exception is the entertaining account at the beginning of Part Fourth of the history and local peculiarities of Shaston.

Later in the Part the schoolteacher Richard Phillotson goes to Leddenton to ask the advice of his friend Gillingham about the action he proposes to take in allowing his wife Sue to leave him and go to live with Jude. In his answer Gillingham raises the possibility of a communal response to such a resolve:

'It will upset all received opinion hereabout. Good God – what will Shaston say!' (p. 243)

We soon discover what Shaston will say, and the chaos of the public meeting which Phillotson calls to protest against his dismissal by the school committee 'on account of his scandalous conduct in giving [his] tortured wife her liberty' is Hardy's commentary on the communal response. At first glance the 'farcical yet melancholy event' seems an excrescence on the novel, at best comic relief; but on closer consideration it establishes two of the positions Hardy is trying to argue through the novel about the nature of community.

It is Hardy's harsh conclusion that in the eighteen-nineties whatever community exists, the force holding it together is a rigidly conformist social view. Whether he held that times had changed from the times that used to be, or whether he now felt that his earlier novels were foolishly optimistic, he proposes in his last novel that surviving (urban) communities are exclusive not inclusive, that instead of finding a space for a witch and an idiot, they would drive them off. Anything outside their narrow experience is to be shunned, exiled, anything outside their conventional rules: 'All the respectable inhabitants and well-to-do fellow-natives of the town were against Phillotson to a man' (p. 260). The ultimate conclusion to which this proposition tends is that society is fate, that society destroys the individual who in some way dissents from its rules. Also, and more painfully, as the end of the novel shows, it destroys the exceptional individual who attempts to conform.[7]

Amidst all this hostility to the unusual, Hardy, perhaps building on an idea from Dickens's *Hard Times*, suggests that there is, against all odds, a possible community which is still open enough, unprejudiced enough, to accept individuals on their merits:

somewhat to his surprise, some dozen or more champions rose up in [Phillotson's] defence as from the ground.

It has been stated that Shaston was the anchorage of a curious and interesting group of itinerants, who frequented the numerous fairs and markets held up and down Wessex during the summer and autumn months. Although Phillotson had never spoken to one of these gentlemen they now nobly led the forlorn hope in his defence. The body included two cheap-jacks, a shooting-gallery proprietor and the ladies who loaded the guns, a pair of boxing-masters, a steam-roundabout manager, two travelling broom-makers, who called themselves widows, a gingerbread-stall keeper, a swing-boat owner, and a 'test-your-strength' man. This generous phalanx of supporters and a few others of independent judgment whose own domestic experiences had been not without vicissitude came up and warmly shook hands with Phillotson. (p. 260)

It is true that the nature of the support provided by these people provokes laughter in the reader and distress in Phillotson, and if this is where Hardy's allusions to fairground and market folk ended the reference might be dismissed as local colour. But Hardy goes on to use an Agricultural Show as the location for the only episode in the novel that stands for the otherwise unrepresented time that Jude and Sue spend in happiness producing and raising a family. When they are subsequently forced to leave Aldbrickham, Sue says:

> 'I wish we could both follow an occupation in which personal circumstances don't count,' she said, smiling up wistfully . . . .
> '. . . I ought to take to bread-baking. I grew up in the baking business with aunt, you know. But even a baker must be conventional, to get customers.'
> 'Unless he keeps a cake and gingerbread stall at markets and fairs, where people are gloriously indifferent to everything except the quality of the goods.' (p. 322)

Two and a half years later we see Sue (successfully) selling Christminster cakes at Kennetbridge fair. Hardy suggests without stressing the matter that there is a community where all that counts is what you do, how well you do it, which is free from the narrow destructive constraints of the convention-bound communities that thrive elsewhere. It is no coincidence that this community is (unlike those approved communities of *Under the Greenwood Tree* and *Far From the Madding Crowd*) not rooted in one dear perpetual place, but itinerant. The rooted place has become in *Jude the Obscure* an outpost of conventional exclusivity, whose inhabitants live in fear of contamination by the unorthodox and the exceptional.

One of the ways in which it is possible to distinguish between *Jude the Obscure* and all of the other texts that Hardy designated 'Novels of Character and Environment' is also emblematic of the breakdown of community as Hardy understood and explored it, and of the potential contemporary significance of a rootless existence.[8] *Jude* is essentially a railway novel, rather than a horse and foot novel. *Tess* has as much of a peripatetic character as *Jude*, but the journeys in that novel are mostly by cart or on foot. Roads and paths run through villages, past the fronts or backs of houses, are an essential element in the life of communities, connecting lives along their length. Their shapes are a reflection of generations of human custom. Railway lines are alien to the community, arbitrary intrusions taking the straightest most level route through whatever natural feature is in their way, tunnelling, viaducting, embanking and cutting. Where a road sinks below the fields on either side through the pressure of innumerable feet and the erosion of a thousand years, a railway cutting is dug out in a week or two. The railway passenger is carried at relatively considerable velocity from point to point without chance of contact with the environment passed through. With great rapidity this development accellerated the destruction of traditional preindustrial communities.

Hardy has this class of perception in common with all of the high Victorian novelists:

> The great western highway from London passes through [the town], near a point where the road branches into two, merely to unite again some twenty miles further westward. Out of this bifurcation and reunion there used to arise among wheeled travellers, before railway days, endless questions of choice between the respective ways. But the question is now as dead as the scot-and-lot freeholder, the road waggoner, and the mail coachman who disputed it; and probably not a single inhabitant of Stoke-Barehills is now even aware that the two roads which part in his town ever meet again; for nobody now drives up and down the great western highway daily. (p. 303)

Passages which imply a similar attitude can be found in *Great Expectations, Vanity Fair, Doctor Thorne* and *Felix Holt,* to mention only one of several works by each writer in which the demise of the coach, and thus of the road, and the communities it nourished, is regretted. In the context of Hardy's writing it is amusing to note that the only other of his novels in which the railways play an important part, indeed a crucial part, is his first, *Desperate Remedies* (1871).

Hardy was quite clear about the imaginative and the real impact of the railway, and took thematic pleasure in showing how many moments in the lives of his characters in this novel are shaped by the mechanics of the railway time-table:

> He would meet her at Alfredston Road, the following evening, Monday, on his way back from Christminster, if she could come by the up train which crossed his down-train at that station. (p. 184)

Or there is the earlier episode in which Sue spends the night away from the Melchester Training College, with all the scandal that entails, because she and Jude underestimate the time it will take them to reach a railway station to catch their return train.

We are given an excellent example of the casual unconcern about distance that the railway provokes when Jude and Arabella get into a train for Aldbrickham at 9.40 p.m., just to go off for the night together, and come back to Christminster the next morning (p. 191). And this spur-of-the-moment there and back journey acquires extra significance when the same day Jude and Sue travel in a similar direction:

> He released her hand till they had entered the train, – it seemed the same carriage he had lately got out of with another – where they sat down side by side, Sue between him and the window. He regarded the delicate lines of her profile, and the small, tight, apple-like convexities of her bodice, so different from Arabella's amplitudes. (p. 195)

The superimposition of Sue upon Arabella in the railway carriage, with its erotic notation, becomes a prefiguring of the more potent later superimposition of Sue on Arabella, when she finds herself with Jude in the same room at the inn at Aldbrickham that he and Arabella had shared.[9]

But the most powerful of all the images of railway travel is that of Little Father Time on his journey to his father, alone and separate:

> In the down train that was timed to reach Aldbrickham station about ten o'clock the next evening a small, pale child's face could be seen in the gloom of a third-class carriage. He had large frightened eyes, and wore a white woollen cravat, over which a key was suspended round his neck by a piece of common

string, the key attracting attention by its occasional shine in the lamplight. In the band of his hat his half-ticket was stuck. His eyes remained mostly fixed on the back of the seat opposite, and never turned to the window even when a station was reached and called. On the other seat were two or three passengers, one of them a working woman who held a basket on her lap, in which was a tabby kitten. The woman opened the cover now and then, whereupon the kitten would put out its head, and indulge in playful antics. At these the fellow-passengers laughed, except the solitary boy bearing the key and ticket, who, regarding the kitten with his saucer eyes, seemed mutely to say: 'All laughing comes from misapprehension. Rightly looked at there is no laughable thing under the sun.' (pp. 289–90)

The boy's isolation seems intensified by the idea of the train as a capsule of folk being drawn at some speed by a machine on an invariable route through a landscape with which they have no contact. Even within this cocoon the boy makes no contact; feels no sense even of temporary community with fellow passengers. Ultimately the significance of railways in the image-structure of the novel is focussed in Sue's idea that the station (not the barn as in *Far From the Madding Crowd* or the cathedral) is the cen-trally symbolic building of modern civilization, a civilization which holds within itself the destruction of the long-established concept of community, and which even yet has not established a wider, national or global idea. All things, from love-affairs to war, were altered by the railway, an alteration which the aeroplane has only intensified.

It is with the entry of Little Father Time into the narrative that the question of community is finally polarized. When Jude and Sue first hear of his existence, and consider what to do, Jude responds with characteristic wide-reaching idealism:

The beggarly question of parentage – what is it, after all? What does it matter, when you come to think of it, whether a child is yours by blood or not? All the little ones of our time are collectively the children of us adults of the time, and entitled to our general care. That excessive regard of parents for their own children, and their dislike of other people's, is, like class-feeling, patriotism, save-your-own-soul-ism and other virtues, a mean exclusiveness at bottom. (p. 288)

Setting aside the selfish gene, Jude envisages a global commitment to the globe's children (and at the same time provides the appropriate criticism for Sue's 'save-her-own-soulism' at the end of the novel). In this he was indeed ahead of his time, and maybe such selflessness will always remain an impractical dream. Nevertheless, a hundred years after Hardy wrote this passage, it begins to seem that if the globe has a future then it will be achieved only through global cooperation on the scale that Jude imagines. We might say that he has made his perception of what he lacked in Mellstock and Marygreen expand to fill the world.

If the first thought occasioned in the novel by Little Father Time's existence is a global extension of the idea of community, the last stimulated by his suicide proposes its total collapse. This is Jude's account of what the doctor, who examined the bodies of Little Father Time and the other nameless murdered children, said of the motivation behind Little Father Time's acts:

> there are such boys springing up amongst us – boys of a sort unknown in the last generation – the outcome of new views of life. They seem to see all its terrors before they are old enough to have staying power to resist them. He says it is the beginning of the coming universal wish not to live. (p. 355)

Perhaps Hardy does not altogether endorse the idea of a 'coming universal will not to live', perhaps Jude does not, but that any evidently sane person could foresee such an outcome of contemporary social developments and human evolution certainly implies the growth of an equally universal absence of a communal spirit which might relieve some of the burdens from the troubled life of the individual. Sue's turn from Jude to the community of Christians condemns her to perpetual pain. The failure of Jude's search for a community to sustain the individual through loving-kindness ultimately convinces him that in his own case at least, however it may be for the rest of mankind, a wish not to live is the goal to which his life has ever tended.

9

'From the White Sea to Cape Horn': Thomas Hardy and the Wider World

Jude Fawley's vision of a global community of adults caring collectively for a global community of children raises an interesting question about Hardy's position in the development of fiction during the last part of the nineteenth century. Readers and critics of Hardy are accustomed almost automatically to think of him as the creator of Wessex, the half-real, half-imaginary land which it is so much our pleasure to recreate as we read his work, and to see him as an essential element in the pattern of local, regional fiction that spread widest during the later nineteenth and earlier twentieth century, and which includes as other major figures George Eliot and D. H. Lawrence. But what has not often been remarked in studies of Hardy, I think, is that there was during approximately the same period, from the eighteen-seventies onwards, a new concern in fiction and in poetry about the relationship between England and the wider world beyond its shores. The major writers in this movement are Meredith, Stevenson, Gissing, Kipling, Conrad, Forster. The question this chapter attempts to respond to is whether there is any way in which it makes sense to bring Hardy, apparently the archetypal local writer, into relation with this outward-looking trend in English literature.

Some brief historical detail may be useful to begin with, and 1876 is a good date to start from. Hardy had just finished *The Hand of Ethelberta*, and was taking stock of that highly paid failure (highly paid because of the great success of *Far From the Madding Crowd* two years earlier), and was considering the future in a great burst of preparatory reading. It was a transitional time for him, and it was also a transitional time for the country. The crucial symbolic event of 1876 was the crowning by Disraeli of Queen Victoria as Empress of India, thus giving full public rein to the ideas of expansionist Imperialism that had been simmering beneath the surface of English life for several years, ideas stimulated in part by Disraeli himself. The Rothschild-financed purchase of 40 per cent of the Suez Canal shares in the previous year had been another important Imperial milestone (traditional Whig-liberals like Gladstone would have said millstone). The nature and extent of England's commitment to Empire was from now on to be a prominent question in politics in London, and an even more urgent one in the dominions and colonies themselves.

At the same time there was a new order in Europe to be considered. By 1871 the Prussians under Bismarck had decisively defeated Denmark, Austria-Hungary and France, and had become the dominant force on the European continent, uniting the disparate small states of Germany into an empire under the Prussian crown. This new development was given a powerful diplomatic existence at the Congress of Berlin in 1878, at which the newly united German Empire showed its power to arbitrate in European affairs. This Congress inaugurated the complex ballet of alliances and ententes that was performed across the face of Europe, bringing thirty years of uninterrupted peace on the continent, only irretrievably to be broken by the final transformation scene in 1914.

English foreign politics for forty years were dominated by this entanglement of European and Imperial concerns; France, Germany, Russia, Italy and (rather later) the United States, were all competitors for Empire, particularly in Africa, but also in the far East. The rapid industrialization of Germany and Italy, and the recovery of the United States after the Civil War presented England with a different and potentially more damaging threat, to her commercial world-domination.

So this period, during which Hardy was writing his greatest novels and much of his finest poetry, was one of intense self-questioning on the part of England and many of the English, who were forced for the first time in many years to consider critically their role in the world.

As English policy can be divided between European and Imperial interests, so too can the writers who became interested in exploring England's relationship with the wider world, although some, of course, overlap such categorization. The great European of the early part of the period was George Meredith. He wrote to his friend Maxse about the Franco-Prussian war in 1871:

> I am neither German nor French, nor, unless the nation is attacked, English. I am European and Cosmopolitan – for humanity! (*The Letters of George Meredith*, ed. C. L. Cline, [Oxford: 1970] Vol. I, pp. 400–401)

In many of his novels there are significant sections during which the central characters experience life in different parts of Europe, and are changed by those experiences; *Vittoria* is devoted to the topic of revolutionary Italian nationalism.

Gissing, like Meredith, was powerfully moved by Italy, but it was the remains of Classical Rome and Naples that went deepest to his heart during his long-delayed first journey there in 1888–9. His novel *The Emancipated* is mostly set in Italy. Meredith has scarcely a word to say about the Empire, and in a way this marks him out as being a survivor from an earlier generation. Gissing's last novels, on the other hand, written around the turn of the century, have plenty to say on Imperial issues, especially as they appear to be affecting ordinary people. Here, to show what I mean, is a brief extract from *The Whirlpool* (1897): Rolfe, the novel's central character has just been reading Kipling's *Barrack-Room Ballads*:

> The Empire; that's beginning to mean something. The average Englander has never grasped the fact that there was such a thing as a British Empire. He's beginning to learn it, and itches to kick somebody, to prove his Imperialism. The bully of the music-hall shouting 'Jingo' had his special audience. Now comes a man of genius, and decent folk don't feel ashamed to listen this time. We begin to feel our position. We can't make money quite so easily as we used to; scoundrels in Germany and elsewhere have dared to learn the trick of commerce. We feel sore, and it's a great relief to have our advantages pointed out to us. By God! we are the British Empire, and we'll just show 'em what *that* means!' (ed. Patrick Parrinder [Cranbury, N.J.: 1977] p. 450)

Gissing claimed that this was spoken with 'quiet sarcasm', and a Rolfe has already intensified the irony with a clear-sighted prediction of the first world war:

It's a long time since the end of the Napoleonic wars. Since then Europe has only seen the sputterings of temper. Mankind won't stand it much longer, this encroachment of the humane spirit . . . . We may reasonably hope, old man, to see our boys blown into small bits by the explosive that hasn't got its name yet. (pp. 449–50)

Is there anything in Hardy that seems to show such interests, such sensitive attention to contemporary issues? Is there anything which we might compare with Kipling's evocation of the small wars of empire and those who conduct them? Is there anything comparable with Conrad's savage indictment of Imperial exploitation in *Heart of Darkness* or *Nostromo*? Is there anything one could find to connect Hardy with the critique of English society that Forster offers though a comparison with Italian society in *Where Angels Fear to Tread* and *A Room With a View*? How can we relate Hardy – Hardy of Wessex – to the wider world?

The quotation in the chapter's title offers a starting point for investigation. It comes from *The Woodlanders*, that novel of Hardy's which, together with *The Return of the Native*, offers the reader the most enclosed environment of all rural environments, remote even from the nearest small market town, let alone London or Berlin or Calcutta. Yet Hardy sees it as essential to his purpose in *The Woodlanders* to point out to the reader during the course of the first three chapters both that the intensity of the personal relationships he is about to present is equal in power and significance to those presented in the greatest international dramas, and that the 'lonely courses' of two of his characters 'formed no detached design at all, but were part of the pattern in the great web of human doings then weaving in both hemispheres, from the White Sea to Cape Horn' (p. 18).

Part of my argument, embodied in this quotation, is that where Meredith continually imagines his essentially English actions within a European framework, and where Conrad's English protagonists find their identities modified or reinforced in a colonial context, Hardy is anxious for his readers to be constantly aware of the global, even the universal (in a literal as well as a figurative sense) significance of his deliberately circumscribed actions.

Consider that other archetypally limited environment Egdon Heath. It is no coincidence that in the middle of the first chapter which places the Heath at centre-stage, and which deliberately sets out for the reader the heath's long and effective resistance to the transforming hand of man, there is the following passage:

> Fair prospects wed happily with fair times; but alas if times be not fair! Men have oftener suffered from the mockery of a place too smiling for their reason than from the oppression of surroundings oversadly tinged. Haggard Egdon appealed to a subtler and scarcer instinct, to a more recently learnt emotion, than that which responds to the sort of beauty called charming and fair.
>
> Indeed it is a question if the exclusive reign of this orthodox beauty is not approaching its last quarter. The new Vale of Tempe may be a gaunt waste in Thule: human souls may find themselves in closer and closer harmony with external things wearing a sombreness distasteful to our race when it was young. The time seems near, if it has not actually arrived, when the chastened sublimity of a moor, a sea, or a mountain will be all of nature that is absolutely in keeping with the mood of the more thinking among mankind: and ultimately, to the commonest tourist, spots like Iceland may become what the vineyards and myrtle-gardens of South Europe are to him now; and Heidelberg and Baden be passed unheeded as he hastens from the Alps to the sand-dunes of Scheveningen. (pp. 4–5)

This intrusion of narratorial speculation has upset many critics, but I feel certain that Hardy saw it as an essential corrective to the isolation and insulation that the Heath is going to provide for the fiction upon which the reader has just embarked. Such narratorial analysis has been seen by many critics as part of the novel's obtrusively 'educated' framework of reference and allusion, directed by the novelist at the urban book-borrowing public, and as a consequence irrelevant to the novel's real issues; but it really is not so. This account, in European terms, of the connection between the physical nature of the Heath and a fundamental contemporary human concern, can be associated with the equally celebrated account later in the novel of Clym's physical appearance, in which he too is seen as representing a phenomenon essentially modern, and is thus more deeply associated with the Heath. But the underlying point that Hardy is making in these narratorial excursions (as he does in other ways throughout the novel) is that though the action of the novel may seem parochial, it is indeed rather representative of the most modern, the most advanced concerns, not perhaps in this instance of global humanity, but at any rate of western civilization.

It is not, it must be said, however, a characteristic of Hardy's finest fiction, that (as do many of his contemporaries) he sends characters abroad in order to test the values of the culture they leave behind in England, or indeed take with them across the channel or the Atlantic. The exception is *Tess of the d'Urbervilles*, in which we do actually see Angel Clare in Brazil, for a page or two of chapter 49. Though it is true that Hardy makes no attempt to represent anything specific about Brazil to us – Angel might have been with Marlow in the Congo, or with the great contemporary traveller Isabella Bishop in China for all the detail of the environment that we get, especially when compared with, say his evocation of the vales of the great and little dairies in the same novel. Yet, in giving us a brief, unsatisfying glimpse of Angel, disillusioned, ill, on the way home after a futile experiment, Hardy focusses on some important issues. One I have already alluded to: on this uncomfortable mule-journey towards the Brazilian coast Angel has for a time a large-minded companion, who has been for much longer a world-traveller. This shadowy figure is, in the context of the whole of the literature of the period, a representative man, one of that kind of Englishman met with much more frequently in Conrad or Kipling or Stevenson, or even in later Gissing, whose reactions to English society and morality encourage him to find occupation anywhere but England, anywhere that his particular knowledge – commercial, geological, engineering, agricultural – places him at an advantage over the natives and their current exploiters. This figure turns out good or bad as his nature and the circumstances (and the particular intentions of the author) dictate. It is not just a convention to suggest as Hardy does, that such a man could offer Angel a convincing and powerful new moral perspective, and indeed in the passage in which we learn of the views of this unnamed companion Hardy uses a simile that powerfully reinforces the contrast that he wishes to offer us between self-centred Victorian parochiality and the potentiality of the rest of the world:

to his cosmopolitan mind such deviations from the social norm [as Tess's violation and consequent child], so immense to domesticity, were no more than are the irregularities of vale and mountain-chain to the whole terrestrial curve. (p. 329)

This is a characteristic Hardyan expression of an idea that is found in fiction from Gissing's *The Emancipated* to Forster's *A Room with a View*, and one, of course, that is central to *Tess* itself. There is a strong temptation to dismiss this stranger, indeed the whole Brazilian episode, as no more than an essential narrative device, to provide a means for Angel to come to a right understanding of Tess – note, for instance, how the stranger is neatly killed off once he has had the desired effect on Angel. But if we think, just for a second, about even this detail, we find how active is Hardy's insight, for this utterly casual death and burial, no more than a few hours' pause for Angel on his flight from the promised land, is powerfully emblematic of the fate facing so many of the Wessex characters about whom Hardy writes.

Though there is in the novels of Character and Environment no other attempt to represent (however tenuously) foreign parts, yet in almost all of them emigration is considered or achieved. Hardy meticulously records in 'The Dorsetshire Labourer' the migration of people from the land, and in his fiction he embodies one of the resources they were driven to. Gabriel Oak thinks of California, Clym Yeobright is in Paris, Donald Farfrae is off to America, Tim Tangs takes Suke to New Zealand, the Donns go to Australia. Hardy isn't particularly interested in exploring the pressing economic or social motives for their leaving England, but we do feel that the decision wasn't particularly anguishing for any of them, that it was more an adventure, if anything. And yet, in these same few pages from *Tess* we have been looking at, Hardy offers a brief and poignant insight:

> The crowds of agricultural labourers who had come out to the country in his wake, dazzled by representations of easy independence, had suffered, died and wasted away. He would see mothers from English farms, trudging along with their infants in their arms, when the child would be stricken with fever and would die: the mother would pause to dig a hole in the loose earth with her bare hands, would bury the babe therein with the same natural grave-tools, shed one tear, and again trudge on. (p. 328)[1]

It is outside these privileged novels that we get more material to assess Hardy's response to abroad; emigration and going for a soldier or a sailor were the only ways the poor could expect to experience other cultures than their own, (unless we take a more microcosmic view than I am currently doing and consider that Bath or Bournemouth, not to say London, offers a different enough culture for the rural workfolk to experience the radically other). The professional and upper classes, however, do travel. We might consider (in chronological order) Stephen Smith earning fame and fortune as an architect in India, Henry Knight futilely examining the architecture of Europe; Ethelberta finding no escape from her suitors in Normandy, her brothers Sol and Dan examining French construction techniques in Paris; Paula Power manipulated around Europe by a conspiratorial entourage, but ultimately finding her true love on a beach in Normandy; Sir Blount Constantine hunting lions and Swithin St Cleeve hunting constellations in South Africa; Pierston contemplating Roman antiquities.

Few of these episodes are of central importance to the novels in which they occur. Nor is it possible to base on them a claim that Hardy is, like Meredith or Conrad, a cosmopolitan novelist with well developed ideas about various political and social relationships between England and the rest of the world. What is of interest is that in sending these various characters abroad for the reasons that he does, Hardy conforms to, or rather, forms part of, a pattern in Victorian literature.

For instance, one of the chief reasons that many characters in many Victorian novels and narrative poems go abroad is to attempt to escape or forget unhappy or unfortunate romantic experiences. Travel, the confrontation of different cultures, the putting of distance between the self and the problem, was a perennially offered cure (an idea brilliantly rendered, for instance, by Trollope in his masterpiece *He Knew He Was Right*, or by Meredith in *Diana of the Crossways* or *One of Our Conquerors*), and almost always the cure fails, since one of the lessons the great Victorian writers have to teach is that without some fundamental transforming impulse, you cannot leave fragments of your personality behind you, however far you travel in the attempt to evade it. Henry Knight, Ethelberta Petherwin and Paula Power all discover this (there is a strong resemblance, I think, between Knight and Claude, the central character of Clough's superb narrative poem *Amours de Voyage*). On the other hand, Hardy shows with Swithin St Cleeve that when the journey to escape emotional trauma is allied to another powerful purpose – in his case an astronomical one, then the experience of abroad may be effectual – at least until you come home again. Whether such apparently successful escape from a deeply felt emotion is to be approved of is, however, doubtful; and Hardy allows his narrator considerable hostility towards the Swithin who is able to erase his love for Viviette from his consciousness in favour of 'a wheelbarrow-load of astronomical data'.[2]

Stephen Smith offers a representative example of another familiar later Victorian character, the child of rural or urban workfolk making good in the Empire. Smith has, of course, exceptional advantages from the start, in that he was sent (like Grace Melbury) away from his home to a good school in Exeter, but his reception by Parson Swancourt once his ancestry is known at Endelstow Rectory makes it clear that, however well-educated, he will have a hard time thriving in England. Remote Bombay, where no-one knows his ancestry, offers him a much fairer chance of advancing through talent alone (though, to keep matters in perspective, Hardy doesn't show us India at all, and Kipling ten or fifteen years later was to make clear to everyone that class was as potent a factor in Anglo-Indian society as at home – Hardy might have been on slightly safer ground in Australia or South Africa, where one's ancestry really was less important).

Hardy was very much a novelist of his time, and we should not be surprised that he shared, to a perhaps underestimated degree, some of the interest shown by most turn-of-the-century writers in ideas about relations between the English and abroad. Hardy's formal conservatism as a novelist also meant that he was not prepared – perhaps even not able – to experiment very far with his fiction in directions that would have allowed him to realize much more fully the prospect offered us at the beginning of *The Woodlanders* of a global, almost universal context for his narrative.

George Eliot, in the celebrated opening of chapter fifteen of *Middlemarch*, makes vividly the point about the relationship between later Victorian fiction and the life it presented and interpreted. In this passage Eliot invokes Henry Fielding as one of the colossi of English fiction and, referring specifically to the chapters that introduce each book of *Tom Jones*, goes on to lament that a hundred and twenty years after Fielding's death, the pace and density of life have increased to such an extent that his relaxed and broad perspective is no longer possible:

We belated historians must not linger after his example; and if we did so, it is probable that our chat would be thin and eager, as if delivered from a camp-stool in a parrot-house. I at least have so much to do in unravelling certain human lots, and seeing how they were woven and interwoven, that all the light I can command must be concentrated on this web, and not dispersed over that tempting range of relevancies called the Universe.

It is the coincidence of the web-image, pervasive throughout *Middlemarch* but not so common in Hardy, that justifies a speculation that in the passage from *The Woodlanders* from which the title of this chapter is taken, Hardy is directly responding to Eliot. I am sure that he found the universal range of relevancies increasingly tempting at this stage in his career as a writer, and that after three further efforts at resisting the temptation, in *Tess of the d'Urbervilles, Jude the Obscure* and *The Well-Beloved*, Hardy gave in. What we get as a result of this capitulation to the temptation offered by the universal frame is not more novels, but a substantial fragment of his poetry, and above all, *The Dynasts*.

In *The Dynasts* at last Hardy was able to present human actions not just from the minutely realistic point of view of the later Victorian novel, but also from a perspective so remote that differences between England and abroad became irrelevant (as Hardy ultimately believed they were), a point of view from which it was possible to encompass both the White Sea and Cape Horn. This is the play's second stage-direction:

> The nether sky opens, and Europe is disclosed as a prone and emaciated figure, the Alps shaping like a backbone, and the branching mountain-chains like ribs, the peninsular plateau of Spain forming a head. Broad and lengthy lowlands stretch from the north of France across Russia like a grey-green garment hemmed by the Ural mountains and the glistening Arctic Ocean.
> The point of view then sinks downwards through space, and draws near to the surface of the perturbed countries, where the peoples, distressed by events which they did not cause, are seen writhing, crawling, heaving, and vibrating in their various cities and nationalities. (p. 13)

It is through his stage directions that Hardy instructs us most clearly in the transformation of scale that his vision demands; this, for instance, is how we are asked to envisage the battle of Leipzig:

So massive is the contest that we soon fail to individualize the combatants as beings, and can only observe them as amorphous drifts, clouds and waves of conscious atoms, surging and rolling together; can only particularize them by race, tribe, and language. Nationalities from the uttermost parts of Asia here meet those from the Atlantic edge of Europe for the first and last time. By noon the sound becomes a loud droning, uninterrupted and breve-like, as the sound from the pedal of an organ kept continuously down. (*Part Third*, pp. 78–9)

Hardy's sense of the smallness of the world, its interconnectedness and interdependence, of the futility of nationalistic or dynastic ambitions in the face of this perspective, is really a very modern one. Hardy has no sympathy for such dynastic warfare, and in this massive drama as much as in the brief famous lyric 'In Time of 'The Breaking of Nations'', he balances against it the activities and values of ordinary lives. All human endeavour when seen from so remote a controlling perspective as that in *The Dynasts* seems futile, but poised against such an account is Hardy's vivid representation of the individual combatant, who, whether Captain Hardy supporting the dying Nelson or Hussar Sergeant Young at bivouac on the eve of the battle of Vitoria, recalls with deep affection the life of the home from which war has driven him. The remote but total control that is exercised over the action by the Immanent Will, renders the significance of the local and the individual more powerful, but also more poignant.

Perhaps it is not entirely frivolous to suggest that in *The Dynasts* Hardy offers a very early critical model for those who have become dedicated to the idea of global integration, the Earth itself as living organism, Gaia even: a world in which nationalities, politics, wars are irrelevant, indeed a world which is itself, as Jude Fawley envisaged it, a community. As in so many respects, Hardy's most characteristic and mature view turns out to have been finely anticipatory.

Notes

1. The story 'The Distracted Preacher' (1879) has a similarly real topographical and historical environment.

CHAPTER 1: *UNDER THE GREENWOOD TREE* OR THE MELLSTOCK QUIRE?

1. The leaf is reproduced in facsimile between pp. 112 and 113 of the first volume of Hardy's autobiography, *The Early Life of Thomas Hardy*, published under the name of his second wife Florence in 1928. The manuscript itself is in the Dorset County Museum in Dorchester.

2. The exception is the group of substantial changes that Hardy made to the historical and environmental elements in the narrative. The notes to the World's Classics edition of the novel point out the most important of these alterations.

3. There is something of the same attitude perceptible when John Upjohn in *The Woodlanders*, reflecting on what might have happened to the superior doctor Fitzpiers when he fell asleep on horseback on his way home, says: 'you might ha' been a-wownded into tatters a'most, and no brother tradesman to jine your few limbs together within seven mile!' (p. 161)

4. It should not be surprising, considering the titles of the novels, to find aspects of *Under the Greenwood Tree* repeated in *Far From the Madding Crowd* written two years later. We would expect the later novel to be similarly remote from centres of urban sophisticated culture, and to adopt a similarly pastoral mode of perception. And indeed there is also in *Far From the Madding Crowd* a similar concern with the right way to do things, such as sleeping in a hut, making a proposal, getting a job, quenching a fire, dipping, shearing and curing sheep, saving a rick. However this fascination with how (or how not) to do things diminishes considerably towards the end of the later novel, as the power of the individuality of the four main characters pushes all else aside.

5. Hardy reserves his account of that perpetual nineteenth-century concern, the clash between the exceptional individual and the functioning society for *The Return of the Native* and some subsequent novels. His approach to this question (examined in Chapter five of this study) is directly related to J. S. Mill's *On Liberty*.

6.   It is interesting in this context that in 1912 Hardy added *pocket* in
     place of *world*, a financial for a social distinction.

CHAPTER 2:   HARDY'S DANCES

1.   In most of his novels that centre on the life of rural workfolk there
     are similar occasions to be marked by a dance. In *The Return of
     the Native* the Yeobrights hold a traditional Christmas dance in
     which they wait upon their guests, and May-Day is celebrated
     with a dance; in 'The Three Strangers' Shepherd Fennel and his
     wife hold a dance to mark the christening of their child; in *The
     Mayor of Casterbridge* Elizabeth-Jane's wedding is confirmed in a
     dance, while both Henchard and Farfrae feel that an appropriate
     way to commemorate 'a national event' is by a dance. In *Tess of
     the d'Urbervilles* Whitsun is marked by a dance, and the community
     expressed through the dance can incorporate the alien Angel Clare
     for the time. It is only in *The Woodlanders*, and more strikingly in
     Jude the Obscure, that dance is not a measure of the stability of the
     fundamentals of that society. In *The Woodlanders* the only dance is
     one in which Giles Winterborne attempts to help on his suit for the
     hand of Grace Melbury by providing a Christmas party for her and
     her family. Giles has asked Marty South's opinion about the efficacy
     of the party, and she replies:

> 'Is there to be dancing?'
> 'There might be, certainly?'
> 'Will He dance with Her?'
> 'Well, yes.'
> 'Then it might bring things to a head, one way or the other –
> I won't be the maid to say which.'

The occasion turns out a disaster, for Giles (unlike the tranter or Mrs
Yeobright) is unaccustomed to hosting such parties, and when the
Hintock Band begins to play:

> Grace had been away from home for so long, and was so drilled
> in new dances, that she had forgotten the old figures, and hence
> did not join in the movement. Then Giles felt that all was over.
> As for her, she was thinking, as she watched the gyrations, of a
> very different measure that she had been accustomed to tread
> with a bevy of sylph-like creatures in muslin in the music-room
> of a large house. (p. 75)

It is characteristic that Hardy should have Giles recognize his defeat
in the fact that Grace will not dance the traditional figures of the

country-dances, but dreams of the waltzes and polkas that she has learned in a different environment, early examples of the closed-couple dances that will usurp the country-dances almost universally by 1914.

In *Jude the Obscure* there are no dances, just as there is no sense, even at Marygreen, of a rural culture, and, as Chapter 8 of this book attempts to show, no sense of community whatsoever. Weddings are funerals, and in western culture at least, even in Ireland, there is not normally dancing at wakes.

2. 'The Egalitarian Waltz' in *What is Dance?* ed. Roger Copeland and Marshall Cohen (New York: Oxford University Press, 1983) pp. 521–32.

3. It is an indication of the essentially rural nature even of the county-town Casterbridge that at the wedding-dance of Donald Farfrae and Elizabeth-Jane Newson in *The Mayor of Casterbridge* the guests dance country dances, not waltzes.

4. The climax in Hardy's writing of the connection between music and dance is in 'The Fiddler of the Reels', and the crisis of the story needs to be read in full to experience the almost magical effect Mop Ollamoor's fiddling has on Car'line Aspent:

> . . . at that very moment a five-handed reel was proposed, in which two or three begged her to join.
>
> She declined on the plea of being tired and having to walk to Stickleford, when Mop began aggressively tweedling 'My Fancy-Lad,' in D major, as the air to which the reel was to be footed. He must have recognized her, though she did not know it, for it was the strain of all seductive strains which she was least able to resist – the one he had played when she was leaning over the bridge at the date of their first acquaintance. Caroline stepped despairingly into the middle of the room with the other four.
>
> Reels were resorted to hereabouts at this time by the more robust spirits, for the reduction of superfluous energy which the ordinary figure-dances were not powerful enough to exhaust. As everybody knows, or does not know, the five reelers stood in the form of a cross, the reel being performed by each line of three alternately, the persons who successively came to the middle place dancing in both directions. Car'line soon found herself in this place, the axis of the whole performance, and could not get out of it, the tune turning into the first part without giving her opportunity. And now she began to suspect that Mop did know her, and was doing this on purpose, though whenever she stole a glance at him his closed eyes betokened obliviousness to everything outside his own brain. She continued to wend her way through the figure of 8 that was formed by her course, the fiddler introducing into his notes the wild and agonizing sweetness of a living voice in one too highly wrought; its pathos running high and running low in endless variation, projecting through her

nerves excruciating spasms, a sort of blissful torture. The room swam, the tune was endless; and in about a quarter of an hour the only other woman in the figure dropped out exhausted, and sank panting on a bench.

The reel instantly resolved itself into a four-handed one. Caroline would have given anything to leave off; but she had, or fancied she had, no power, while Mop played such tunes; and thus another ten minutes slipped by, a haze of dust now clouding the candles, the floor being of stone, sanded. Then another dancer fell out – one of the men – and went into the passage in a frantic search for liquor. To turn the figure into a three-handed reel was the work of a second, Mop modulating at the same time into 'The Fairy Dance,' as better suited to the contracted movement, and no less one of those foods of love which, as manufactured by his bow, had always intoxicated her.

In a reel for three there was no rest whatever, and four or five minutes were enough to make her remaining two partners, now thoroughly blown, stamp their last bar, and, like their predecessors, limp off into the next room to get something to drink. Caroline, half-stifled inside her veil, was left dancing alone, the apartment now being empty of everybody save herself, Mop, and their little girl.

She flung up the veil, and cast her eyes upon him, as if imploring him to withdraw himself and his acoustic magnetism from the atmosphere. Mop opened one of his own orbs, as though for the first time, fixed it peeringly upon her, and smiling dreamily, threw into his strains the reserve of expression which he could not afford to waste on a big and noisy dance. Crowds of little chromatic subtleties, capable of drawing tears from a statue, proceeded straightway from the ancient fiddle, as if it were dying of the emotion which had been pent up within it ever since its banishment from some Italian or German city where it first took shape and sound. There was that in the look of Mop's one dark eye which said: 'You cannot leave off, dear, whether you would or no!' and it bred in her a paroxysm of desperation that defied him to tire her down. (*Life's Little Ironies* pp. 180–82)

Car'line soon collapses, and Mop takes their illegitimate daughter and disappears for ever. Though Hardy is careful to suggest that the power of the music over Car'line may derive partly at least from her own highly-strung, impressionable, weak-willed nature, and though, as we have seen with Margery and the drum polka, everyone responds in some degree to the rhythmical intensity of dance-music, nevertheless the overwhelming impression is of the supernatural power of Mop's fiddling over Car'line's body.

5.   The following discussion owes much to Sondra Fraleigh's superb book *Dance and the Lived Body: A Descriptive Aesthetics* (Pittsburgh: University of Pittsburgh Press, 1987), abbreviated henceforward as *Fraleigh*.

6. Hanna, Judyth Lynne *To Dance is Human: A Theory of Nonverbal Communication* (Austin and London: University of Texas Press, 1979), p. 66.
7. See also, for instance, 'The Fiddler' and 'At a Pause in a Country Dance'.

CHAPTER 3: *THE RETURN OF THE NATIVE*: CHARACTER AND THE NATURAL ENVIRONMENT

1. Hardy seems to have a similarly split vision of Casterbridge in *The Mayor of Casterbridge*. See below, pp. 75–6.
2. Blackbarrow, an imaginary name, was replaced by Rainbarrow, the real name of the topographical feature on which Hardy based his descriptions, in the revision of the novel he made in 1895 as part of the move throughout the novel's history of revision towards demystifying its environment. The World's Classics edition of the novel excludes revisions made after the publication of the first edition.
3. For another example of how Hardy understands the relationships between his characters and the natural environment, see pp. 105–6 below.

CHAPTER 4: *THE TRUMPET-MAJOR, A LAODICEAN* AND *TWO ON A TOWER*: THE MAN-MADE ENVIRONMENT

1. As already noted on pp. 7–8 above, in 1895 Hardy wanted to integrate *The Trumpet-Major* with Wessex, and so replaced most of the real place-names he had originally felt were appropriate for this historical romance with Wessex place-names – thus Weymouth became Budmouth, Exeter became Exonbury. However, he also desired at the same time to make the fictional topography accord as precisely as possible with that observable on the ground. The village of Overcombe, where most of the action takes place, was imaginary (in that Hardy made it from fragments of different places in the neighbourhood of Weymouth) and thus had to remain Overcombe. As an element in this original environment-construction, Derriman's house, called Overcombe Hall, was modelled on the existing Poxwell Manor. In accordance with Hardy's almost mechanical procedures in the 1895 revision Overcombe Hall became Oxwell Hall, and some directions and distances were changed in both 1895 and 1912 to accommodate the alteration.
2. Norman Page's description of the tower is in his *Thomas Hardy* (London, 1977) pp. 111–12.
3. Perhaps too carefully patterned Michael Millgate has suggested in *Thomas Hardy: His Career as a Novelist* (London, 1971) pp. 189–91.

CHAPTER 5:   *THE MAYOR OF CASTERBRIDGE*: THE FATE OF MICHAEL HENCHARD'S CHARACTER

1. In *Thomas Hardy: The Forms of Tragedy* (Detroit, 1975), Chapter 4.
2. Two of the three novels that Hardy wrote after *The Return of the Native* – *A Laodicean* and *Two on a Tower* – also contain studies of women whose lives are also conditioned by their lack of access to power in a male-dominated environment, despite the fact that one is rich and the other aristocratic. Paula Power's name is thus fundamentally ironic, and though Lady Viviette Constantine loves and is loved in return, male authority determines her subsequent unhappiness and death.
3. Elaine Showalter's fine essay 'The Unmanning of the Mayor of Casterbridge' reaches a similar conclusion by a different route. The essay is in *Critical Approaches to the Fiction of Thomas Hardy*, edited by Dale Kramer (London and Basingstoke: Macmillan, 1978) pp. 99–115.
4. See, for instance, the first chapter of David Enstice's *Thomas Hardy: Landscapes of the Mind* (London and Basingstoke, 1979) with its reliance on A. Lindsay Clegg's *A History of Dorchester, Dorset* (London, 1972), and almost every substantial commentator on the novel.
5. Another aspect of the urban nature of Casterbridge is the rapidity with which gossip spreads through the community: 'By this time the marriage that had taken place was known throughout Casterbridge; had been discussed noisily on kerbstones, confidentially behind counters, and jovially at the Three Mariners' (p. 217). The actions of prominent people in the town are speedily and intimately discussed by the workfolk and out-of-workfolk of the town. Similarly, at the beginning of the next chapter: 'The retort of the furmity-woman before the magistrates had spread; and in twenty-four hours there was not a person in Casterbridge who remained unacquainted with the story of Henchard's mad freak at Weydon Priors Fair, long years before' (p. 218). Gossip is one of the many potential agencies of events that the novel empowers, as for instance when inaccurate gossip about Farfrae's intentions with regard to purchasing a seed shop for the bankrupt Henchard creates enmity in the ex-mayor where none was intended (p. 241).
6. The incident is a triumph of a different sort for Henchard too, in that he does not use his authority to attempt to crush the woman, but at once accepts the inherent validity of her claim.
7. It is then a reasonably harsh criticism of Susan and of conventional morality when the narrator adds: 'Mrs Newson would have rewarded the old woman as far as her small means afforded, had she not discreetly borne it in mind that it was by this unscrupulous person's liquor her husband had been degraded.' (p. 25) Elizabeth-Jane's concern for respectability, the anxiety of saving herself and her mother from categorization by observers as 'the lowest' must share in this criticism.

8. This speech echoes Thomas Leaf's unintentionally comic story at the end of *Under the Greenwood Tree*, in which a man is supposed to make a thousand pounds through a kind of natural multiplication. Henchard actually does it, though we have no details about how he does it. His achievement might also lead a reader to imagine that the tendency of this novel is to attack the institution of marriage.

9. There is a strong flavour of Blake underpinning the idea of energy in both Mill and Hardy: 'Energy is the only life, and is from the Body; and Reason is the bound or outward circumference of Energy. Energy is Eternal Delight. Those who restrain desire, do so because theirs is weak enough to be restrained; and the restrainer or reason usurps its place & governs the unwilling. And being restrain'd, it by degrees becomes passive, till it is only the shadow of desire' (from *The Marriage of Heaven and Hell*). Energy, defined in the *OED* as 'vigour of action, utterance, etc. Hence as a personal quality: The capacity and habit of strenuous exertion', has its earliest record in Coleridge 1809–10; but the word was in the air at the end of the eighteenth century as descriptive of painting and so on.

10. The narrator comments that 'Any suspicion of impropriety was to Elizabeth-Jane like a red rag to a bull. Her craving for correctness of procedure was, indeed, almost vicious' (p. 216). With regard to Farfrae a good example of his adherence to social conventions is on p. 307, where Henchard thinks how he could alienate 'the correct' Farfrae from Elizabeth-Jane by revealing her bastardy to him.

11. This novel defines 'practical jokes' as something rather more sinister and dangerous than I am used to considering them; there is also a considerable number of them. As well as telling a man his daughter is dead when she is alive, threatening to sell your wife is a joke (though actually doing it is not) (p. 14); making a man ride to work half-naked is a joke (p. 100); getting a potential husband's daughter to live with you is a joke (p. 150); a bull charging two women intends a practical joke rather than murder (p. 207), and the same is true of Henchard wrestling Farfrae (pp. 235, 239); Henchard's reading aloud of Lucetta's love-letters is a joke (p. 251, and Lucetta herself calls it 'horse-play' p. 249); some people think the skimmity ride 'too rough a joke', and for Jopp 'it was not a joke, but a retaliation' (p. 268). This extensive list might provide the basis for a study of playfulness in Hardy.

12. There are thirteen places in the novel where God is named, and Henchard is responsible for ten of them (the others are Christopher Coney, Joyce and the landlady of Peter's Finger). From the oath he swears before God in the church near Weydon Henchard uses the name freely, telling Farfrae to 'pray to God' that he may never suffer fits of desperate gloom (p. 78), saying to himself that God knows whether Lucetta will be contented to be put off with a cheque now Susan has returned (p. 81), using the exclamation 'Good God' twice to introduce chastisements of Elizabeth-Jane's Dorset speech and humble actions. As he looks forward to the day when his oath will be fulfilled, he says 'then I mean to enjoy myself, please God.' When

he has Farfrae's life in his hands, and the Scotsman tells him to take it as he has long wished to, he replies 'that's not true! . . . God is my witness that no man ever loved another as I did thee . . . '

Apart from his oath-swearing, we never see Henchard in church (though as a churchwarden presumably he must go), and it is hard to imagine him there. The narrator repeatedly stresses Henchard's superstitious nature, and it would be possible to say that his frequent reference to God is an instinctive superstitious attempt to ward off evil consequences rather than a deeply held belief in the Christian God's power in the world. A different reading might suggest that Henchard is more open to the supernatural, more naturally religious, than any other character in the novel. As usual the ambiguity leaves us free to choose, to construct our own meaning.

13.   The Napoleonic allusion also directs one's thoughts immediately to *The Dynasts* and the Immanent Will.

CHAPTER 6: *TESS OF THE D'URBERVILLES*

1.   It seems from early cancelled readings in the first part of the manuscript of *Tess of the d'Urbervilles*, and indeed from earlier titles for the novel (see *Tess of the d'Urbervilles*, ed. Grindle and Gatrell [Oxford: Clarendon Press, 1983], pp. 3–4) that the prominence of the d'Urberville theme in the novel was a late addition to Hardy's ideas about his heroine, thus marking it out as a contribution of the second Thomas Hardy metaphorically identified later in this chapter.

It is possible to find this preoccupation with decayed aristocracy in other of Hardy's works, in the character of Troy in *Far From the Madding Crowd*, whose probable pedigree as a bastard of the Earl of Severn was added in the proofs for the novel's serialization in *Cornhill*, in the presumed lord-of-the-manor ancestry of the Melburys in *The Woodlanders*, in the specific noble connections of Edred Fitzpiers added for the Wessex edition of the same novel, in the de Stancys of *A Laodicean*, in the remote noble ancestor added in revision for the first collected edition of Hardy's work to the background of *The Return of the Native*'s Eustacia Vye, or at numerous places in *A Group of Noble Dames*. The assumption in the following chapter that the d'Urberville theme was a private obsession of Hardy's is based on this observation.

2.   For another view of Alec d'Urberville (and Angel Clare) see Robert Heilman's 'Lemuel Gulliver and Tess Durbeyfield: Houyhnhnms, Yahoos, and Ambiguities' newly collected in his *The Workings of Fiction* (Columbia, MO, and London, 1991) especially pp. 152–61. Heilman is one of Hardy's most perceptive critics, and all the relevant essays in this collection are excellent reading (or re-reading).

CHAPTER 8:   SEX, MARRIAGE AND THE DECLINE OF TRADITIONAL COMMUNITY IN *JUDE THE OBSCURE*

1.   See also:

> In short, as if materially, a compelling arm of extraordinary mus-
> cular power seized hold of him, something which had nothing
> in common with the spirits and influences that had moved him
> hitherto. This seemed to care little for his reason and his will,
> nothing for his so-called elevated intentions, and moved him
> along, as a violent schoolmaster a schoolboy he has seized by
> the collar, in a direction which tended towards the embrace of a
> woman for whom be had no respect and whose life had nothing
> in common with his own except locality. (pp. 40–1)

2.   As for instance when she gets Jude drunk in order to remarry him.
     The narrator comments: 'How Arabella had obtained money did not
     appear but she ordered a liqueur each, and paid for them' (p. 395).

3.   It is perhaps as a consequence of this young man's high chivalrous
     restraint, as prescribed by the highest code of Victorian society, that
     Sue can tell Jude 'I have no fear of men . . . I have not felt about
     them as most women are taught to feel – to be on their guard against
     attacks on their virtue; for no average man – no man short of a
     sensual savage – will molest a woman by day or night, at home
     or abroad, unless she invites him' (pp. 152–3). I suppose we are to
     think of Alec d'Urberville as a 'sensual savage'.

4.   It seems quite likely that Sue (if she thought about the sexual
     implications of marrying the schoolmaster at all) initially saw
     Phillotson as a father-figure, and as being too old to want to put
     the kind of sexual pressure on her that her leader-writer did. And
     thus his wanting her to make love with him is triply bad for her
     – because she doesn't love him, because she finds him physically
     repulsive, and because there is for her a psychological element of
     incest in the idea. For 'gross' see also p. 150 below.

5.   Sue is deeply self-centred, as Arabella sees during her conversation
     with Sue in her room at the Prince Inn: "Ah, yes – you are a oneyer
     too, like myself,' said Arabella, eyeing her visitor with humorous
     criticism' (p. 283). This self-centredness leads her into a number of
     such casual cruelties. Another acute example is the demands that Sue
     makes of Jude during the preparation for her wedding. She is not
     deliberately cruel, though the pain she inflicts on Jude is sharp; we
     might interpret her actions as revenge for his being married already
     and not telling her (as indeed the whole project of the marriage
     seems to be); but the narrator makes clear that in this instance she
     is acting as 'an epicure of the emotions' who drags Jude through the
     wedding rehearsal so that she can experience 'new sensations'. She
     apologizes afterwards, after the pain has been caused. Later she feels
     bad because she has left Phillotson and he has become ill; because

she wishes to exorcise her guilt she returns to him for an afternoon, unthinking of the pain she is giving him. The sensitivity she feels, the rushing to save people, or to be with them, the writing of relenting letters after face to face rejection, all these are attempts to preserve others' love for her, or to put herself right with herself. Where Jude helps others out of deep sensitive fellow-feeling, Sue gestures help to others out of deep sensitive self-concern. Such examples can be multiplied until they climax in the great and cruel betrayal of Jude at the end of the novel in order to save her own soul.

I have said or implied that little of this is deliberate, but Hardy is carefully ambiguous; there is room in his presentation of this aspect of Sue for a reader justifiably to identify her as a sado-masochist, deliberately putting herself in positions where she will suffer, and at least partly conscious of the pain she inflicts on those around her.

6.   It is right that Arabella is granted the final insight into Sue, and we accept what she says not just because it echoes our own fears, but because Arabella too is concerned alone with self, and this fundamental harmony with Sue lends her statement authority.

7.   In this conclusion may also be found an echo of J. S. Mill's account of the fate of the man of character referred to extensively in Chapter 5 above. It might further be worth reflecting on the question of whether Mill considered that there could also be a place in contemporary society for the woman of character – or indeed whether he would have considered such a concept possible. Sue herself invokes the *Of Individuality* section of *On Liberty* on p. 235, asserting to Phillotson her right of independence of thought and action:

> She or he, 'who lets the world, or his own portion of it, choose his plan of life for him, has no need of any other faculty than the ape-like one of imitation.' J. S. Mill's words, those are. I have been reading it up. Why can't you act upon them? I wish to, always.'

It is perhaps also worth noting of Sue's ambition to 'ennoble some man to high aims' (p. 158) that she has no thought of finding high aims herself, or of seeking comradeship, community with other women.

8.   One might compare Hardy's account of this question with Forster's in *Howards End*, 1908.

9.   It is worth considering in passing the utterly characteristic Hardyan phrase 'apple-like convexities'. Thus abstracted from its context the phrase seems almost ridiculously pedantic, but when put back into its sentence the distanced abstract 'convexities' and 'amplitudes' lend a real vividness to 'small, tight, apple-like'. It does not seem to me to be ridiculous to relate this to Keats's technique in the 'Bright Star' sonnet, in particular, to his 'ripening breast'. Sue's breasts are compressed, hard, unripe as yet. And the plural in 'amplitudes' is good; the sentence is almost witty. And even in this novel of

deracination Hardy cannot help observing his creations in terms of their unacknowledged but rooted connection to the natural world.

CHAPTER 9:   'FROM THE WHITE SEA TO CAPE HORN': THOMAS HARDY AND THE WIDER WORLD

1. It is perhaps worth noting in passing that Rolfe, the central character in Gissing's *The Whirlpool*, once worked in the office of an emigration agent. Gissing writes that 'it became one of his functions to answer persons who visited the office for information as to the climatic features of this or that new country, and their physical fitness for going out as colonists. Of course there was demanded of him a radical unscrupulousness, and often he proved equal to the occasion . . . ' (pp. 22–3).
2. See above pp. 60–61.

Index

Note: Hardy's works are listed under individual titles